Legacy of a Freedom School

Legacy of a Freedom School

Sandra E. Adickes

LEGACY OF A FREEDOM SCHOOL

First published in 2005 by
PALGRAVE MACMILLAN™
175 Fifth Avenue, New York, N.Y. 10010 and
Houndmills, Basingstoke, Hampshire, England RG21 6XS
Companies and representatives throughout the world.

PALGRAVE MACMILLAN is the global academic imprint of the Palgrave Macmillan division of St. Martin's Press, LLC and of Palgrave Macmillan Ltd. Macmillan® is a registered trademark in the United States, United Kingdom and other countries. Palgrave is a registered trademark in the European Union and other countries.

ISBN 978-1-4039-7213-2

Library of Congress Cataloging-in-Publication Data is available from the Library of Congress.

A catalogue record for this book is available from the British Library.

Design by Newgen Imaging Systems (P) Ltd., Chennai, India.

First edition: November 2005

10 9 8 7 6 5 4 3 2 1

Transferred to Digital Printing in 2008

Contents ᕲ

Introduction: Legacy of a Freedom School ⌁

In 1963, when I was an English teacher in a New York public high school, I volunteered to participate with approximately thirty other teachers in a "Freedom School" project our union sponsored in Prince Edward County, Virginia. The county's school board there had closed schools in 1959 rather than comply with the Supreme Court's decision in *Brown v. Board of Education* mandating integration. While we were teaching basic math and language skills to youngsters in classrooms set up in the county's rural black churches, the Student Nonviolent Coordinating Committee (SNCC) was planning to launch a major civil rights project the following year in Mississippi. In August, organizers from SNCC came to Prince Edward County to tell the volunteer teachers about plans for the summer project and the Freedom Schools that were to be one of its components; I decided to volunteer to teach in Mississippi.

We volunteer teachers understood that not all white people in Prince Edward County, had favored the closing of the schools and that the decision was under reconsideration. However, second thoughts about school segregation by white people in Virginia were not shared by their counterparts in Mississippi, where segregation was enforced with a religious zeal.

The 1954 *Brown* decision, with its declaration that "racial segregation in public education is unconstitutional," represented a significant victory for the NAACP, which had presented the case before the Supreme Court, because it vindicated the organization's legalistic approach to opposing segregation. However, the Court's 1955 implementation of the *Brown* decree made a concession: Without setting a date for the end of segregation, the Court ordered the lower courts that had originally heard the cases "to require that the defendants make a prompt and reasonable start toward compliance" with the *Brown* decision. In effect, this action placed the responsibility for achieving desegregation on the complainants. Confident the law was on their side, state leaders of the Mississippi NAACP directed branches to take steps to end school segregation.

However, in July, 1954, two months after the first *Brown* decision, a group of Mississippi businessmen adopted the NAACP's strategy and organized the Citizens' Council in order to use legal means to *preserve* segregation. When parents, at the direction of NAACP branches, filed petitions with school boards, the Citizens' Council chapters in those cities responded by publishing the names of petitioners in newspaper advertisements and on placards in store windows. The immediate result was that petitioners with white employers lost their jobs; independent black businessmen were refused delivery of goods by distributors, were denied credit and loan renewals by banks, and were boycotted by white clients. This campaign of economic harassment devastated the desegregation activists, many of whom were forced to leave the state. Spreading from the Delta, Citizens' Councils grew into the semi-official Committee of Public Safety, organizing all over Mississippi to proclaim unswerving devotion to the principles of white supremacy and state sovereignty. In Virginia, one county had defied *Brown*; in Mississippi, the entire state had resisted, and the segregated school system remained solidly in place.

In 1963, SNCC workers, who had been active in voter registration in Mississippi since 1960, responded to the injurious segregated school system by adopting a proposal to include Freedom Schools in the summer project. These schools were envisioned as places where students could ask questions about matters that interested them, such as voting and freedom rides, without being thrown out of class. In recognition of the fear of dismissal that restrained teachers in the segregated schools from exploring controversial topics, and also noting that the per capita expenditure in Mississippi for black students was one quarter of that for white students, the proposal recognized that help (in the form of one thousand volunteers from outside Mississippi) was needed to fill an intellectual void in the lives of young black Mississippians and to enable them to express their own questions, needs and demands.

SNCC leadership formed a Summer School Committee and charged it with responsibility for establishing schools and creating curriculum that would serve as a first assault on the state of semi-illiteracy that segregation had inflicted on the black youth of Mississippi. A remarkable conference of SNCC workers and professional educators convened in New York in March, 1964 to produce a course of study for the Freedom Schools. The work of that conference resulted in the "Citizenship Curriculum," which, according to the introduction, began on the level of the students' experiences in their everyday lives and built to a "more realistic perception of American society, themselves, the conditions of their oppression, and alternatives offered by the Freedom Movement."

This curriculum presented educational alternatives to the students through a sequence of units designed to enable students to understand their own heritage as African Americans; to evaluate the basic conditions of their lives in terms of schools, housing, health care, and job opportunities; to compare those conditions with those of whites in the South; to recognize that the living conditions of blacks and whites in the North had the same disparity; and thus, with the understanding that "escape" to the North was pointless, begin to envision ways to change the conditions where they lived through participation in the nonviolent Freedom Movement.

I entered Mississippi on July 4th, 1964, assigned to teach in Palmer's Crossing, a suburb of Hattiesburg that I quickly recognized as a closely knit community of forthright, determined people who, living in relative isolation from the white communities of Hattiesburg, relished their spirited independence. For six weeks I taught English, with emphasis on African-American literature and history, at the Priest Creek Baptist Church Freedom School to high school students who were seasoned activists, eager for the subjects that had been withheld from them, and ready to use what they learned to continue their struggle. Fortunately, I had acquired skills as a teacher that enabled me to provide these teenagers with what they needed: a respectful appreciation of them, an interest in their experiences and beliefs, and a pedagogical style based on questioning them and welcoming their questions.

During that tumultuous summer, my students delighted in reading for the first time works by black authors, having discussions, writing essays, role playing events in African-American history; producing a newsletter; debating other Freedom School students, presenting a play, and holding a model political convention. "Our school," I wrote after the summer, "was by any definition a fine school—no attendance sheets, absentee postcards, truant officers, report cards—just perfect attendance."

Near the close of the session, I accompanied six students on what was, in effect, a graduation trip: a visit to the Hattiesburg library in order to get library cards. Their request was denied, they were told, on the grounds that the Citizens' Council had decreed that the libraries not be integrated. However, the students' spirits were not dampened, for they knew, that they had been transformed by their Freedom School experience and would ultimately go on to make changes in their society. They returned to their segregated schools in the fall, energized by the experiences of the summer and with increased confidence because of their achievements.

Most of the students of the summer of 1964 went on to college, often to black colleges like Mississippi's Jackson State. Moreover, they were a generation in the vanguard of change. Schools in Hattiesburg and other Mississippi communities were gradually integrated with respect to both students and teachers, and black high school students accepted higher education as a normal rite of passage. In 1968, the University of Southern Mississippi in Hattiesburg renounced segregation, and Freedom School students who had vowed as children to go there enrolled at USM. In Mississippi at last, *Brown* was the law of the land. Of course, much more needed to be done to fulfill the goals of the Freedom Movement, but most of my Freedom School students followed the precepts of the Civic Curriculum and have remained in Mississippi to bring those changes into being.

In a recent letter from a former Freedom School student, one whom I accompanied on that quest for library cards and who is now a hospital dietitian in Vicksburg, wrote that she would be "eternally grateful" to "the Movement for exposing me and the others to a whole new world of knowledge." However, she believes that the descendants of the Freedom Movement activists "know nothing about the struggle for equality we endured."

I have written this book to honor those who struggled in the Freedom Movement and to record one of its extraordinary successes. The Freedom School experience enabled students to achieve goals that had not seemed possible before that summer, and also allowed them to continue in the Freedom Movement, making beneficial changes for generations that followed. We often sang, "Deep in my heart I do believe that we shall overcome one day." They did overcome. The knowledge that I was part of a struggle that has made life permanently better for great numbers of people has brought me enduring pride and satisfaction. I also believe, as for years I have been saying to students, that the best thing one can do when one is young is to become involved with a movement dedicated to making life better for others.

1. Movement Beginnings in Hattiesburg ⌒

When I arrived in Hattiesburg's shabby bus station on July 4th, 1964, the sight of the city's quiet business district of mid-sized office buildings and shops brought to mind the cliché "sleepy southern town." It was a mistaken impression, for as civil rights historian Neill McMillen later observed, if "the good and God-fearing" white people of Hattiesburg would not tolerate incursions by "scruffy flame-throwers from outside," they were equally rigid in their denial of the rights of citizenship to people with black skin.[1] And, as I would learn later, if they disdained the raw brutality of the unreconstructed Delta region, they exercised an exquisite cruelty in denying those rights.

Situated about one hundred miles north of the Gulf Coast, Hattiesburg—the seat of Forrest County in Mississippi's Fifth Congressional District—was first known as Twin Forks, then as Gordonville, until it was given its final name by the city's first mayor, William H. Hardy, in honor of his wife, Hattie. The city had been incorporated with a population of approximately 400 in 1884, the same year that what is now the Southern Railway System was built from Meridian through Hattiesburg to New Orleans. In the post-Reconstruction era, people of Scotch, Irish, and English ancestry came from Georgia and the Carolinas, drawn by the vast areas of virgin pine timberlands. The advent of the railroad advanced the growth of the timber industry, but the greater lumber boom arrived in 1897 with the completion of the Gulf and Ship Island Railroad through Hattiesburg from Gulfport to Jackson—now part of the Illinois Central System. The formation of the transportation intersection, together with the industrial growth in the rural South, resulted in the designation of Hattiesburg as "Hub City." When the timber industry expanded from the 1890s through 1919, owners and managers built impressive homes, a number of which are still standing. At first, they were built close to the depot, then in the southeast edge of Hattiesburg and southwest of town.[2]

However, Hattiesburg also had its wild side, with houses of ill fame, gambling, public drunkenness, assault and battery, and horses running wild in the streets. Jail did not tame the criminals, for the city was obliged at times to pay for "repairs on the calaboose." In 1898, an extra policeman was added to the force, and the next year two more policemen were hired to patrol the city. In 1908, Forrest County—named for Nathan Bedford Forrest, a founder of the Ku Klux Klan—was created, with Hattiesburg designated as the county seat. After World War I, as the timber industry declined, new industries were developed that produced turpentine, chemicals, metal products, apparel, food products, building materials, household appliances, and many other items.[3]

The African-American community that had been established after the Civil War also expanded, and between 1895 and 1910, a major business district for the black community developed on Mobile Street, in the northeast area of the city. African-American residents lived in communities to the south and east of this section. Two other significant African-American communities were the Kelly settlement, a farming community to the northwest of town, and Palmer's Crossing, a hamlet to the south.[4]

In the 1960's, the population of Hattiesburg was around 35,000. About one-third of the city's residents were African American; approximately 38 percent of these residents were home owners and 62 percent were renters of housing, two-thirds of which was not in good condition.[5] Although Hattiesburg was not known outside the city as one of the state's more violent communities, violent incidents were known to have occurred nearby.

In 1959, Mack Charles Parker, in jail in neighboring Poplarville awaiting trial on the charge of raping a white woman, was abducted from his cell, beaten, and shot to death. In 1962, Roman Duckworth, a corporal in the United States army, was shot on a bus as it pulled into Taylorsville, his hometown north of Hattiesburg.[6] And like their peers throughout Mississippi, black children and teenagers in Hattiesburg were haunted by the murder in 1955 of Emmett Till, a fourteen-year-old Chicagoan visiting relatives in the Delta hamlet of Money, because he was said to have whistled at a white woman, the wife of a grocery store owner. The two men who killed him—the woman's husband, Roy Bryant, and his half-brother, J. W. Milam—were tried by a jury that declared them "not guilty" within sixty-eight minutes. In 1956, in return for cash, Milam and Bryant admitted to *Look* reporter William Bradford Huie that they had killed Emmett Till.[7]

Over the years, the many lynchings of blacks in the South had not significantly touched the conscience of Americans, but the lynching of a fourteen-year-old boy profoundly shocked them. In Mississippi, teenagers were perhaps those most stricken by his brutal death. The newspaper articles and pictures of Till's bloated body after it was retrieved from the Tallahatchie River caused Joyce and Dorie Ladner of Palmer's Crossing to wonder how anyone could have killed a boy so close to their age. They wept for him as they would for one of their brothers and vowed to work for change when they were older.[8] But children too young to remember the murder of Emmett Till were also threatened by it. Josie Brown, nine years old in the summer of 1964 when she attended Freedom School at Mt. Zion Baptist Church, recalled her mother warning her brother Arthur, "Remember Emmett Till."[9]

Although the Gulf Coast cities to the south of Hattiesburg were known as "moderate," Hattiesburg in the early 1960s was rigidly segregated. The schools were racially separated, but the separation was far from equal, and black students could not go on to higher education at Mississippi Southern College (now the University of Southern Mississippi). The "public" library served whites; blacks had access only to a small storefront with a limited number of outdated books in the Mobile Street area. Buses were segregated, with curtains to separate the races. Water fountains and bathrooms came in twos; black drivers were not permitted to use restrooms at gas stations. Black diners could not sit down at tables; they were required to go to the rear of a restaurant to buy food. Black people were not permitted to swim in the city's pools; they had to go to a segregated pool twenty miles away in Laurel. Few working-class black families earned more than $3,000 a year as service employees or workers at local industries and mills.

The black middle class consisted of ministers, teachers, farmers and entrepreneurs. This last group, members of the lively Mobile Street business community, had an economic base in the black community that enabled them to join the Hattiesburg movement with relative freedom from fear of reprisals by white employers or customers. Significant participants were Glodies Jackson and his partner in a television repair shop, J. C. Fairley. Fairley had joined the Civilian Conservation Corps at Camp Shelby during the Depression, was drafted into the army during World War II, and became a leader of the Hattiesburg NAACP in the post-war years. Among the women who emerged as activists were beauty shop owners Peggy Jean Connor and Pinkey Hall; the midwife named for the Biblical feminist heroine Queen Vashti, Mrs. Vassie R. Patton; and property owner and business woman Mrs. Lenon E. Woods, whose entrepreneurship had yielded uncommon knowledge of the men of Hattiesburg's white power structure.

The Hattiesburg civil rights movement was spurred by the memory of the abusive and ultimately lethal treatment of one of Hattiesburg's black citizens. Clyde Kennard, an army veteran with seven years of distinguished service as a paratrooper, was a student at the University of Chicago in the late 1950s, when, because of his stepfather's poor health, he returned to Mississippi to run his family's farm. He then attempted several times to enroll at the all-white Mississippi Southern College. An account of the state's treachery against Kennard is given by John Dittmer in *Local People: The Struggle for Civil Rights in Mississippi*. Kennard's efforts to get a college degree from a white institution attracted the attention of the Sovereignty Commission (a secret police force created by the Mississippi state legislature in 1956), who assigned Zack Van Landingham, a former FBI agent, to work on the case. Van Landingham's report made clear that Kennard was highly regarded for his intelligence, courtesy, and "desire to better the negro race in Mississippi," but Kennard's exemplary character references did not deter Van Landingham from launching an ultimately fatal dirty tricks campaign. Mississippi Southern president William D. McCain met with Kennard, and Kennard, perhaps believing that McCain recognized his merit and would admit him to the college, trusted McCain. However, McCain never intended to admit Kennard, as he later admitted, on the grounds that by remaining president of Mississippi Southern College he would accomplish more than by losing his job over a "silly martyrdom for one Negro."[10]

Landingham recruited a minister, the Reverend R. W. Woullard, to head a committee of other compliant black leaders—a principal and an English teacher from the Palmer's Crossing school, and two principals in the Hattiesburg school system—to dissuade Kennard from applying to Mississippi Southern. Kennard received the visitation committee, but remained firm in his intention to attend Mississippi Southern. In the meantime, Governor James P. Coleman, a committed but seemingly moderate segregationist, was succeeded by Ross Barnett, a zealous and openly repressive segregationist. The tactics used against Kennard became vicious and dirty.

In 1960, an illiterate young warehouse worker, Johnny Lee Roberts, was arrested for stealing five bags of chicken feed, worth about twenty-five dollars, and depositing it on the Kennard farm. Roberts claimed Kennard had planned the robbery, and Kennard was arrested and brought to trial. Roberts was so confused and inconsistent a witness that the district attorney had to feed him his testimony as to how Kennard had planned the robbery. Roberts received a suspended sentence, and was immediately rehired by the employer whose feed he had stolen. The jury took ten minutes to convict Kennard, and the judge imposed the maximum sentence: seven years in Parchman penitentiary.[11]

At Parchman, Kennard was made to work from dawn to dusk on the penitentiary's cotton plantation. Despite his fatigue, he used his Sundays to teach reading and writing, while also writing letters for illiterate inmates. Meanwhile, NAACP lawyers worked to get Kennard's sentence reversed on appeal; however, the Mississippi Supreme Court upheld the sentence. The NAACP appealed to the United States Supreme Court, where Thurgood Marshall argued the case, but in October, 1961, the Court left standing the Mississippi Supreme Court's decision.[12]

In 1962, Kennard experienced abdominal pains; he was taken to the University of Mississippi Hospital where he was diagnosed with colon cancer and underwent surgery. The hospital staff recommended parole because of poor prognosis for his recovery. Nevertheless, Kennard was returned to Parchman. At this point, a campaign was launched to obtain his freedom. Joyce Ladner, then a Tougaloo student who had been a member of Clyde Kennard's NAACP youth council chapter in Hattiesburg, organized a student demand for Kennard's release. *Jet* magazine picked up the story, and national leaders including Martin Luther King and Dick Gregory demanded that Kennard be set free. Fearing the unfavorable publicity that would follow Kennard's death in Parchman, Governor Ross Barnett ordered Kennard's release in the spring of 1963. Wasted away, Kennard immediately went to Chicago for further surgery, but it was too late. Kennard died at age thirty-six on July 4, 1963.[13]

Kennard's friend and neighbor Vernon Dahmer was one of the earliest leaders in the Hattiesburg movement; he had been active in politics since the early 1950s. In 1958, he and Medgar Evers assisted in the formation of a youth chapter of the NAACP, with which Clyde Kennard had also worked.[14] Dahmer—light-skinned because of his white father, George Dahmer, and white grandfather, John Kelly, a plantation owner and namesake of Kelly settlement—was a farmer and owner of a general store and sawmill. As a man of property and steward of an ancestral homeland, Dahmer had the confidence necessary—despite being surrounded by white neighbors extremely hostile to a movement for civil rights and jealous of his success as a farmer and businessman—to be an activist in the Hattiesburg chapter of the NAACP. Deeply troubled that Kennard's imprisonment meant the loss of his family's farm and the dispossession of Kennard's mother, Dahmer sought to honor Kennard's sacrifice by organizing a special voter registration meeting. Dahmer was proposing an undertaking that would challenge members of his community to overcome their fear of the Forrest County registrar, Theron Lynd, a 300-pound, former football player who had not allowed a black person to vote since 1959. The pervasive intimidation surrounding disenfranchisement of African-Americans had reduced the Hattiesburg chapter of the NAACP to a handful of members.[15]

Nevertheless, Dahmer rose in his church, Shady Grove Baptist, one Sunday in the spring of 1962, and urged the congregation to risk having a meeting at the church because the federal government was now supporting the effort by suing Lynd to register black voters. Dahmer had supplied Justice Department lawyers with names of qualified black voters who had been rejected and unqualified white voters who had been accepted. Dahmer, a respected church trustee and generous contributor, carried a persuasive message to the congregation. Then Reverend Woullard responded from the pulpit that politics had no place in church. Woullard preached persuasively on the wages of sin, and offered a substitute motion that Dahmer be expelled from Shady Grove, along with his three closest supporters and all their immediate families. Woullard's motion carried. Dahmer led his family, his supporters and their families out of the church that stood upon land donated by his family.[16]

Shortly after his expulsion from Shady Grove church, Vernon Dahmer attended a meeting of NAACP chapter presidents in Magnolia, sixty miles west of Hattiesburg . The NAACP leaders were addressed by Bob Moses, a New Yorker and doctoral candidate at Harvard University who, moved by accounts of lunch counter sit-ins in Greensboro, North Carolina, had left his graduate studies and job teaching math at Horace Mann High School in New York City in 1960 to work with the Student Nonviolent Coordinating Committee (SNCC), an organization that had evolved from the spread of lunch counter sit-ins by students in fifteen cities in five southern states.

At the meeting, Moses pleaded for sponsorship of two nineteen-year-olds from Pike County, Mississippi, whom he had recruited and trained to be field secretaries. The NAACP leaders, who viewed Moses's efforts as harmful rather than productive, were unresponsive to his plea. However, Dahmer agreed to take the two young men, Curtis Hayes and Hollis Watkins, into his home. In a short time, Hayes and Watkins would find that Dahmer, who drove himself and his children very hard, expected them to earn their keep when they had run out of money. Hayes and Watkins were working half of the day at Dahmer's sawmill and the remainder of the day on voter registration until June, 1962 when a grant from the Voter Education Project established by the Southern Regional Council materialized.[17] Before the summer ended, Hayes left Hattiesburg to go to Jackson, but he had found the time spent in Hattiesburg rewarding for himself and Watkins, "for this was our first time working out in the field with an individual project. It was amazing how the people accepted us 'two little children trying to do a man's job' and out of this sympathy came their willingness to help."[18]

Hollis Watkins, inspired by the work of SNCC staff in other parts of the state, had come into Hattiesburg as a field secretary, "proud, determined, prepared to take on the world if necessary," and remained there for three months in order to set up meetings to discuss voter registration.[19] Reverend Woullard had foreclosed the Baptist churches in Hattiesburg to such meetings, but Watkins had better luck when he turned to the Methodists. An informational meeting was held at St. James Colored (afterward Christian) Methodist Episcopal Church in downtown Hattiesburg, where Hollis Watkins talked to the two dozen people who attended about the raised expectations brought by the Freedom Rides and the sit-ins. He also explained the mechanics of the voting tests, and described the process of escorting small groups to the courthouse and dealing with Theron Lynd's confrontations.[20]

The event credited with beginning the Hattiesburg movement occurred later in the summer of 1962 at St. John Methodist Church in Palmer's Crossing, where the Reverend Leonard P. Ponder, at considerable risk, had been persuaded by women leaders of his church to open St. John for Hollis Watkins to organize a voter registration drive. Six people raised their hands in response to Watkins' request for volunteers to take the registration test at the Hattiesburg courthouse; four of these became involved in the Hattiesburg movement. Reverend Ponder was the first Hattiesburg minister to open his church to a Freedom School in 1964; Mrs. Virgie Robinson, at seventy, walked on a picket line, sheltered volunteers, cooked meals, and went to jail; Reverend J. W. Brown worked as a school bus driver and remained an activist until his death; and Victoria Jackson Gray, a wife, mother of three children, and businesswoman, became a leading activist and candidate for the United States Senate.[21]

Victoria Jackson Gray Adams has described herself as "blessed to have been born into a family of great property owners." Her great-great grandfather settled in the Hattiesburg area and homesteaded two hundred acres. Her grandfather instructed his family, "When Jessie [her grandmother] and I close our eyes, hold on to our land, for once you have your land, you have your independence."[22] After attending the local schools, she enrolled in Wilberforce College for one year before returning to Mississippi to marry Anthony Gray, a career military man. Later, with her three children, Gray moved to Germany when her husband was stationed there during the Korean War. The Gray family returned to Hattiesburg in 1955, and for the next six years, Victoria Gray operated a franchise of a cosmetics firm, "and not doing too bad by Mississippi standards." She was a leader in her church and head of a local PTA, but Gray was not invited to join, nor did she consider joining, the male-dominated Hattiesburg branch of the NAACP. Nevertheless, her social conscience prodded her to look for ways to promote change.[23] Of the night at St. John in 1962, Gray has said, "When I raised my hand, I knew the rest of my life would not be the same." The change came quickly; Gray closed her business and "joined the Movement because I had been waiting for it all my life." When Watkins left Hattiesburg to join the SNCC Delta project in September, Gray took over as project leader.

In 1963, Gray went for a week to a Southern Christian Leadership Conference workshop that Septima Clark of the Highlander Folk School had set up in Dorchester, Georgia. Highlander workshops brought together local leaders and provided them with skills that would enable them to develop leadership skills in others when they returned home.[24] When Gray went back to Hattiesburg, she established the Citizenship Education Program in the community, recruiting her students from the Hattiesburg churches for her literacy program. Gray taught her students, most of whom were older adults, basic skills such as writing their names and addresses; she also taught them to read, using the Mississippi Constitution and the Mississippi voter registration form. Each session ended with the singing of "We Shall Overcome." At her first session, Gray looked around at her six students: her "sixty-plus-year-old cousin" and her "eighty-plus-year-old godmother" and four others nowhere near her age, and thought, "*We shall overcome?*" But this group and others Gray recruited did overcome. The pride and confidence the students gained from the literacy program enabled them to walk the courthouse picket line, and face jail with no bail in order to gain the right to vote.

From her groups of literacy students, Gray recruited teachers to go to Georgia for training and to return and recruit new groups of students. These literacy teachers—Peggy Jean Connor, Helen Anderson, Ruth Campbell, Virgie Robinson, Minnie Sullivan, and others—became, in Gray's words, "the heart of the Hattiesburg Movement." Reverend Ponder's courageous example of opening his church to the Movement was not immediately followed, because while much of the city's black population were responsive to the Movement, the black clergy remained resistant. However, the ministers' recalcitrance was eventually overcome, because the literacy cohorts Gray had recruited from their congregations demanded they open their churches to the Movement.

In the spring of 1963, voter registration faltered statewide; to strengthen the campaign, the Student Nonviolent Coordinating Committee ("Snick"), the NAACP, and the Congress of Racial Equality (CORE) agreed to unite as the Council of Federated Organizations (COFO). In Hattiesburg, recruiting volunteers for voter registration by teaching literacy class by class and canvassing household to household took much time and energy; fewer than 150 people had attempted to register, and there had not been mass meetings or marches to the courthouse. Moreover, Theron Lynd continued to be the principal obstacle to black suffrage, for despite a federal injunction, he refused to register black citizens as voters. In the summer of 1961, the Justice Department filed another suit against Lynd, and the next year, in *United States v. Lynd*, asked the federal courts to prohibit Lynd from discriminating against black voters. Lynd evaded judgment against him because Federal District Judge Harold E. Cox, an ardent segregationist appointed by President Kennedy at Senator Eastland's urging, ruled against the federal government. The Fifth Circuit Court of Appeals overturned Cox and issued an injunction against Lynd, prohibiting him from continuing to discriminate against black voters and ruling him subject to contempt proceedings if he did not comply. Nevertheless, Lynd remained defiant.[25]

In July, 1963, a three-judge panel of the Fifth Circuit Court of Appeals upheld an earlier judgment against Theron Lynd ordering him to register blacks on the same standards required for whites. In an August 1963 memo to civil rights leaders, Bob Moses pointed out that the Fifth Circuit Court's decision was "the first such order handed down in Mississippi," and it was crucial for the civil rights organizations in Mississippi "to launch a concerted drive in [Forrest] county to register Negroes before the 1964 elections." In recognition of the importance of Hattiesburg in the struggle for suffrage, COFO sent SNCC workers John O'Neal and Lawrence Guyot—Tougaloo College graduates—and Carl Arnold—a lawyer—to Hattiesburg to work full time in building the movement.[26]

On September 23rd, John O'Neal reported to COFO headquarters in Jackson that as Hattiesburg was slated to become headquarters for organizing the 5th Congressional District, he hoped that the number of people "passing through these gates" would stimulate the people living full time in Hattiesburg and shatter some of the "provincialism which is as much a part of that hallowed 'southern way of life' as is segregation." O'Neal thought that a "plateau" had been reached in Hattiesburg, and that "a congenial atmosphere" had been established that would enable the project to "move into another phase of development." He foresaw six things necessary to achieve success:

> the capacity to create an active and interested student group, an increased number of people actually going out to canvass which is the fulcrum of the whole program, the successful development of block club [sic] with effective and significant programs, and in support of these fundamental things, I think of a mass meeting program on a regular basis, the Citizenship Education Program and the Newsletter.[27]

Carl Arnold, in his September 25th report, credited O'Neal with having established "a solid foundation of people going down every day to register and come to the office for help in preparing for the test" Arnold also reported that Hattiesburg had many young people, "and of course, young people make up the most solid militant group."[28] Gerald Bray, another worker assigned to Hattiesburg, reported to COFO that he found Hattiesburg "fantastic material for a beautifully organized shift from the old to the new," and that the Mobile Street office on October 4th "must be a sort of cultural oasis."[29]

John O'Neal did not remain in Hattiesburg; nevertheless, the things he had cited as necessary for success were in progress.

Voter registration efforts were strong, the Citizenship Education Program was growing, and COFO staff was publishing a newsletter, "Voice of the Movement." At a time when Joyce and Dorie Ladner were activists at Tougaloo College, another generation of students in the two Negro high schools in Hattiesburg were being mobilized through the newsletter, mass meetings, and flyers. One of these flyers, addressed "Attention Students," questioned the ability of teachers at Earl Travillion Attendance Center to teach the United States Constitution without pointing out "the misuse of its precepts here in Mississippi," or to "speak out for justice and freedom" if they were not "concerned enough . . . to register and to vote." The flyer acknowledged that the teachers at Travillion feared loss of their jobs, but claimed that most of the teachers at Hattiesburg's Rowan High School were registered voters.[30]

In an effort to bring major change to Mississippi, COFO organized an independent political party, the Mississippi Freedom Democratic Party in March, 1963. In November, COFO launched a statewide "Freedom Vote" campaign on behalf of MFDP candidates: Aaron Henry, a World War II veteran, pharmacist and NAACP leader from Clarksville ran for governor, and Ed King, a white Methodist minister and chaplain at Tougaloo ran for acting governor. The campaign's purpose was to demonstrate that fear rather than apathy was the reason only 20,000 of 450,000 eligible African Americans were registered voters. During the three days of the mock election, groups of registrars, including approximately seventy student volunteers recruited from Yale and Stanford, traveled to collect ballots from people in homes, churches, businesses, cafes, beauty parlors, and pool rooms. The goal was to gather 200,000 votes; despite the harassment and arrests of canvassers, 83,000 votes were collected.[31]

Plans for a summer project involving the recruitment of large numbers of white student volunteers, which had been considered and argued over since mid-summer, were settled in a meeting in Greenville following the Freedom Vote. Supporters of the plan were pragmatic, arguing that in two years of activism, SNCC had registered very few voters in Mississippi, and black Mississippians they had recruited had been killed, beaten, imprisoned, expelled, or harmed in other ways, but if white volunteers were to come to

Mississippi in large numbers, the nation would be concerned with their safety, and harm to them would probably draw federal intervention. Opponents objected to the transfer of resources from projects outside Mississippi to the summer project and were concerned that the emerging indigenous black leaders would be humbled in the presence of a horde of articulate, white Northerners. Convinced that "a larger response" than SNCC had been able to provide was needed to stop the "the growth of white violence," Bob Moses "threw all . . . [his] weight" behind the summer project.[32] Gradually an agreement was reached to launch the summer project, with voter registration at its center. However, in recognition of the need to provide community services to local people, the concept of community centers was accepted as a necessary component. A proposal to establish "freedom schools" developed by Charlie Cobb out of his work with the youth of Greenville received enthusiastic community support, and plans for Freedom Summer went forward.[33]

Shortly after the Greenville meeting, the Mississippi staff, then numbering fifty full-time workers, met in a planning meeting at SNCC's office in Jackson. The state was divided along congressional lines and workers elected a project head in each district. Lawrence Guyot, who had become state chairman of the Freedom Democratic Party, was elected head of the 5th district. Guyot was determined to force a "showdown" with Lynd. There had been little movement since the Freedom Vote, and Guyot believed that the black community of Hattiesburg was not going to move, according to words quoted by COFO's Mendy Samstein, "until they see his ass put in jail." In addition, all the 5th District registrars had been watching the Lynd situation; according to Samstein, "if Lynd has nothing to fear from the justice department and from defiance of court orders, then neither would they." A showdown would therefore "force the government to put up or shut up."[34]

The showdown in Hattiesburg called for a "Freedom Day" on January 22nd, 1964, directed at mobilizing the black community for a mass demonstration at the courthouse, where local people would picket with signs urging "register to vote" and "one man—one vote." Hattiesburg COFO staff worker Mike Sayer anticipated that the demonstration would bring "increased resistance by local authorities, which means arrests on a large scale for our voter-inners."

Capitalizing on the event required an intense communications effort to contact national newspapers and radio and tv networks, and develop material to hand to the news people "we hope will just be swarming all over the place." Sayer foresaw the Freedom Day launching the entire 1964 program: the spring primaries, the freedom registration, the freedom primary and freedom general election, the participation of the Freedom Democratic Party at the Democratic convention, and the summer student program.[35]

The COFO staff's communications effort succeeded in drawing the hoped-for swarms of reporters, as well as approximately forty clergy flown in by the National Council of Churches and numbers of national and state civil rights leaders. On the evening of the 21st, a crowd of four hundred gathered in St. Paul's African Methodist Episcopal Church, while many stood outside. Lawrence Guyot, the speaker who drew the most enthusiasm from the audience because of his steady, months-long preparation for the event, offered practical advice to the pickets: conceal money in shoes; bring toothbrushes for jail but leave behind pencils or anything that might be thought of as a weapon; use the nonviolent techniques he had described for reducing injury from attacks by police or white mobs. Guyot assured them that whatever happened would be over quickly, because civil rights demonstrations in Mississippi never lasted more than fifteen minutes.[36]

On the cold, rainy morning of January 22nd, eighty demonstrations lined up in front of the Forrest County courthouse, as a phalanx of auxiliary police marching three abreast lined up between them and a crowd of white spectators. But when the pickets refused to obey a series of commands to disperse, the police turned to face the jeering bystanders, thereby protecting the demonstrators from attack and enraging the segregationists.[37] As historian Howard Zinn, who was on the scene, observed, "something unprecedented was taking place in the state of Mississippi: a black and white line of demonstrators was picketing a public building, allowed to do so by the police."[38]

Many media representatives were disappointed by the lack of confrontation, for without violence, their stories lacked interest. However, black observers who had feared arrest crossed the street to join the pickets, some of whom were inspired to take the voting test in the courthouse, where Theron Lynd was accepting applications one by one.[39] Because of the tirelessness of the COFO workers, over a hundred black men and women had come to register. Only a handful of those who got through the courthouse door passed the test; nevertheless, Howard Zinn summed up Freedom Day "as a kind of quiet victory and everyone was commenting on how well things had gone."[40]

Of course, there were reprisals. Bob Moses was arrested for breach of the peace and sentenced to sixty days in jail; Lawrence Guyot was arrested on charges of corrupting minors through his speeches and sentenced to six months in jail; Victoria Gray's husband was fired from his job at the city water works; and several people who were recognized on the picket line lost their jobs as well.[41] Mrs. Pinkey Hall was a "brave soldier." She joined the picket line, but when she went to work in a white home the next day, her employer told her she "couldn't use her anymore" because a neighbor had called to report that she had seen her on the picket line. Mrs. Hall responded, "Take your job and do what you want to do with it," and walked out.[42] Through this kind of stubborn defiance, the Hattiesburg movement gained momentum. The first group of clergy who came to Hattiesburg inspired other groups of clergy to follow them in shifts, and thus maintain a picket line that encircled the courthouse throughout the spring and into the summer.[43]

A significant number of the pickets were students, who, far from being corrupted, were empowered by Guyot's speeches and the organizational efforts of the COFO staff. Impatient with their segregated schools, these young people were energized by the challenge, even when they were arrested. "We spent our weekends in those days," former Freedom School student Shirley Anderson recalled in 2000, "by leaving school, going to the courthouse, then going to jail." The students were well prepared for the experience they would embrace in the summer.

2. Creating Mississippi Freedom Schools ✍

I went to Douglass College, the women's college of Rutgers University, in the stifling McCarthy era when women students were "campused," that is, confined to their dormitories, for staying out past curfew. In those years, a demand for better dining hall food drew little support, because students feared their signatures on a petition—any petition—would one day ruin their careers.

Sexually active women were considered subversive. Rutgers University fraternity men were said to inform the Dean of Women about Douglass students whose behavior at house parties they considered inappropriate. When Douglass students complained to the dean that a close friend of mine was flaunting her sexuality in the Douglass student center, the Dean took action, forcing my friend to leave college in her senior year. (The Rutgers boyfriend was not penalized, but a Douglass faculty member who defended my friend was fired).

After I graduated in 1954, a member of what *Time* magazine labeled "The Silent Generation," I foundered in several dead-end, "Help Wanted, Female" jobs before making a career choice I had resisted for years because it was one of the few choices open to me. Mostly I had refused to follow the path of students I considered intellectually uninvolved: "fall-back" education majors, as in "God forbid he should drop dead, I'll have teaching to fall back on." I became a teacher.

My first assignment was teaching English in a vocational high school for girls in the Yorkville section of Manhattan, where an earlier population of German and Irish immigrants housed in tenements had been replaced by middle-and upper-income, native-born Americans living in high-rise luxury apartments. The suburban New Jersey middle-class high school I had attended provided resources and activities: a campus, an auditorium, and a cafeteria; a stadium, gymnasiums, hockey fields, and tennis courts; competitive sports teams (even in those pre-Title IX days, for girls) and cheerleaders; a student newspaper, plays, clubs, and dances. In contrast, the vocational high school students experienced New York's meanness. After traveling by subway from the Bronx or Harlem, they passed unfriendly area residents to enter a treeless, lawnless fortress where they were to be trained in one of four vocational tracks: secretarial studies, nursing, beauty culture, or needle trades.

Students in the secretarial studies program had the best academic records and a spirit of elitism that was cultivated by the teachers in charge. These girls had positive attitudes about themselves, got good grades, and were assured of job placement after graduation. The nursing program ranked second, although it was not clear what post-high school job opportunities existed for these students. As part of their training, nursing students staffed a nursery school maintained by the high school. The director of the nursery school tried to recruit working-class minority children, but the the only children to benefit from the program were the neighborhood's young upper-middle-class offspring, often accompanied by their nannies, who came to the school to be tended half the day by African-American and Puerto Rican teenagers.

Students in the beauty culture program were enthusiastic about their training in hair care; however, their opportunities were limited because African-American girls had difficulty getting jobs in beauty shops owned by Puerto Ricans. Puerto Rican girls, in turn, had difficulty getting jobs in shops owned by African Americans, and both groups were excluded by white-owned beauty shops. Girls for whom all hope had been abandoned were sent to the bottom-ranked needle trades program, where they would train on obsolete sewing machines for work in a declining industry. The woman in charge of the program, no doubt as despairing as her students, frequently screamed at the girls or sent them out of the room to stand in the hallway.

The school lacked a kitchen, so hot lunch was not served, and thin sandwiches with monotonous fillings were brought in everyday.

Many of the students were from welfare-recipient families; after the parents filled out a form declaring themselves paupers, their daughters would be issued a lunch card entitling them to the Dickensian quota of one sandwich per day. My first patrol—that is, an assignment beyond classroom teaching duties—required me to go into the bathroom during their lunch period and poke my head into the stalls to see that the girls were not smoking. I was often chided for not showing sufficient zeal in performing this task. Many of the students had emotional problems, family problems, problems with the law, out-of-wedlock pregnancies, but the school provided no effective guidance counseling or access to psychological assistance.

I did not find role models to follow in my first year of teaching. Most of my colleagues were older women who had taught for years in classrooms they had arranged as second homes, shared bag lunches with the same people each day, and maintained a detachment from the students. The principal had died the previous year, and the acting principal created an indelible image for me with her frequent reminders at faculty meetings that "you cannot leave a class when there are thirty bodies in a room." The chair of the English department, an intelligent middle-aged woman frustrated about capping her career at an undistinguished vocational school, at times referred to the students as "garbage." Another teacher in the department, a man who had turned to teaching after disappointment in another career, savored the school's lack of distinction, remarking to me one day that, "You could hide out here for years, Sandra, and no one would find you." He was cynically amused by the students, whom he considered slightly above the level of plant life. He mocked my concern for them: "You just love the underdog, Sandra, and the dirtier their faces, the more you love them."

I was a conscientious but not very skilled teacher in that first year. Mentoring was not a practice known at that time, and even if it had been, I could not have found one teacher among that faculty who could have or would have assisted me. More than a mentor, I needed a cohort, a group of people near me in age and career level, who could ask questions, pose ideas, and learn from each other as peers. When the head of the English department told me at the end of the school year that there was not a position for me in the 1961 academic year, I left without regret. My cynical colleague's assessment of the school as a permanent hiding place proved false; the Board of Education belatedly recognized its obsolescence and closed the school.

I quickly got another job at Benjamin Franklin, the first academic high school in East Harlem. The building—a neo-Georgian structure in upper Manhattan overlooking the East River and the Franklin Delano Roosevelt Drive—was little more than twenty years old at the time, but it was inconveniently located and already obsolete, with classrooms subject to the highway din. Moreover, it was a pariah, by reputation the worst academic high school in New York City. Until 1959, all the students were male, most of them Italian-American; then, during a period of declining enrollment, girls were admitted, and the school population, which rose to 2,700 during my four years there, became 97 percent African-American and Hispanic. In those days, students could graduate with a general diploma or the diploma designed by the New York State Board of Regents, which required students to take four years of English, three years of math, science, and social studies, two years of a foreign language, and to pass Board-designed examinations. The majority of students at Benjamin Franklin were tracked into the general curriculum, where they took easy versions of hard subjects, and were not required to study a foreign language, or take a Regents examination. Only 10 percent of these students went on to college.

Again, I encountered a sense of hopelessness and boredom. The English department chairman made available such texts as *Old Yeller, The Yearling,* and an anthology of short stories about rural and suburban life. I had been reading books by African-American authors and wanted to offer my students a work by Richard Wright or James Baldwin; the chair instead offered me the biography of the prizefighter Floyd Patterson as a text relevant to the students' lives. Aware of being patronized, the embarrassed students covered books they carried on buses and subways so that the titles would not be seen by students at "good" schools. I tried to compensate for inadequate texts by reproducing short articles, essays, and poems (Gwendolyn Brooks's "We Real Cool," for example). Occasionally, however, I did grab appropriate texts from the book room: an honors class enjoyed *Romeo and Juliet,* and other classes found

All Quiet on the Western Front relevant during the early days of the Vietnam War.

Very little in the education courses I was taking at this time was memorable or helpful, but I learned how to plan a developmental lesson. According to this format, a teacher begins with a motivating question designed to elicit a keen response from the students that will lead directly to the "aim" of the lesson, usually stated in the form of a question. The teacher then proceeds to ask "pivotal questions" based on the material the students have been assigned to read. These questions are designed to promote "socialization"; that is, one student makes a statement relevant to the assigned material, and this comment provokes a strenuous response from another student, and then another, resulting in a stimulating discussion. Midway through the discussion, the teacher makes a "medial summary" of what has taken place, further discussion is designed to ensure classwide understanding of the topic, and the teacher elicits the statement that answers the original question. The discussion is then extended toward connecting what has been established as true for the particular material to other material or to life situations. This is known as the "outcome." I am certain that the developmental lesson would be effective if students have read an assignment and have come to class prepared to engage in discussion about it, but that was not my experience.

I spent hours preparing lessons, but my pivotal questions did not pivot, usually because for a variety of reasons most students had not read the assigned material. The few students who had read the assignment risked being mocked by their classmates if they responded to questions, so I usually had to abandon the plan and improvise. When I could not get responses to the assignment, I would ask direct questions about their opinions on anything: questions often, seldom, or not at all related to the text; a current event, a favorite musician, sports figure, anything to keep a leaden silence, or worse, the hum of separate conversations, from overtaking us. Once I had the students expressing their opinions, I worked to get them to listen to each other's point of view. I felt I had succeeded if I could select a comment that a number of students could respond to and then create a volley, bouncing a statement with a point of view or concept from one to another, probing with "what-do-you-think" questions, until a true discussion, or "socialization" took place. When I found the right comment, question, or response that could move them from anecdote to concept to thesis, I would say, "Now I'd like you to spend the next ten minutes writing a paragraph on . . . ." A collective groan would go up, but the silence that followed signaled the energy of students thinking and putting thoughts on paper.

Among the faculty, I again found cynicism, expressed vividly by one teacher to a newcomer: "You'll like it here; you don't have to do any work." However, I did find a cohort at the high school, a group of mostly young teachers who also became my friends. We partied together, went to films and plays together—sometimes with groups of students—but we also shared our concerns about being effective teachers. We asked each other for help and offered each other suggestions for good practices. We worked to create a meaningful classroom experience and encouraged promising students to find their strengths and establish goals. Our pleasure when we led students to an appreciation—even an excitement—about their studies, and to a consideration of education beyond high school was often blunted when promising students were forced by a parent's loss of job, desertion of family, illness, or death to abandon their plans.

Another obstacle was lack of support. A colleague who declared, "When I close my classroom door, I shut everything else out. I'm in charge," failed to recognize that she could not control what the students faced when that classroom door opened again, and the students went on to other, less able and caring teachers, or to their homes and community. With a complacent administration and a lethargic faculty, a band of dedicated teachers' best efforts will produce only limited gains. One veteran teacher spoke of how good the school had been in its early years under its first principal, Leonard Covello. I read Covello's book, *The Heart Is the Teacher*, and learned that under Covello's tenure, the school had been open day and evening; teachers and students interacted with the community and involved parents took classes and assisted in their children's education.

I was becoming increasingly and stressfully aware of New York's educational, economic, and social inequity—and of the racism at its roots—but, along with my concerned colleagues, I did not know how to improve the situation. Many New Yorkers at the time were complacently certain that economic and social conditions for black people in the North were generally good. Activism was muted, but my Methodist upbringing had instilled in me a commitment to social justice that required me to act where I could. During the first strike called in New York on behalf of District 1199—a union representing mostly minority hospital workers—I marched on its picket line. I became a "checker" for an organization that uncovered discrimination against minority tenants; on weekends I would pair up with an African-American woman and we would separately respond to advertisements for rental apartments. We would later report the manager's or landlord's response—uniformly positive for me and negative for my partner—back to the organization. I felt these were isolated and not very effective efforts, but soon a major national event led to my participation in a significant struggle against injustice.

The 1954 Supreme Court ruling against segregation in *Brown v. Board of Education* ignited a resistance movement in the South; in Prince Edward County, Virginia, segregationists organized as the Defenders of State Sovereignty and Individual Liberty established the Prince Edward Educational Corporation and launched a subscription drive to support private schools for white children.[1] In mid-1959, Prince Edward County administrators closed all the public schools, and in September opened the Prince Edward Academy and admitted only the county's white children. A number of options were offered to the black students shut out of school. Special courses designed for upper-level high school students were offered at Kitrell College near Henderson, North Carolina. A number of children attended charity-run, elementary-level educational centers. For children whose parents were willing to send them out of state, the American Friends Service Committee arranged for them to board with Northern families, both black and white, and attend integrated schools. And an unknown number of children were "bootlegged" to schools in other counties.[2] However, the great majority of black children in Prince Edward County were without schooling altogether, to become "part of a Lost Generation whose formal education ended abruptly, or never began."[3]

In the spring of 1963, I responded when Richard Parrish, an African-American officer of the United Federation of Teachers (UFT), recruited teachers for a "freedom school" project in Prince Edward County. After the school year ended, thirty UFT teachers and sixteen Queens College students, led by their professor, Dr. Rachel Weddington, journeyed to Farmville, Virginia, where, with funds contributed to the UFT for our sustenance, we shared bedrooms and boarded at the homes of local African-American families. Supported by the community led by Reverend L. Francis Griffin, we set up elementary-level classes in the rooms of eight local black churches. Throughout the summer, the UFT teachers, the Queens College students, and Dr. Weddington met regularly to plan curriculum and teaching methods. Although the curriculum included small-group study of basic mathematics and remedial English skills, the emphasis of the Freedom School curriculum was on analyzing the social conditions under which the students lived and, through discussion and questioning, identifying the obstacles to their progress and envisioning ways to overcome them.

Although I had not taught young children before, the children I was assigned to teach who had not yet entered school responded to our basic reading-writing-arithmetic curriculum. However, the curriculum overwhelmed the students—two or three boys as I remember—who had been shut out of the school for four years. They looked up in dismay when, among younger and smaller children who were quickly acquiring skills, they were confronted by words they could no longer recognize and arithmetic problems they could no longer solve. Embarrassed, ashamed, and seeing themselves as sinners rather than the sinned against, the shut-out students often gave up the attempt to reacquire skills they had lost.

Reverend Griffin had made us aware that children who had started school prior to the closing would be more damaged than children who had not attended school, but I had not anticipated the extent of harm that deprivation had caused these students. Although I worked with them, I lacked the skills to restore their confidence. They needed one-on-one counseling, and I regret that beyond encouraging them to come to school and providing them just the amount of individual attention that would not cause them further embarrassment, I could not do not much in three weeks' time to remedy their loss. Indeed, a study of the impact of school closings on black children in Prince Edward Country conducted by

Dr. Robert Green and a team from Michigan State University found that short-term remedial programs such as we had established had only "minor effects."[4]

By 1963, the school closings had taken a heavy toll on the the county's black children; the children sent to out-of-state schools were deeply homesick and the children in the educational centers had experienced deterioration in terms of quality of instruction and physical plant. The black community's mood of resistance had sharpened, and, under the leadership of Reverend Griffin, they staged demonstrations. I attended one of the mass meetings, and afterward witnessed a confrontation outside the church that revealed the black community was not entirely unified. An old man was surrounded by several teenagers, who were in a heated argument with him. I did not hear what the argument was about, but someone nearby explained to me that the young people were the old man's grandchildren, angered because he was a "Tom" who regularly informed on black activists to Farmville's white power structure, and would, they knew, report to his bosses what had been said and done at the mass meeting. However, sustained pressure within the community and from the NAACP was having an effect, and in September 1964, Prince Edward County administrators reopened the schools and admitted all students. Of the children who had been denied education for five years, Dr. Green's study predicted that such deprivation would have "irreversible effects" and that their skill development "would never attain a normal level."[5]

We worked hard during our weeks in Farmville, but there were diversions. With Dr. Weddington as our leader, a group of us went one Saturday into Richmond, where we enjoyed looking at paintings in the Museum of Fine Arts. The civilized experience made us forget we were in the heart of the Confederacy, but we were sharply reminded of our situation when we attempted to have dinner together at a Chinese restaurant. When the Chinese proprietor angrily refused to serve an integrated group, we left, unaware that two plainclothed policemen, who had been in the restaurant when we entered, were following us in a car. We tried to eat at another Chinese restaurant where the proprietor was willing to serve us, but the plainclothes policemen came into the restaurant and instructed him not to serve us. Again we left, and outside the restaurant, the policemen told us that we should get out of town before something happened to us, because "cars in Richmond drive very fast." We quickly got into our cars and drove away, with the policemen following us all the way out of Richmond.

On another excursion, the entire Freedom School group—teachers and students—went by bus to a lake outside of Farmville, because black people were refused access to swimming pools and lakes in the town. It was a very pleasant day, made more satisfying by the awareness that our beach and lake access were upstream from the segregated beach in Farmville. I heard someone say that the beach and the surrounding trees had been created by the Civilian Conservation Corps during the Depression. My father had been away from home for a year when I was young—like J. C. Fairley in Mississippi—working on a CCC project. However, my father never wanted to speak of it, out of the shame of being out of work that afflicted so many men in that time. I wanted to believe that he had helped to build this lovely resort. (Even under the New Deal, the races were separated, and my father could never have worked in the same CCC project as Fairley.)

We volunteers spent most evenings entertaining ourselves on one or another front porch. One evening as I approached the home where Norma Becker, a junior high school social studies teacher was staying, I saw a tall, young, African-American man speaking to my colleagues. He was Ivanhoe Donaldson, a Michigan State University student–turned staff member of SNCC, describing plans for a mobilization in Mississippi the following summer over the issues of voter registration and inferior, segregated schools. Norma and I stayed long to talk with Ivanhoe; the conversation would lead to our commitment to organize New York City teachers to participate in a "freedom school" project in Mississippi in the summer of 1964.

In late autumn, Norma and I began to prepare for Freedom Summer. We met with the Human Relations Committee of our union to request sponsorship of our proposal to recruit teachers for schools at safe sites in Mississippi and to raise funds to support our project. Anticipating possible objections, we had prepared our presentation carefully, but to our surprise, the committee quickly approved our proposal and passed it on to the union's executive committee, which also gave us its approval. During the winter Norma and I were actively involved in recruiting teachers and raising funds for books, supplies, car rentals, and our support in Mississippi. We were also in regular communication with the SNCC staff in New York and in Jackson, Mississippi about plans for the summer.

During the time Norma and I were in Farmville, Virginia, Charlie Cobb, a Howard University student, was director of a COFO project in Greenville, Mississippi; his partners in the "operation" were, in addition to other COFO workers and college volunteers down for the summer, members of the Greenville Student Movement who had been "recruited off the block, in the pool halls, and out of the cafes and juke joints, and were probably the wildest crew of working freedom fighters in the state." The crew had "toned themselves down considerably over the past couple of months," although they continued to test the COFO staff with a taunting comment—"You're nonviolent, huh?"—accompanied by a threatening gesture that was followed by laughter. Cobb's respectful, purposeful recruitment of these students had transformed them from what today would be called "at risk" young people into dedicated workers, and Cobb prophesied that "one day, some day," they would be leaders of the movement.[6] Cobb's appreciation of the talents of students, who had been subjected to an educational system "geared to squash intellectual curiosity" flowed into a formal proposal he put forward later that year that included a statewide system of freedom schools within the summer project then being planned. Cobb envisioned a six-week program in July and August for tenth and eleventh graders that would provide them with 1) skills "they are not learning in high schools around the state," 2) a "broad intellectual and academic experience," and 3) "a basis for state-wide student action such as a school boycott."[7]

Cobb foresaw the freedom school curriculum dealing with several areas: 1) supplementary education, such as grammar, reading, math, typing, and history; 2) cultural programs in dance, art, music appreciation drama, and writing; 3) political and social science relating to their own society; and 4) films and other special projects such as a student newspaper and a statewide freedom school conference. "If we are concerned about breaking down the power structure," Cobb reasoned, "then we have to be concerned about building our own institutions to replace the old, unjust, decadent ones which make up the existing power structure."[8]

Persuaded by the support Cobb's proposal drew in communities with adult activists and high school students in the COFO-sponsored Mississippi Student Union, the COFO staff decided to include the program in the summer project, and a Summer Steering Committee consisting of Cobb, Mendy Samstein, Penny Patch, and Lois Chaffee, was created to establish the Freedom School component of the summer project.[9] Lois Chaffee was charged with organizing a curriculum conference, which, with funding from the National Council of Churches, would be held in New York City on March 21st and 22nd. Assisted by Jim Monsonis and Julia Prettyman in SNCC's New York office, Chaffee located a meeting place, identified good people to invite ("hard-working people who know about curriculum, especially if they're in the New York area and won't cost us anything"), arranged housing for out-of-towners, and planned eating arrangements ("we'd like to spend as little of our money on food as possible, but people have to eat").[10] Chaffee learned that Ella Baker of Southern Christian Leadership Conference was planning to attend the conference. She invited Baker, who had gathered sit-in leaders to a meeting Raleigh, North Carolina in 1960 for what became the founding of SNCC, to chair the conference because Baker's skill in getting "people thinking in the right directions, in a very few minutes" would avoid having "a bunch of good minds spend two days . . . thinking great thoughts but not actually producing a curriculum."[11] And thus, with material enclosed in an undated letter from Chaffee—an agenda, instructions, a proposed daily schedule for the Freedom Schools, a preliminary curriculum outline, and the Freedom School prospectus—53 conferees gathered in the District 65 Union Hall on Astor Place on Saturday, March 21st.[12]

The participants included Art Thomas and Robert Spike of the National Council of Churches; Staughton Lynd from Spelman College's History Department; Noel Day from Roxbury, Massachusetts, designer of the curriculum for the February 1964 Freedom Day protest against segregated schools in Boston;

Septima Clark and Bayard Rustin of SCLC; Dr. Rachel Weddington of Queens College; Dr. Robert Green of the University of Michigan; Myles Horton of the Highlander School; Velma McLin, a remedial reading specialist in the Tougaloo College Education department; Ira Landess, Norma Becker and me from the UFT; and John O'Neal, Charles Cobb, Robert Moses, Dona Moses, Mendy Samstein, and Lois Chaffee from COFO. For two days (with time out, after all, for much needed breaks and noon meals), the conferees divided into four groups, and following an outline, planned curriculum for improving students' educational needs in four basic areas:

(1) Leadership development—to provide students with the history of the struggle for social and economic justice; to educate them on the goals of the civil rights movement; and to develop their skills in public speaking, dealing with the public, managing finances, canvassing, and keeping financial records and report.

(2) Remedial academic program—to improve reading, writing, and math skills; to supplement students' knowledge of American history, economics, and politics; to introduce students to art, music, and literature; and to enable students to use scientific methods.

(3) Contemporary issues—to introduce students to more sophisticated views of current issues; to enable them to see local problems within the context of national problems; and to acquaint them with research techniques.

(4) Non-academic curriculum—to enable students to form networks with peers; to enable students to develop organizational and leadership skills in voter registration, student publications, and student government; and to develop their skills in expressing themselves informally in creative writing, spontaneous discussions, drama, and talent shows.[13]

We spent the first day developing general course outlines in each area and the second day working on the content; members of each group were charged with responsibility for submitting conference reports to Lois Chaffee within a week. The Leadership group divided into two sub-committees. One subcommittee developed the outline for the curriculum that, with the addition of an introductory lesson on the Amistad, became the "Guide to Negro History," and the second group developed the outline for what became the "Citizenship Curriculum."

I was a member of a group that had originally been established to prepare a remedial curriculum, but we decided that we preferred to develop a list of resources and procedures that could be included in a general course of study. I was charged with creating material for developing language skills, and submitted a paper in which I emphasized the importance of "cohesiveness and cooperation" among Freedom School teachers and advocated that they work as a team to integrate academic skills with actual experiences.

> If . . . the group of students plan to canvass, the language arts phase of the program could concentrate on an appropriate verbal skill, the social studies area could be devoted to the study of the population to be canvassed in terms of economic, social, religious factors and the implications of those factors, the math area could be given over to statistical breakdown, charts, etc.

I stated that the value of the Freedom School experience "will derive from what the teachers are able to elicit from the students in terms of comprehension and expression of their experiences. The classroom groups will be small; the social interaction between teacher and students will be as important as academic instruction."

I included a list of suggestions for procedures and activities to enhance reading and writing skills. Suggested verbal activities included informal discussion, with students reporting events, summarizing the day's activities and discussing issues from different points of view; reading aloud, developing verbal skills in real life situations, such as asking directions and giving instructions; and developing persuasive skills through improvisations of real life situations.

Suggested writing activities included summaries of discussions, endings to stories, reports for newspapers, persuasive handbills, business and social letters, and poetry. Recommended reading activities included reading newspaper reports, magazine articles, and short stories. Activities for improving reading comprehension included substituting selected words from an article with words of similar meaning, or having students derive meanings of words from their context.

I also suggested a number of related activities to improve students' skills: drawing pictures to illustrate stories, poems, and experiences; listening to stories and poems; teaching one another; holding problem-solving discussions; following instructions, as in a recipe; drawing and reading maps; interpreting tables; using indexes and tables of contents; attempting short homework assignments and tests; and when "attention lags," switching to another kind of activity.

Ira Landess provided ideas for some games for developing skills. One I liked involved clipping words, sentences, and paragraphs from magazines or newspapers and using them to write a story about a picture taken from a magazine; the words were to be pasted on a piece of paper, with no other words being written. Another of Ira's suggestions was to adapt games such as Twenty Questions to summarize class activities, "or just make a break if a session gets dull."

With respect to pedagogy, I urged that classroom activities "not be dealt with as fragmented, isolated parts of a program; one activity should flow naturally from another." I warned against flooding students with information in the lecture mode; "the formal classroom is to be avoided," I insisted, for "questioning is the vital tool. . . . . Questioning is the path to enlightenment."[14]

My report, with some editing; a math diagnostic and a set of increasingly difficult math problems; and suggested outlines for teaching physics, chemistry, astronomy and biology completed the academic curriculum.[15] Of course, volunteer teachers adapted the curriculum to the needs of the students, improvised, or brought their teaching materials with them.

In the workshops, people were diligent about developing material of high quality for Freedom Schools students. However, when the conference met as a whole, Norma and I were unsettled by the impression we both received that at least some of the COFO staff regarded the schools as training grounds for activism, as subordinate to the function of canvassing for voters. Our commitment to the educational purpose of the Mississippi Freedom Schools was derived from our experience in New York. Both Norma and

I taught in schools that served primarily minority students and understood the importance of making students serious about their roles as learners. Our concern for providing a good educational summer program was intensified by having witnessed in Prince Edward County the damage done to students who had been shut out of school.

I offered to share my apartment with a conferee, and Lois Chafee arranged for Velma McLin to be my guest. Because of flight problems, she did not arrive until after 2 a.m. Half asleep, I showed her to her room and returned to bed. We shared some meals together, but, in the intensity of the conference, did not spend much time getting to know one another. Shortly after the conference, I received a note from Velma, thanking me for having her as a guest, and stating that she had never in her life received such kind treatment from a white person, and had not thought it was possible. That my basic bed-and-breakfast hospitality was ranked so high in her experience saddened me.

Shortly after the curriculum conference, Lois Chaffee and John O'Neal asked Staughton Lynd to be administrator of the Freedom School program.[16] In the weeks following the conference, a vast amount of curriculum material was sent to the Jackson COFO office, including lesson plans for teaching science, English language skills, social studies, and mathematics. With the good manners of a well-bred radical, Chaffee promptly wrote thank-you letters to all the conference participants.[17] However, as "a bit of a worrier," she also wrote nagging letters to those who were tardy in submitting curriculum. She ended these letters with the sentence, "I hope this reaches you just as you're finishing, so you can send it off with an especially strong feeling of righteous satisfaction."[18]

The Summer Program Committee took all the material that was submitted, and, as Liz Fusco, a volunteer teacher in Ruleville who succeeded Lynd as Freedom School administrator after the summer, later wrote,

[t]he curriculum for the proposed schools became everyone's concern. I understand that Lois Chaffee, Dona Moses, Mendy Samstein, and Casey Hayden, as well as Noel Day, Jane Stembridge, and Jack Minnis worked on and argued about what should be

taught, and what the realities of Mississippi are, and how those realities affect the kids, and how to get the kids to recognize themselves
as human beings. And then, I understand, Staughton Lynd came in
to impose a kind of beautiful order on the torment that the curriculum was becoming.[19]

The many curriculum drafts recorded on the SNCC microfilms
reveal the passion the young Summer Project Staff members
brought to their Promethean task while surviving on less than ten
dollars a week, living in disordered quarters, working under threat
of attack, and traveling in danger of arrest. In daylong and night-
long sessions, guides, lesson plans, and case studies were criticized,
amended, discarded, and rewritten in a mission to create an educational model capable of raising the consciousness of the black youth
of Mississippi "that begins on the level of the students' everyday
lives . . . and builds up to a more realistic perception of American
society, themselves, the condition of their oppression, and the alternatives offered by the Freedom Movement."[20]

However, the process of creation, when it ended at last, was followed by a rushed, often futile, effort to print the documents in
time for distribution to the volunteer teachers before or during orientation sessions scheduled for late June. Part of what Staughton
Lynd wrested from the Committee was enclosed in a letter of
acceptance—a second letter with additional curriculum materials
was promised—to volunteer Freedom School teachers from Lynd
and his assistant, Harold Bardinelli. The first of the letter's six
enclosures was a memo from the Summer Project Staff, "Overview
of the Freedom Schools," advising volunteers that each school
would be located in a church, store front, or home, and consist of
five to fifteen teachers and twenty-five to fifty students. Teachers
would be involved in academic work, recreation and cultural activities, and leadership development. The Summer Project
Committee hoped that students would be "involved in the political
life of their communities," with teachers "free to participate in these
activities." A typical day's schedule would likely be "concentrated
individual work" from 7 to 9 a.m., academic work from 9 to noon,
non-academic work, such as recreation, cultural activities, and
"some tutoring," in the afternoon; then the evening from 7 to 9

could be devoted to voter registration activities, or a special event, perhaps a visiting folk singer; and then the teachers were expected to develop a weekly schedule and a daily lesson plan.[21]

The second enclosure, "Notes on Teaching in Mississippi" was a collaborative effort to prepare young college student-volunteers for a challenge they had never faced. Jane Stembridge wrote that the purpose of the Freedom Schools is "to help the students begin to question"; and warned that because the students "will have in common the scars of the system" they have been taught not to trust; and the key to the volunteers' successful teaching will be "honesty and creativity." Charlie Cobb wrote that learning for black students in Mississippi "means only learning to stay in your place" and that "silence is safest"; nevertheless, students were waiting to "reach out and meet, and join together, and to change." Mendy Samstein instructed the volunteers that the effectiveness of the Freedom Schools depended on their resourcefulness, honesty, "ability to relate sympathetically to the students . . . and to create an exciting 'learning' atmosphere." The most concrete part of the document was Noel Day's "Remarks to the Freedom School Teachers About Method."

The first section, "Teaching Hints," provided basic stratagems such as preparing for each lesson; relating material to the students' experiences; providing easily visible visual aids and allowing students to help develop them where possible; summarizing a lesson at the end of a session and at the beginning of the next; keeping the atmosphere informal and the language simple; and avoiding being too critical at first, and not allowing any expression of hostile or aggressive feelings to be passed over. In the second section, "Discussion-Leading Techniques," Day recommended opening discussions with questions that should be simply and clearly phrased, in easily understood language, and "not answerable by 'yes' or 'no'." Day explained that the best types of questions explored an emotional response ("how did you feel when?"), investigated motivation ("why would you do that?"), and responded to others' reactions ("what do you think about what Bob said?"). Some of Day's other useful recommendations for inexperienced teacher volunteers were: to summarize occasionally what has been said; to encourage participation by using small groups and appointing silent students as reporters; and to change activities, particularly those involving physical movement, when interests lag.[22]

The third enclosure with the acceptance letter was an impossible-to-fill list of materials and equipment, some of which were "must bring," some were "try to bring," and some were "try to send for distribution to the schools." The "must bring" list included, in addition to pencils, ball-point pens, and lined paper pads, a first aid kit, one item of sports equipment, a typewriter, typing paper, and one "quire" of four-hole stencils for an A.B. Dick or Gestetner mimeograph machine. The "try to bring" items included a blackboard, chalk, bulletin boards, a camera and film, and a dictionary, and books of interest to high school students. The "try to send" items included a mimeograph machine with stencils, paper, ink, and correction fluid; tape recorders and tape; film projectors and films; strip projectors and film strips; poster construction paper and rolls of newsprint; and envelopes in bulk.[23]

The last three enclosures contained general information on the Mississippi Summer Project: a statement of the need to raise at least five hundred dollars to support each student volunteer; a description of the COFO program as a cooperative effort by SNCC, CORE, SCLC, and the NAACP to function politically in Mississippi through statewide and district organizations; and background on the Mississippi Freedom Democratic Party and its plans to challenge the seating of the Mississippi delegation at the 1964 National Democratic Convention in Atlantic City.[24]

Another mailing on May 20 from Lynd and Bardinelli stated that because of the large number of volunteers, two orientation sessions would be held at Western College for Women in Oxford, Ohio: the first on June 21 and the second on June 27. (Another orientation session was later set up in Memphis which the New York City teachers and other teacher volunteers attended.) The letter informed volunteer teachers that the curriculum materials were being printed, but would not be available until the teachers arrived for orientation; however, it assured volunteers that the list of the six units of the curriculum included in the letter, together with the overview and teachers' notes they had previously received, would be of some help. The letter instructed the volunteer teachers to follow "a question-and-answer method and use the curriculum as a guide from which they "should feel free to depart."[25] The units of the Civic Curriculum, set forth an incremental structure, with each unit building on the information of the previous unit, were listed as:

1. An examination of the student's situation in Mississippi
2. Consideration of the situation of the Negro in the North
3. Survey of some myths and inconsistencies in the dominant "white culture"
4. A study of the power structure of Mississippi and of the power of the Dixiecrats in Congress
5. Comparison of the plight of the poor Negro and the poor white
6. The Movement

The volunteers were assured that case studies would be provided as background information "to help make your presentation of these topics more concrete and vivid." These included a statistical analysis of black Mississippians' housing, health, education and economic status; an analysis of the Mississippi power structure; a study of freedom rides and sit-ins; and case studies on the civil rights bill and school boycotts in the North. Other curriculum materials promised were on "remedial and specialized instruction in conventional academic subjects, and the widest possible exploration of the arts." The volunteer student-teachers were asked to bring any materials they could assemble on the topics of the citizenship curriculum, along with novels, magazine pictures, teaching aids, and ideas for creative work with small groups.[26]

An introduction to the curriculum added two sets of questions intended to be reintroduced at "appropriate points" in the units in order to evaluate the effectiveness of the curriculum and teaching methods, and to provide "students with recurring opportunities for perceiving their own growth in sophistication." The Basic Set of questions was:

1. Why are we (teachers and students) in Freedom School?
2. What is the Freedom Movement?
3. What alternatives does the Freedom Movement offer us?

The Secondary Set of questions was:

1. What do "white people" (the majority culture) have that we want?

2. What do "white people have" that we don't want?
3. What do we have that we want to keep?[27]

The Civic Curriculum contained in the May 20th letter from Lynd and Bardinelli, in another version contained seven units. Unit I, "Comparing the Students' Reality With Others," began at the base of the students' reality: their schools. Students were asked to move from basic questions about the number of grades their schools had, the conditions of the textbooks, and whether they had access to a library and gymnasium to questions about what they learned, what number of students went on to college, and what kinds of jobs they were prepared for. The unit then invited them to examine the conditions in the white schools and the reasons why those schools were better. Explorations of housing, employment, and medical facilities continued the process of examining differences between conditions for Negroes and those of whites and exploring the reasons for those differences.[28]

Unit II, "North to Freedom," established that conditions for whites with respect to schools, housing, employment, and medical facilities in the North were better than conditions for Negroes: The conclusion, therefore, was that "migration to the North is not a basic solution."[29]

Unit III, "Examining the Apparent Reality," explored the limitations of the "better life" whites enjoyed: they were not taught about other cultures in their schools, nor did they realize that not all people in this country enjoyed freedom and justice.[30]

Unit IV, "Introducing the Power Structure," developed awareness of the Southern power structure's manipulation of the myths of white superiority and Negro inferiority and maintenance of seniority by Southern members of in Congress to maintain political and economic power.[31]

Unit V, "Poor Negroes and Poor Whites," examined the Southern power structure's maintenance of control through Jim Crow laws and the perpetuation of myths that kept Negroes and whites from joining together in their own interests.[32]

Unit VI, "Material Things versus Soul Things," addressed the inadequacy of "pure materialism" to create a better world.

The unit established that to build a good society, ethical values in individuals were necessary.[33]

Unit VII, "The Movement," explored the history of the sit-ins and the freedom rides and foretold that the Negro people of Mississippi would change society through learning in freedom schools what is never taught them in segregated schools; through demanding the right to vote; and through supporting Freedom Democratic Party candidates for office.[34]

The Committee's third important curriculum package, Guide to Negro History, included a series of lessons provided by the Amistad Society that began with a synopsis of the Amistad mutiny. Subsequent lessons dealt with the cultural and political life in Africa before the destructive impact of the slave trade, the conditions on the ships that transported the slaves, slave revolts, the abolition movement, and analyses of the Amistad case and the court system.[35]

The Amistad lessons provided background for a detailed four-part study of the history of African Americans in the United States. Part One of the curriculum, "Origins of Prejudice," made the claim that because of the Founding Fathers' economic dependence on slavery, slaves were regarded as property, and thus slavery was protected in the United States Constitution. Part Two, "Negro Resistance to Oppression," recounted major slave revolts in this country and presented the conditions of slavery through passages from the accounts of Frederick Douglass, Harriet Tubman, and Booker T. Washington.[36]

Part Three, "Reconstruction (1865–1877) and the Beginning of Segregation," presented the accomplishments of Reconstruction—the Thirteenth, Fourteenth, and Fifteenth Amendments; education and enfranchisement for blacks—and attributed the failure of Reconstruction to lack of support from the Supreme Court and President Andrew Johnson's policy of 1865 to restore power to the secessionists. The struggle of Thaddeus Stevens and Charles Sumner to preserve Reconstruction was described and myths about Reconstruction—that the South was overrun by federal troops and illiterate Negroes were given the vote, for example—were refuted.[37]

This section of the Negro History Guide was revelatory, for it documented the well hidden history of Mississippi's rescission of the freedmen's gains in the post-Reconstruction era through four plans. Plan 1 (1865–1867) gave black people the right to marry and to inherit property, but denied them the right to vote, thus keeping them in a state of docile dependence on white employers. Under Plan 2 (1867–1874), a constitutional convention provided for universal manhood suffrage, public education, property rights for women, the end of imprisonment for debt, and the outlawing of discrimination in public accommodations. However, the economic subjugation of black people was not ended, for they were still subject to arrest for vagrancy and dismissal by employers for meeting in their own self interest. Plan 3 (1874–1890) began with the overthrow by white reactionaries of the constituted state government, followed by a period of violence against and intimidation of black people. Under Plan 4 (1890–1964), a constitutional convention disenfranchised blacks without violating the Fifteenth Amendment by requiring a poll tax and a demonstrated ability to read the state constitution; similar voting regulations were adopted throughout the South and were upheld by the Supreme Court in *Williams v. Mississippi* in 1898.[38]

While the details of the summer program were being worked out by the COFO staff in Jackson, SNCC staff workers—Betty Garman, Carol Rogoff, and Dinky Romilly in Atlanta; Julia Prettyman and Jim Monsonis in New York—coordinated the establishment of "Friends of SNCC" groups in cities and on campuses across the country. These groups raised money for SNCC and also collected contributions of novels and poetry by black authors, books on African and African-American history, mathematics, science, and language arts for the community center libraries and Freedom Schools that were then sent down to SNCC staff, along with food and clothing they arranged to be shipped down to community leaders.[39]

Staff in SNCC's regional offices in Boston, New York, Philadelphia, and Atlanta, along with Friends of SNCC groups, actively recruited on campuses volunteers for the Freedom Schools and voter registration drive. Students who responded were asked to supply, on four-page applications, information about their education and work experience, their local newspapers, community organizations, Congressional representatives and Senators, their skills, areas of interest in the summer program, their previous arrests if any, and the names of five references.[40] Friends of SNCC groups recruited ministers, psychiatrists, civic leaders, and academics to interview the volunteers and evaluate favorably volunteers with experience in community work, health care, or the arts. Interviewers also looked for a strong belief in the civil rights movement, a willingness to admit doubts and fears about going to Mississippi, and an understanding that risks involved jail and beatings. Volunteers who were excessively nervous, or who held extremely dogmatic views could be hazardous to themselves as well as to others and were to be rejected.[41]

To support the 1,000 or more volunteers expected in Mississippi, the SNCC network arranged for legal assistance needs in the summer from the Law Students Project, the Lawyers' Constitutional Defense Committee, and the National Lawyers Guild. At COFO's request, a Medical Committee for Human Rights was established that channeled physicians, psychiatrists, nurses, and dentists to serve volunteers and local people in Canton, Clarksdale, Greenwood, Hattiesburg, Meridian, Jackson, and McComb. The National Council of Churches recruited four hundred ministers to work around the state on a rotating basis as counselors to volunteers.[42]

As time neared for the summer project to begin, Betty Garman sent a memo exhorting the Friends of SNCC groups to intensify their fund-raising efforts because "the situation is desperate." Garman asked the groups for names of people willing to receive emergency calls "in the middle of the night if necessary, and collect if necessary," and to send lists of radio and TV stations and newspapers "that give regular and fair coverage to civil rights events" who would receive collect calls from the South for "a newsworthy incident."[43]

All these activities indicate the intense anxiety within SNCC about bringing down 1,000 volunteers to a hostile and dangerous situation. Meanwhile, Norma and I were involved in recruitment, raising funds for our support and car rentals, preparing instructions, and arranging for shipments of books and supplies. We were pleased with the response. Forty teachers answered our summons for volunteers, and people inside and outside the teaching community made generous contributions. A number of teachers at the high school where I taught were responsive; however, I shall never forget the question, indicative of the spirit of the time, that one male colleague asked me: "When are you going to use all that energy, Sandra, to take care of some man?"

On a Friday in June, Norma and I, anxious because we had not had clear directions from the COFO staff, flew to Jackson to find out where we were leading the forty teachers who had volunteered to staff the Freedom Schools. We were met by two COFO workers, Penny Patch and Eric Johansson, and brought to the COFO office on Lynch Street. The glass windows of the office had been completely smashed on a previous evening, but fortunately no one had been injured. When and if money became available for a carpenter, the front would be boarded up. The workers in the office sat at desks or at cubby holes built again the wall, telephoned or typed, or just wandered about. We knew Ivanhoe Donaldson from the previous summer in Prince Edward County, and had been in contact with Charles Cobb, Penny Patch, and Mendy Samstein—coordinators of the summer project—since February, but now we were confronting them in the chaos that was their way of life.

Norma and I persuaded Mendy to put down the telephone that seemed attached to his ear and drive us to a local restaurant where we pressed him to tell us what was expected of the volunteer teachers in the summer.

"Oh, for example, you might get to know people by going out to the field to pick cotton."

"But we're teachers. You don't seem to understand that teaching, even under the most informal of conditions, requires preparation and time to think. You seem to expect that we'll get up at six, go out and do chores, teach all morning, turn out lessons during the noon recess, provide recreation in the afternoon, go out to do voter registration work, and go to rallies in the evening."

"No, but you have to be flexible. You have a Northern structured, organizational point of view. There will be time for preparation, but you won't be effective if you isolate yourself from the community. You have to get to know the people, go to meetings with them, go to church with them."

"What if you're Jewish?"
"I'm Jewish and I've made my peace with the situation. If you
    want the program to be successful, you have to go where the
    people are. And religion is the center of their lives."
"Are we expected to participate in the voter registration drive?"
"That's up to you. You may be challenged. Your students may
    wonder why you aren't out there with them."

Norma and I were alarmed. The conflict between the Freedom
School program and the voter registration drive that had been evi-
dent at the curriculum conference was reappearing. However, as we
talked, moving from the restaurant to the "Freedom House" apartment where the staff lived, arguing until 2:30 a.m. (4:30 a.m. New
York time), we began to understand that the key word was "flexible."
We volunteer teachers would have to meet the educational needs of
our students while at the same time creating personal bonds with
them and their parents. Our resources as human beings were as
important as our gifts as teachers, and when we had adapted what
we had to what was needed, a Freedom School would "happen."

After Norma and I spent the rest of the night in the staff's
Freedom House, we rented a car on Saturday morning, and
Ivanhoe drove us out to Tougaloo College. Norma visited Hellen
O'Neal, who had been working on a literacy project there, and I
visited Velma McLin. Lois and Penny had wanted to come with us,
but were told to remain at the office. The broken windows were evidence of external danger, but white female workers were made to
bear the brunt of enforced circumspection.

In the afternoon, a group of COFO staff and volunteers,
Ivanhoe among them, boarded a bus for Washington to urge that
federal protection be provided during the summer. Norma and I
again dragged Mendy from a telephone and—at our insistence—
with Penny, drove to a town where one of our centers would be
located. A truck had arrived with cartons of books, and we helped
people the unload them into the community center. On the way
back to Jackson, Mendy described the possible locations for
schools. We agreed on six, possibly seven locations (eventually there
were eight) where the support of the black community was strong,
where facilities and housing were available, and where the threat of

harassment was not great. When we returned to the COFO office, Norma pulled out the applications from the UFT volunteers, and we made tentative assignments, attempting to mesh the personalities and skills of individuals with each other and with the needs of the communities as Mendy described them. We included at least one driver in each group.

Then we dragged Mendy away from the telephone, got Penny and Bill (another volunteer), and returned to the restaurant where we had eaten the night before.

"What about the vigilante groups that have been forming?" Norma asked.

Penny giggled.

"What's so funny?"

"Nothing's funny. People have been killed; there will be violence, we can't make predictions, and I'm giggling."

By this time I had taken on a Southern point of view— disorganized and unstructured—and I was beginning to understand how one dealt with this bizarre world: I giggled.

We spent the night in Hellen O'Neal's house because Norma had refused to spend another night in the disorder of the Freedom House. Ron Kennedy, a volunteer from the University of Illinois, drove us there and returned for us the next morning. He had spent the night in the COFO office; for security, someone stayed there every night. We said goodbye, left a note for Mendy, who was still sleeping, and drove to the airport.

We had an hour stopover in Atlanta, so on Saturday we had called Staughton Lynd, who came to the airport with his wife, Alice, Howard Bardinelli, and Harold's friend Diane Hill. They brought materials that had evolved from the March curriculum conference, and we discovered that Staughton was our ally in support of the educational function of the schools. The Freedom Schools, Staughton had made clear to the COFO staff, were to have status in and of themselves and were not to serve merely as an adjunct to political activities.

Norma and I met with the New York volunteers before our departure for Mississippi, and with a clear conscience, reported our findings and shared with them our sense that our mission, though dangerous, had a truly important educational purpose. We had all received a copy of a recent memo from the Summer Project Committee advising us to have bond money ready in the event of our arrests; informing us of the orientation sessions that would be held prior to our entry into Mississippi; urging us to contribute funds to the project; and pointing out that the leadership reserved the right to "deselect" any summer worker during orientation or "to ask people to leave Mississippi at any time during the summer."[44]

The seriousness of the venture we were undertaking was reinforced at a meeting for volunteers sponsored by the National Council of Churches at their imposing, corporate-seeming headquarters on Riverside Drive. The message that the SNCC leaders were emphasizing was the risk and danger involved in volunteering for service in Mississippi and, they assured us, withdrawing from the project was a reasonable choice. Their message added to the pressure Norma was already feeling, for her mother pleaded with her not to go to Mississippi, inflicting guilt by reminding Norma of her responsibility to her two young children. Norma was torn, but believed she could not in good conscience withdraw because she had persuaded others to risk themselves. Without dependents to be concerned about, I had already weighed the risk and was not frightened by the SNCC leaders' message. Never having seen the collegiate volunteers for the summer project, I was more involved at the NCC meeting in studying a number of Ivy Leaguers at the gathering who asked questions, then often responded to the answers with comments or other questions. These young men impressed me with the way they wore their privilege and confidence like a second skin.

In the days before we left New York, Norma and I were busy with last-minute preparations that included renting cars for use in the projects where UFT volunteers would be serving: Greenville, Gulfport, Hattiesburg, Holly Springs, Jackson and Meridian. (McComb, not originally designated as a UFT project because of its dangerous situation, was later added when a New York teacher volunteered to go there.) Norma wisely designated the UFT as the organization authorizing the rentals to avoid difficulty with local police officers in the event drivers were stopped and questioned.

In late June, immediately after the end of the school year, thirty-six New York teachers (four teachers would leave for Mississippi later) traveled by car or by Greyhound bus to Memphis, joining with other volunteers for a three-day orientation session at LeMoyne College. The UFT had sent out press releases, and city newspapers wrote articles about our mission. As we were departing on an endeavor not attempted since Reconstruction, a crew from a local television station gathered around us at the bus terminal, and a reporter sneeringly instructed, "Now, get out your musical instruments."

The volunteer students, whose classes ended earlier than the New York teachers' school calendar, went for their orientation at Western College for Women in Oxford, Ohio. A significant number of parents of Western College for Women students did not approve of the college's hosting the Freedom Summer orientation, with the result that enrollment at Western College dropped in the fall; the college was eventually closed, and its campus was absorbed within Miami University.

On our first night at LeMoyne, Elaine Weinburger, the director of the orientation, described the position of the white Mississippians: "In their eyes, they are Christian, God-fearing people; they are good citizens, and you are invaders." We all knew by then of the disappearance of the civil rights workers James Chaney, Andrew Goodman and Michael Schwerner. Our understanding that they had been killed cast a pall over the sessions, but I don't believe any volunteers withdrew from the project. Elaine spoke of Mickey Schwerner, attempting to tell us about a time riding with him and his wife Rita in "that blue station wagon." She did not finish the anecdote; the thinly held control broke, and she stopped speaking.

During the orientation sessions, we were to learn the political structure of Mississippi, including the character of the black and white communities with which we would be dealing, and how to cope nonviolently with the verbal and physical abuse we might experience. In a memorable session on non-violent resistance, we practiced rolling into a fetal position while protecting our heads in order to deal with a physical attack. We watched a role playing demonstration by Ivanhoe Donaldson as a sheriff and Curtis Hayes as a prisoner. We were riveted when Ivanhoe repeatedly asked questions: "Nigger, what you doin' here?" "Don't you say 'Sir' when you're spoken to?" "How's your mammy?" "How's your sister?" Ivanhoe was visibly ambivalent about his role, while Curtis's replies in a soft voice, with the required "Sir" held one beat, revealed his complete absorption.

On our last night in Memphis, we volunteers experienced a much-needed pleasure: a convivial meal at the 4-Way restaurant in the black community, where we devoured wonderful hamburgers and shared laughter-filled conversations having nothing to do with the Mississippi project.

Saturday, the Fourth of July, I left Memphis on a Greyhound bus for Hattiesburg with fellow UFT volunteers Ira Landess, Barbara Schwartzbaum, and Stan Zibulsky. Nowhere on the ride into the state did I see signs of celebration of our nation's birthday: no parades, no backyard family gatherings, not even an American flag. We passed a billboard on the highway that bore an endorsement by President Kennedy of support for mental health. Someone had hurled a can of black paint at the billboard, spattering it all over the late president's image. We stopped for lunch in Philadelphia, MS, which seemed as friendly as its name until one read the sign in front of the bus station: "White waiting room only by order of the Police. Philadelphia, Miss.," and remembered this was the town where Chaney, Goodman, and Schwerner had disappeared, and, we had no doubt, been murdered.

We new arrivals watched and listened as Mr. Dahmer showed us his cotton plants.

3. First Weeks of a Memorable Summer ᔐ

When we arrived at the Hattiesburg bus terminal in mid-afternoon, I telephoned the local COFO office to let the staff know of our arrival, and then called the COFO staff in Memphis to let them know we had arrived safely. Within minutes, Reverend Bob Beech, a volunteer with the Delta Ministry Project, arrived in a car to take us to Vernon Dahmer's farm for a picnic, the first sign I had seen that day of an event honoring our nation's independence. After months of soliciting funds, books, and other resources, and recruiting teachers, and planning curriculum—gripped at times with fear for my own and others' safety—I was astonished by the happiness I witnessed and experienced at that picnic. The photos taken by the photographer Herbert Randall, who remained in Hattiesburg through the summer, reflect the explosive joy at this truly revolutionary celebration by the COFO workers, summer volunteers, and those members of the black community, young and old, who had joined the Movement.

We new arrivals met and talked with people, ate catfish deep-fried in large dome-bottomed iron pots, watched and listened as Mr. Dahmer showed us his cotton plants, rode on a tractor-drawn flatbed, and sang freedom songs. It was a glorious and memorable day, but as dusk approached, it was necessary for everyone's safety to settle the question of our lodgings and move out. Victoria Jackson Gray, the candidate of the Freedom Democratic Party running against the Democratic incumbent Senator Stennis, quickly distributed us among her relatives who lived in a suburb of Hattiesburg, Palmer's Crossing, a community of proud, self-reliant people. I was taken to the home of Mrs. Addie Mae Jackson,

Victoria Jackson Gray's aunt, with whom I briefly became acquainted before falling into bed.

Sunday, I went with other volunteers into Hattiesburg to attend services at True Light Baptist Church. I had attended Baptist services in Farmville, Virginia where women were not prominent as church leaders. In True Light, a group of older women, wearing white uniforms, white gloves, and white bands around their heads, ushered congregants to their seats and led the responses to the minister's fiery calls to the people. After delivering his sermon, the minister, Reverend R. D. Ridgeway, took up a special collection for food for the teachers, reminding the congregation that they were "entertaining angels unawares."

The following day (Monday, July 6th), I walked in eager anticipation from Mrs. Jackson's home to the place where, at the Memphis orientation, I had been assigned to teach: Priest Creek Missionary Baptist Church, pastored by Rev. I. C. Allen. That first day was rather disorganized, but the forty to fifty students, mostly of high school age, were glad to see us and highly motivated to learn whatever we had to teach them. In addition to curriculum materials that had been sent to me, I had brought with me copies of newspaper articles and poems, tape recordings of greetings to the students from my New York City students, and books donated by publishers that had been sent to me in Hattiesburg through the UFT. I did not know what I would teach until I had an opportunity to plan with my colleagues, Joe Ellin, a philosophy instructor at Western Michigan University, and Yale student Bob Stone. That first morning we improvised. We introduced ourselves to the students, told something of what we did and why we came here, and attempted to generate discussions with the students, who were shy at first.

On the second day, we established a routine. The session began with a presentation: Bob Stone, standing earnestly before the students and forming a church steeple with the fingers of his hands, gave a summary of the Amistad revolt. We then broke into groups and dispersed to the Sunday school classrooms for follow-up discussions. Arthur Reese, an African-American school administrator from Detroit, had arrived early in the morning at Priest Creek. We knew that he and his wife Carolyn had been appointed supervisors of the Hattiesburg Freedom Schools, but this was our first visit—an unexpected one—from him. He taped Bob's presentation and the subsequent discussions in Joe Ellin's and my classrooms. At 11:30 we broke for lunch, a marvel of generosity: delicious and filling food donated and prepared for us that day and every day during our six-week session by women from the community.

After lunch that second day, Arthur Reese sat down with us under a tree on the church lawn and played back the tapes. Then he began a lengthy and harsh criticism of Bob, chiding him for talking too long and not making his presentation concrete. He criticized Joe for not directing his class's discussion. By contrast, he was full of praise for the way I had engaged the students in dialog. I was embarrassed and annoyed that he had complimented me while subjecting my colleagues to a dressing-down. When Arthur Reese said that he expected us to attend "mandatory" weekly or twice weekly meetings at St. Paul's Church in Hattiesburg, I explained that it would be difficult for us to get into Hattiesburg; we had no car and would have to travel by bus into town for a meeting and then travel back to Palmer's Crossing in time for our evening classes with the adults. But Arthur Reese made no concession. Had he approached us in a different way, I might have made more of an effort to attend the meetings. However, Joe Ellin did not share my reaction; although he conceded that Arthur and Carolyn Reese had some ideas that "seemed a bit rigid," he thought that "maybe they provided good ballast to the 'free spirits' of many of the rest of us."[1]

The initial encounter with Arthur Reese dampened my spirits, but that mood vanished in subsequent days because teaching in the Freedom School was so exhilarating. Like Joe, I was inspired by the high energy of the people of Palmer's Crossing that surged up in church meetings and in Freedom School. However, Joe's wife Nancy, who had also volunteered to teach, found herself foundering at the True Light Baptist Church Freedom School, where she was assigned to teach elementary students. Bill Jones, one of the UFT volunteers, showed her how to make a lesson plan, but when she tried to use it, the lesson ended after ten minutes. So Nancy took responsibility for setting up a library on Mobile Street. She spent hours in a hot room sorting, cataloging, and shelving books, as well as setting up a check-out system. The Ellins disagreed about the value of the library: Joe thought "it was quite a good library by the end of the summer," but Nancy was frustrated because she found herself shelving "a lot of books that nobody would ever read."[2]

Joe Ellin recalls that one thing that continues to stick in his mind is the difference in our teaching techniques; he remembers that my students were "very active participants"; he can see "hands waving all over the room." Joe recalls "being rather shocked" at how "directive" I was, more or less demanding that my class give me the answer I was looking for." By contrast, as a philosophy professor, Joe "wasn't looking for answers as much as discussion."[3] I am pleased that Joe remembers my students as active participants, but I have assured him that I was not looking for one "right" answer; quite the contrary, I was trying to evoke different points of view, in accord with the curriculum I had helped develop at the March curriculum conference, which emphasized that teachers were not to be authoritarian in personality or pedagogy. This method liberated students from the stifling memorization of stale curriculum in their segregated schools. It was the approach I had developed in my teaching, but my Freedom School students responded more enthusiastically than any other group I had ever taught because they had never been permitted, let alone encouraged, to voice their own answers to questions and ask their own questions. And their teachers, whose jobs depended on pleasing the white school administrators, were fearful of any discussion that might open the free flow of ideas. How deeply these students resented teachers and administrators who confined their minds and limited their expression I witnessed one day as I was standing with the students outside the school. The principal of their elementary school walked by without greeting them and as he passed the students spoke of him bitterly, in angry tones I had not heard from them; their scorn for the man reminded of the encounter in Virginia between a compliant grandfather and his angry grandchildren.

The Freedom School curriculum was a revelation to the students, who, in their segregated schools, were issued texts no longer in use in the white high schools, each book issued to them with a label bearing the names of previous users on the inside cover. They never were permitted to study texts by black authors in their English courses, nor to examine in their history classes the system that oppressed them. Mathematics and science texts were obsolete. And the students did not have access to books in the Hattiesburg Public Library, which served only whites. To borrow books, they would have to go to an out-of-the-way storefront downtown, where, as in the case of the schools, the books were discards from the white library. Therefore, after I opened the boxes of copies of James Baldwin's *Go Tell It On the Mountain* and *Black Boy* by Mississippi native son Richard Wright, I was as thrilled as the students to be placing in their hands crackling stiff, never-before-owned books, which were, indeed, as good as gold to them. Doug Tuchman once said of Hattiesburg that if one left money behind, it would be in that place the next day, but a book left behind would disappear in seconds.

As Freedom School became a matter of daily routine, the curriculum that had been designed for high school students had to be adjusted to a student body that ranged literally from eight to eighty. The schedule remained the same: mornings from 8:00 to 11:00, and evenings from 7:30 to 9:30, with meetings or community activities in the afternoon. The school day began with all the students gathered together as one of us gave a presentation based on the Guide to Negro History, after which we dispersed to classrooms for small-group discussion of the presentation. The students then divided again into individual subject areas; I taught English, Bob Stone taught history, and Joe Ellin taught math. We had to make one adjustment, however, when the temperature rose (as it inevitably did each morning) to ninety degrees and above, we moved our classes outside the church and sat in circles under the trees. Jimmella Stokes, Sam Williams, Theresia Clark, Lavon Reed, Shirley Anderson, Gwen Merritt, Charles Bester, Diane and Carolyn Moncure, and Curtis Duckworth, Jr. came regularly to my English class. In a very short time, they were fulfilling the goals set for the Freedom Schools, making their own experience part of the curriculum, analyzing and challenging the basic precepts of their society. I did not know then that this spirit was not typical of all Freedom Schools in the rest of Mississippi, but I did realize in a short time that Palmer's Crossing was special.

I enjoyed walking to the Freedom School in the evenings when the air was cooler, the red dust of the roads did not bite my legs, the sky was pink and purple, and young children ran out to call my diphthonged name: "Sa-yendy." The twenty adults who came to Freedom School in the evening enjoyed discussing their lives with each other and putting the past into perspective. They were more aware than the students were of the struggle necessary for mere survival and often viewed the past with longing rather than scorn. In contrast to the eagerness of the young students to change the status quo, people in their sixties, seventies, and eighties recalled with nostalgia the days of their youth. They savored in particular memories concerned with the provision of food. Many of them had lived in homes where vegetables were grown; this was still true, but what was common in the past was the presence of animals to provide meat for the family, who raised the animals, slaughtered them, and dressed them. The close communal living, the production of all that was consumed, brought people close to one another. Life in those years seemed to these elders a happy time.

Jimmella Stokes informed me that the hamlet was named Palmer's Crossing because of the railroad track that separated "up the hill" from "down in the crossing." There were no paved streets, street or traffic lights, or signs. At the center of the hamlet was a post office, a gas station, a furniture store, a drug store, a clothing store, a grocery store, and an ice house. All of the stores were "salvage" stores and, with the exception of the gas station, all of the businesses were owned by a white man named Hudson. The gas station was owned by a white man, well known as a Klansman, named Burkett. Neither proprietor lived in Palmer's Crossing. The community's main entertainment attraction was the Hi-Hat Club, where well known performers such as B. B. King and Tina Turner had appeared.

Jimmella also provided me with a description of the class structure of the community's black population. In her view, Palmer's Crossing's middle class consisted of families who owned a grocery store or a farm. At the upper level of the community's working class were two-parent families with a mother who worked as a cook in one of the white restaurants and a father who was employed in one of the lumber, tin or resin mills. On a lower level were poor two-parent families in which the mother worked as a maid in the home of a white family and the father worked as a janitor. On the lowest level were poor single mothers who were either unemployed or working as maids in a white hotel or in a jail. With little education, these women had to take any job offered in order to get support from the Department of Welfare, which, at the time amounted to $80.00 a month, no matter how many children were involved; food stamps and Medicaid did not exist at the time. The segregated Charity Hospital in Hattiesburg provided medical care to the poor.

According to Jimmella, most people in Palmer's Crossing did not have indoor plumbing before the early 1960s, as was the case with the school she attended in her first four years of elementary education. In her fifth year, she attended the brand new Earl Travillion Attendance Center, which served grades one through twelve; however, the books issued to the students were not new.

I became acquainted with the people of Palmer's, beginning with my host, Mrs. Jackson, who was retired from work as an institutional cleaner in a local hospital and a local radio station; never, as she told me emphatically, "in folkses' homes." Her daughter had died, and she had brought up her daughter's children: Mary, who lived with her, and a son who had moved out. She was proud of the home and car that she earned by her labors. I ate most evening meals with her, often fish she had caught on trips to Gulfport, and sometimes her specialty, sweet potato pie. (I had not eaten before, nor have I eaten since, sweet potato pie as good as hers.) I admired Mrs. Jackson and understood what she appreciated about herself: that, despite the limitations of the system, she had achieved a great deal.

Another woman I admired—and admire still—was Victoria Jackson Gray, who frequently traveled in behalf of the Methodist Church and Freedom Democratic Party. One morning I witnessed her saying good-bye to her youngest child, Cecil—known to all of us as "Ceecee"—who was crying. As I watched her comfort her son, I wondered where she got her strength. One evening, as I was passing Shirley Anderson's home, I saw Victoria Gray sitting with Shirley's mother Helen on the porch, snapping string beans. I joined them on the porch and snapped a portion of beans. I did not join their conversation, nor did I attempt to follow it. What I was keenly aware of was that each comment or question they addressed to each other began with the salutation or ended with the valedictory "Mrs. Anderson" or "Mrs. Gray." In a society where black women were never addressed or noted—not even in telephone directories—as "Mrs.," these women were using these terms as words of love and respect for each other.

I learned of other women leaders in the hamlet. Betty Steppes was a much sought-after midwife. Mrs. Georgia Johnson, a local healer, opened her home to women who enjoyed a lively exchange of gossip while Mrs. Johnson provided hair care and advice on the treatment of health problems. Elnora Knight was a widely known fortune teller, and cars with license plates from states near and far were parked in front of her door on weekends while their owners— usually white—sought her visions.

I followed the SNCC direction to be flexible and joined my students in voter registration efforts. One afternoon I went canvassing with Jimmella, Shirley Anderson, Gwen Merritt, Carolyn Moncure, and a younger Freedom School student, Rita Mae Crawford, who was the best canvasser among us. I enjoyed watching her approach adults, who were at first patronizingly amused by her question, "Have you went to register?" but quickly became defensive when she refused to accept their excuses and persistently demanded that they register to vote.

On Saturday, July 11th, Bob Stone came to tell me Staughton Lynd had asked him to leave Palmer's Crossing to teach in a Freedom School in McComb, which was then considered the most dangerous site in the state. Another teacher who left Hattiesburg that day was UFT volunteer Ira Landess, who wanted to go to McComb to join his friend, Mendy Samstein. After Bob left, George Cohen and Maria Hallett, whose husband Greg taught at St. John, began teaching at Priest Creek.

Hattiesburg was known—sometimes in derision—as a "safe" city; however, violent incidents occurred throughout the summer. On July 2nd, voter registration canvassers had been followed and questioned by men claiming to be state officials; the superintendent of Hattiesburg schools threatened to fire all janitors who participated in civil rights activity, and police stopped a young black girl walking with four white boys. One of the policemen cursed, threatened arrest, and slapped one boy.[4] On July 6th, fifteen to twenty-five teenagers tried to integrate the local drive-in movie theater, and were confronted by the wife of the owner who pointed a pistol at them. Police arrested the group and took them to the "drunk tank" of the Hattiesburg jail, roughing up some of them in the process.[5] On July 10th, Rabbi Arthur Lilyveld, in Hattiesburg with the Ministry Project sponsored by the National Council of Churches, was walking with two white volunteers, David Owen and Lawrence Spears, when two men got out of a pickup truck and attacked them with a tire iron. Rabbi Lilyveld required hospitalization; after receiving treatment for his head injury, Lilyveld said that Jews in Mississippi "should stand up for decency and freedom."[6] The New York COFO staff had worked dedicatedly and usually unsuccessfully for years to get press releases reporting arrests, beatings, and killings of civil rights activists published outside Mississippi; however, a picture of Lilyveld after the attack appeared in New York newspapers the following day, along with an account of an attack carried by wire services.

The day after the attack on Rabbi Lilyveld, word spread throughout Palmer's Crossing that there would be violence that night because members of the "Council"—the White Citizens' Council—were planning to ride. Fearing my presence at Mrs. Jackson's home might make it a target, I told her I would not stay there that night. Along with other people, I spent the night at the home of Elnora and Charlie Knight, jumping at the sound of every passing car and getting very little sleep. But nothing happened; either the rumor was false, or those who would be night riders had changed their minds when they considered the risk to themselves. Palmer's Crossing was isolated from Hattiesburg, and the residents were only theoretically non-violent. Like other Palmer's Crossing homes in similar circumstances, a loaded rifle stood upright by the door of the Knight home, ready, as potential night riders understood, to be used to return fire. Nevertheless, although the White Citizens Council did not come that night or any night while I was in Palmer's Crossing, the community had frequent, harassing visits from two local policemen, Constable F. L. (Cotton) Humphrey and Constable Wilmer Kitchens—known to us as Cotton and Kitchen, who drove slowly through the unpaved roads, the slow-turning wheels of their mud-colored automobile crunching the gravel, their loaded rifles upright and visible as they passed.

On Sunday morning, I went to the nearby St. John Methodist Church. The congregation was smaller than the one at True Light Baptist, and, like Methodist congregations I had known, less exuberant in its worship. The minister, Reverend Ponder, the first minister in Hattiesburg to open his church to the Movement, drew my admiration by exhorting the congregants to "move with the Movement."

In the afternoon, I visited Charlie and Elnora Knight. No seekers of prophesy came while I sat with the Knights on their porch. Mr. Knight had a branch in his hand that he periodically switched at chickens and kittens, all the while complaining to his wife about all the animals he was keeping. He was most upset about the bull that could service only their one cow—she was pregnant anyway—and there were no other cows in the vicinity in need of the bull's skill. The bull, he fretted, was a financial burden, as was the cow whose maintenance exceeded their need of her milk. And, he went on, there were the hens and turkeys; they weren't needed either.

Mrs. Knight said she did not want any of their animals sold because, "I just love having them around."

"Woman," exploded Mr. Knight, "what do you know about it? You don't have nothing to do with their care and feed. I ought to whup your legs."

Later we watched a wonderful storm as the horny bull moaned and the turkeys gabbled. Mr. Knight turned to me and confided, "Now I don't have much book learning, but I have mother wit. For example, I know that if you let a pregnant woman mess with a new-killed hog, the meat will rot. Not many people believe that, but I know it to be so. You don't believe it, do you? I know, too, that you can't let a pregnant girl near a peach tree. We had a gal here like that one time and she wanted some peaches and I said, 'Don't you go there, I'll get 'em for you.' But I guess I didn't get 'em fast enough for her, so she went there and that tree hasn't borne fruit from that day to this. I wrote her a letter and told her, 'Why did you go and spoil that nice tree? Don't you ever come here again.' "

Being in the company of so many brave and dedicated people led me to idealize the black community of Hattiesburg as a unified force of opposition to Southern segregation, with freedom always on their minds and no time for anything but serious matters.

I realized how simplistic my appraisal of the community was when one Saturday night, throngs of people I had never seen before, a population that seemed too large to be contained within Hattiesburg's city limits, their bodies aglow in splendid clothes, rode in crowded cars to attend a concert at the Hi-Hat Club. I saw evidence that the collectivist civil rights movement did not touch the entire population on occasions when I was driven to community meetings through Palmer's Crossing's outer regions, and saw shacks that served as taverns where local men came to drink and settle individual scores. One weekend two men were killed in brawls; one by a knife on Saturday night, the other by a gun on Sunday afternoon. At the high end of Hattiesburg's black community, I learned, was another population that did not participate in the struggle (a word they would have found offensive) for civil rights. These people, according to Jimmella, looked down on the activists; they labeled her and other female teenagers in the Movement "fast," and warned their sons and daughters to avoid them.

However, these factions did not have an impact on our work at Freedom School, which was the center of our lives and we arrived each morning alight with eagerness for that day's discoveries. During one of our discussion sessions, Jimmella Stokes described for the class her participation in Freedom Day in Hattiesburg. The people who had launched the Freedom Ballot campaign by lining up to picket the courthouse or to register to vote were subjected to harassment and intimidation by the police and other white citizens. Three black Hattiesburg bus drivers—John Henry, Bennie Hines, and Reverend John W. Brown—were fired when they tried to register to vote. High school students were arrested and jailed for demonstrating at the court house. Jimmella, who was arrested three times, frightened her mother ("she nearly had a heart attack") on one occasion when she would not call the clerk who signed her release "Ma'am." "I plan to change the state of Mississippi," Jimmella explained. Although her parents may have been disappointed in her, she told the class, "I'm always fighting for my parents' freedom so I won't be worried about my children's freedom."

In my English class, the students made clear to me that they wanted most of all to deal with the novels, especially *Black Boy*. The students identified with Richard Wright, because although they had never known the abuses inflicted on Richard—being fed spoiled food by an employer whose family obliged him to serve them good food; being struck by a bottle thrown by white joy riders; being manipulated into fighting another black boy in one workplace and being attacked by white employees in another—they knew or knew of people who had experienced such abuses. They also knew about the persecution of Clyde Kennard and the lynching of Emmett Till. Moreover, they had their own hurts burned into memory, and our class discussions enabled them to purge their anger. Theresia Clark, for example, recalled returning to Palmer's Crossing on the bus with her seven-year-old sister Linda, who had just had a tooth pulled at a dentist's office. Her mouth full of blood, the child sat down in the first empty seat. The bus driver told her, "Get up, girl, you can't sit there." When she remained in her seat holding her jaw, the driver pulled the bus over to the curb. A white woman protested, "But she's just a child," and the driver replied, "She's still a nigger." When he went toward Linda, she spit blood all over him, and Theresia taunted him by asking, "Now what are you going to do?" The driver returned to his seat and resumed driving.

Richard Wright's autobiography begins with an account of how, out of boredom, he set a fire for which his mother savagely beat him. Wright's language conveys a four-year-old's consciousness, and here and throughout the novel the staccato dialog rings with authenticity. But Wright also describes in lyrical passages the sensual pleasures he knew as a child: the wonder of seeing "a brace of mountainlike, spotted, black-and-white horses clopping down a dusty road; the "languor" he felt when he "heard green leaves rustling with a rainlike sound"; "the cloudy notion of hunger" when he breathed "the odor of new-cut, bleeding grass," the suspense he felt when he heard "the taut, sharp song of a yellow-black bee hovering nervously but patiently above a white rose." Wright's mastery of language enabled him to transcend his bitter beginnings, and his forthright disclosures about dark aspects of himself, such as taking literally his father's command to "kill" a persistently meowing kitten, led the students to reflect on the experiences of their own childhood; his eloquence spurred them to be adventurous with language.[7] Making connections with Wright resulted in essays in our English class that involved the students and me in discussion, reflection, composing, and evaluating, with a steady seriousness of purpose. I read and returned the essays with comments—but no grades. I regret that I was not able to make copies of the papers and keep them.

However, they approached with caution another of Richard's negative actions, the cruel taunting of a Jewish grocery owner, the result of the anti-Semitism, not only of Wright but of the community that "had been taught at home and in school that Jews were 'Christ killers.' " I had heard the thrum of anti-Semitism in Palmer's, but I believed that negative remarks about Jews were made as the people Richard described had made them: thoughtlessly, out of long habit, based on very little knowledge of Jews, despite the existence of a significant Jewish population in Hattiesburg and the presence of many Jewish volunteers in Hattiesburg and in the rest of Mississippi. For reasons they did not make clear, the students did not want to explore that issue.

Whenever I have taught this text, I have drawn my students' attention to Wright's determined pursuit of literature that begins when he reads an editorial in a Memphis newspaper denouncing H. L. Mencken. Wanting to know more about a white man who is hated as much as blacks are hated in the South, he schemes to get access to a library. He is able to borrow books only on behalf of his co-workers in an optical factory, so he enlists the aid of another employee. The man agrees to let Richard use his card; Richard forges a note requesting that the librarian let him have some books by Mencken, and continues the ruse by pretending to the suspicious librarian that the books cannot be for him because he cannot read. Richard is given two books by Mencken and reads one of them, *Prejudices*, through the night. He is shocked by Mencken's "clear, sweeping sentences" and his courage in "using words as a weapon." He is stirred to know more of the writers Mencken writes about so passionately: Joseph Conrad, Dostoevsky, Flaubert, Mark Twain, Stephen Crane, and many others. He forges more notes to borrow more books, for his reading "grew into a passion." Reading Sinclair Lewis's *Main Street* results in his recognition of his boss as George A. Babbitt.[8]

Reading *Black Boy* "opened up new avenues of feeling and seeing" for the students as the books Wright had read had done for him. However, his reading "had created a vast sense of distance" between him and the world in which he lived. His options for living in the South were to organize other blacks—a task he saw as futile—to submit and live as "a genial slave," to transfer his self hatred on to others and fight them, or to forget what he had read and "find release from anxiety and longing in sex and alcohol." Richard goes to the North, his determination to escape strengthened by reading books by Mencken, Sinclair Lewis, and Theodore Dreiser.[9] In contrast to Richard Wright, students in Freedom School were strengthened in their determination by the Freedom School curriculum, as Jimmella Stokes expressed it, "to remain in Mississippi in order to change it."

When we were driven out of doors in the intense Mississippi heat to seek shade under the trees of the church lawn, the students extended the impact of the Negro History and Civic curriculums through role-playing, which became a favorite activity. They enacted situations suggested by the curriculum guides: organizing a union, for example, and the *real* invention of the cotton gin, not by Eli Whitney, but by plantation slaves. However, their most memorable role-playing exercise was the betrayal of a slave revolt, in which Jimmella Stokes and Charles Bester, cringing and speaking words of servility in high-pitched voices, betrayed their fellow slaves to Sam Williams, the "massa." Other students enthusiastically enacted the slave revolt betrayal. I recognized that through the role-play, they vented their anger at adults they believed were too compliant with segregation.

The students at Priest Creek and St. John were excited, almost jubilant, about learning African-American history. However, the revelations of the Freedom School curriculum could have an unsettling effect, as was the case at St. Paul Methodist Church Freedom School in Hattiesburg. A young boy became very agitated one day, and his teacher asked the reason for his distress. He replied that all she had told him about black people having written books and having a glorious history, and about great civilizations in Africa were things he had never heard of before. "I think you're lying," he said, and burst into tears, whereupon his teacher also began to cry. Herbert Randall, who witnessed the exchange, also cried.[10]

Because of the isolation of the community, my contact with other volunteers was limited to those living and working in Palmer's Crossing. In addition to the teachers at Priest Creek, the teachers at nearby St. John were: Stan Zibulsky, George Cohen's wife Jean, Maria Hallett's husband Greg, and Cornelia Mack, from Madison, Wisconsin. The voter registration volunteers I came to know in Palmer's Crossing were Malcolm Zaretsky, a graduate student from Berkeley, California; Stuart Rawlings, a student at Stanford University; Danny Parker and Nick Allis, students at Yale University. Another volunteer in Palmer's Crossing, Lorne Cress from Chicago, was director of the community center.

Occasionally I got a ride from Doug Tuchman, who was "in charge" of the UFT rental car, or took the bus into Hattiesburg. The COFO office, lodged in Mrs. Woods' hotel at 507 Mobile Street, was often crowded, but outside I could stand in front of a window covered by a large poster bearing the face of Victoria Jackson Gray, the Mississippi Freedom Democratic Party candidate for United States Senate, and talk with other volunteers, such as Paula Pace and Dick Kelly, who taught at the Mount Zion Freedom School. Then a group of us might walk across street to the Green Door Cafe and eat wonderful, spicy hamburgers. I did not often get to see the people who staffed the Hattiesburg project. The project director, Sandy Leigh, a 29-year-old former Army officer from Bridgeport, CT. who had attended the Army Language School at Yale University, had been active in the freedom movement since the first sit-ins in 1960. Sheila Michaels, a movement veteran from New York who served as project manager, was always busy keeping records, looking after everyone's security, making arrangements for short-term volunteer support groups of doctors, lawyers, and clergy, and maintaining a cool head to settle disputes. Other people important to the project were Doug Smith, a seventeen-year-old high school student, the deputy project director; Doug's assistant, his fourteen-year-old half-brother, Harold (Poochie) Mobley; Terri Shaw, a reporter from Buffalo, New York, the communications director; Joyce Brown, a college student from New Orleans, the office assistant; Rev. Bob Beech from Minnesota, the director of the Hattiesburg Ministers Project; and Phyllis Cunningham, a nurse from Chicago who established a health care program.

By mid-July, Freedom Summer was flourishing in Hattiesburg, where only the previous November, the project was on the verge of being abandoned However, because of dedicated planning by the

Summer Project Committee and other members of the COFO staff, and the courage of Hattiesburg clergymen and church congregations, an entire system of Freedom Schools had opened, with students eager to attend. Indeed, the response was so enthusiastic, both in Hattiesburg and in other parts of Mississippi, that COFO announced 50 to 100 more volunteer teachers were being recruited for the second session of the summer program.[11]

At this point during Freedom Summer, most of the volunteers were probably not aware of the danger in which those who had opened their homes in the early days of the Hattiesburg movement had placed themselves. All of these local people were courageous, but Mrs. Lenon Woods—who owned the Woods Guest House at 507 Mobile Street—became legendary for her defiant commitment to the Movement and the workers who came to Mississippi to advance it. When David Dennis, a field secretary for CORE, came to Hattiesburg in 1962 to register voters, he stayed at Mrs. Woods's hotel. Dennis recalls that when a group of men came to get him one night at 1:00 a.m., Mrs. Woods stood between them and him and said "they would have to take her first, and she knew they didn't want to touch her because Mrs. Woods had a little bit on everybody."[12] Sandy Leigh recalled another occasion when he was trapped in his office by the police and the fire department. As men turned on searchlights and bellowed through megaphones for him to come out with his hands up, Sandy heard the "the clack, clack, clack, clack, clack of her Minnie Mouse shoes coming down the steps"; the door was thrown open, and

> there was Mrs. Woods, skinny as a rail,
> . . . standing there with her sawed-off shotgun in the door, saying, "Who's out there? Les, is that you? Now you just get to getting. I know it's you. Melvin, is that you? You know I know about you. Now, you just get to getting. Get to getting." And she called out just about every single man in Hattiesburg who was there and they all got to getting . . . . [T]hey got back in their cars and they turned off the lights and they started the engines and they just sneaked away.[13]

In the course of the summer, the volunteers came to regard the people who sheltered and fed them as heroes, and bonds were formed between hosts and guests that lasted for lifetimes: the McFarland family and Doug Tuchman, the Harris family and Paula Pace, Addie Mae Jackson and I were among them.

Seven Freedom Schools operated in Hattiesburg and Palmer's Crossing. In addition to Priest Creek and True Light, Baptist churches sponsoring sessions were Mt. Zion Baptist Church, where Rev. F. L. Barnes was pastor, and Morning Star Baptist Church, where the pastor was Rev. Cloudy Lumzy. The backgrounds of the four Methodist churches where Freedom Schools were held should be explained in order to understand the impact of slavery and segregation on that branch of Protestantism, as well as the differences among them and the name changes that were later made.

The church now known as St. James Christian Methodist Episcopal Church, where Rev. W. M. Hudson served as pastor in 1964, was a branch of the Colored Methodist Episcopal Church established by freed slaves in Jackson, Tennessee in 1870; the name was changed to the Christian Methodist Episcopal Church in 1970. Zion Chapel, where Rev. G. W. Robinson was pastor in 1964, is a branch of the African Methodist Episcopal Church, established in 1787 by African Americans protesting against the inhumane treatment they received from the white congregation of St. George Methodist Episcopal Church in Philadelphia. Methodism's English founder, John Wesley, had vigorously opposed slavery, as had the early leaders of the Methodist church that was established in this country in 1784. However, American Methodists later divided on the issue of slavery, and in 1844, a plan of separation was adopted by the church's General Council, enabling conferences in slaveholding states to remove themselves from the structure of Methodism and maintain segregated churches. In 1968, the United Methodist Church was created, bringing Methodist churches in the South and the North together in commitment to respecting the rights of people of both genders, and of all ages, races, ethnicities, and disabilities. Thus, St. Paul Methodist Church, where Rev. E. E. Grimmett was pastor in 1964, Bentley Chapel Methodist Church, where St. John's Rev. Ponder also served as pastor, and St. John Methodist Church in Palmer's Crossing, became United Methodist churches. Together, these seven churches in Hattiesburg and Palmer's Crossing received more than six hundred students in Freedom Schools, and for this reason Staunton Lynd later called Hattiesburg "the mecca of the Freedom School World."[14]

One afternoon, I had my first encounter with the white community when I took the bus into Hattiesburg to establish an account in a bank on Main Street. The first teller I spoke to saw my New York address and knew I was a civil rights volunteer. She told me I could make only one withdrawal a month from a savings account and directed me across the floor to open a checking account with another teller; as I filled out the form I saw the first woman telephone the second woman. Then the second woman asked me what I did, and I told her I was a teacher.

"How long?"
"*For four years.*"
"Where did you go to school?"
I have a bachelor's degree from Rutgers, a master's degree from Hunter, and will start work on a doctorate at New York University in the fall.
Have you done this sort of thing before?
What sort of thing?
The thing you're doing now.
Yes.
Do you find it interesting and challenging?
Yes.

The second woman sent me across the floor to a third woman because I had cash to deposit.

The third woman looked at the slip, raised her hands and squealed, "507 Mobile Street. Nigger quarters." Then she and the other two woman collapsed into laughter.

My older students provided another image of the white community. Following Kennedy's assassination, they witnessed in silence from their vantage point as waitresses, maids, and hospital attendants as most white people rejoiced at the news of the President's death and made comments like "He needed killing." In contrast, each home I entered that summer had a picture of President Kennedy prominently displayed, usually next to a picture of Jesus.

Voter registration and Freedom Schools drew most of the summer volunteers; however, community centers, a third component, were designed to "encourage deprived Americans in their quest for human dignity and full citizenship" through "four major offensives: Fundamental Needs, Self Help, Youth Programs and Political Programs."[15] In practical terms, these goals were met through distributing food, clothing, and books that had been contributed; and bringing people together for political meetings and entertainment. The Palmer's Crossing community center opened on July 18th, and people came in the same high spirits they had displayed at the July 4th picnic. Norma Becker had come down for a visit from the from Greenville where she had been teaching in a Freedom School under far less satisfactory conditions than I was experiencing because attendance was sporadic and student interest low. However, that weekend, she was greatly cheered by the spirit in Hattiesburg.

On July 22nd, I went to to the mandatory meeting because Staughton Lynd was going to be there. I talked with Staughton at dinner afterward, and he confided that he had found the meeting that Arthur Reese directed heavy and dull, and he wondered where the vitality was. I suggested that he come to the Priest Creek Freedom School to see the model precinct meeting the students were preparing. Staughton said he would come out to meet the teachers in Palmer's Crossing that evening, after we showed the films SNCC staff member Andy Rust was bringing to Priest Creek from the Jackson COFO office. The high school students and adults appreciated the novelty of having films brought to them, although one film about a big-city election campaign did not seem very relevant. Everyone was subdued when the lights came on again, but the energy level was quickly raised when we sang Freedom songs.

Later, the Halletts, Stan Zibulsky, and I enacted a Keystone Cops scenario as we tried to rendezvous with Staughton while Kitchens was in one car and Cotton followed in another. With the constables pursuing us, we drove in circles until Greg finally parked in front of a house near the church. Then he and Stan hid behind the church waiting until the constables left the area. Of course, in this comic confusion, we missed Staughton. However, the next morning he arrived at Priest Creek in company with the Reeses. The model precinct meeting went very well; the students showed great maturity in assuming political roles, and Staughton was very favorably impressed by their work.

On the morning of the 24th, George Cohen gave the master lesson, a presentation on the origins of prejudice. His thesis was that fear and guilt on the part of white people because of their treatment of black people led to discrimination. His conclusion was that the appropriate way for black people to combat prejudice was to prove their worth by always acting intelligently. Maria, Joe, and I immediately protested, rejecting vigorously the idea that black people must be well behaved, compliant, and forgiving in order to gain their rights. Our spontaneous outburst fascinated the students, who had never seen teachers in such strong disagreement with each other. However, I like to think our discourse remained civil, and thus served as a model for argument.

The students were rewarding our efforts with their self-confidence and initiative. While they were mounting a model precinct meeting, a team from Priest Creek and St. John was putting together a newsletter, "Palmer's Crossing Freedom News." An article by Carolyn Moncure on canvassing advised voter registration volunteers that "you won't be doing the job you came to do unless you shock them," because that was "the only way you can have any success in getting the Negroes of Mississippi to act politically." With characteristic maturity, Carolyn went on to advise readers that getting people to register to vote was not as large a problem as "getting them to see themselves as acting politically and getting others to act politically." The Mississippi Project, she concluded, will succeed only when "local leaders, with confidence to act in an effective way, are developed." Theresia Clark wrote that as a child she was "very content," but as she grew older, she realized she was being treated unequally because of the color of her skin. Now that the Civil Rights Law had been passed, she prayed and hoped "for a better America, and a better Mississippi in which to live. Deep down I know that we shall overcome some day. This is my belief and also the belief of my sister and brothers." The front page of the newsletter featured an announcement of the Mississippi Freedom Democratic Party's precinct meeting on Saturday, July 25th in St. John Church, and explained that the MFDP's structure was parallel to the structure of the regular Democratic Party, with precinct, county, and state conventions leading to a national convention. However, an important difference was that the regular Democratic

Party delegates and men like Senators Stennis and Eastland did not represent all the people. Therefore, delegates chosen by the MFDP would also go to the convention, to "tell the world that Senators Eastland and Stennis do not represent *all* the people"; to "ask to be allowed to vote in the National Convention"; and to replace Senators Eastland and Stennis. People over the age of twenty-one were urged to go to the precinct meeting to help the MFDP delegation prove that "many people in Mississippi want to vote but are not allowed to."[16]

By this time, the community was throbbing with political activity. On the 25th, three days after the students presented a model precinct meeting at Priest Creek, about seventy-five people crowded into tiny St. John for the actual precinct meeting. A dance, "Swinging Into Freedom," was held there later that night for teenagers, with many in attendance. The next day a county convention meeting in support of the Freedom Democratic Party's delegation to the 1964 Democratic Convention was held at the Palmer's Crossing Community Center. Along with the long-time activists, a significant number of newcomer, middle-class people attended, because, in Jimmella's view, the Hattiesburg movement was becoming "respectable."

The students at Priest Creek were rehearsing a version of "In White America" that they would perform at the community center on the first day of August. I had an appointment to help them prepare for the performance on July 28th, the day of a "mandatory" meeting in Hattiesburg. When the meeting went on too long, I left to keep my appointment back in Palmer's. Some time later, Staughton called to say that he was coming to Hattiesburg at the request of the Reeses "to iron out the dispute" between the Reeses and the Priest Creek teachers. He spoke admiringly of the work the teachers at Priest Creek had been doing and said he regretted that Arthur Reese was so autocratic. The meeting, with Staughton presiding, was not unpleasant. Carolyn Reese said that she wanted a share of the books that were being sent to me for distribution to other Freedom Schools. Arthur Reese wanted an agreement from all the teachers that they would attend "mandatory meetings." I readily agreed to share the books, but I would not pledge to attend all mandatory meetings.

On the last day of July, when I was scheduled to have a rare night off from teaching, word came that there would be a raid on the schools. I went to Priest Creek and alerted the adults, who scattered to their homes. Then I stood guard with Nick Allis outside the school. By this time, I was too absorbed in and committed to what we all were doing in Mississippi to be frightened by the thought of an attack by racists. Nick and I chatted amiably for hours until it was clear that there would not be an attack that night. However, the rumor of an attack had frightened the adults to the point that their attendance fell sharply; the damage to the valuable evening component of our program was very discouraging.

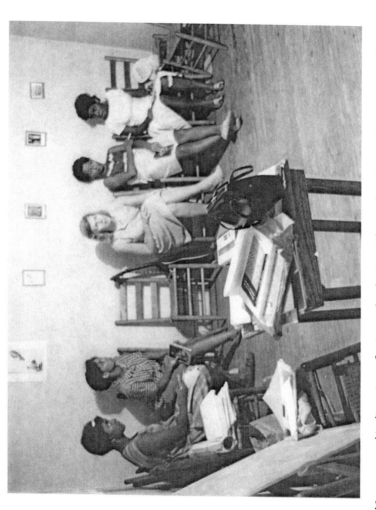

The students and I were engaged in discussion, reflection, and evaluation with a steady seriousness of purpose were taken seriously in Freedom School. Students: Jimmella Stokes, Carolyn Moncure, Ola Mae Leggett, Oatis Neal Harris.

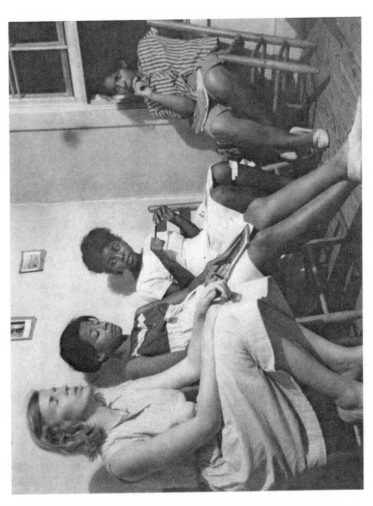

The students were taken seriously in Freedom School. They were encouraged to talk and were listened to. Students: Leggett, Harris, Moncure.

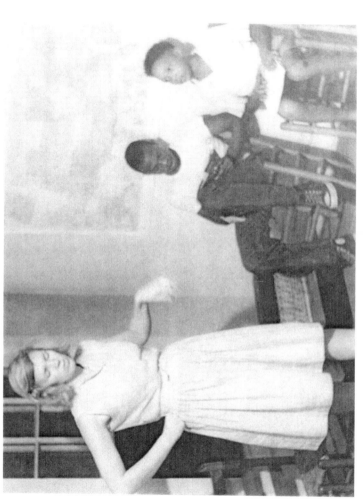

The students were encouraged to think. They were assigned to write. Students: Doug Smith and Curtis Duckworth, Jr.

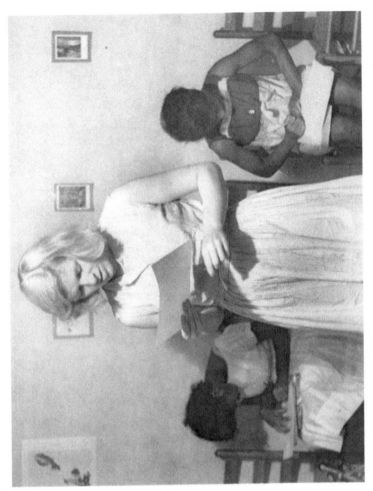

"Their writing was read with attention to idea and style as well as to grammar."

4. An Even[tful August]

By the end of Jul[y] [the Freedom School students, was in high] spirits, liberate[d by the Freedom School curriculum and an] open classroom [atmosphere. Although they had responded] thoughtfully in Englis[h classes to Black Boy, they were less enthusi]astic about James Baldwin's depiction of urban dilemmas in *Go Tell It on the Mountain*. Having at last found a place where they could express long-suppressed ideas about matters closer to their own lives, they wanted to work on subjects less literary and more political. We hastened through the book and turned to projects they found more rewarding: rehearsing *In White America* under Barbara Schwartzbaum's direction with students from St. John Freedom School for a performance at the community center on August 1st. Martin Duberman's drama about the history of black people in this country from slavery to modern times was based on documented words from well-known figures such as Nat Turner, John Brown, Sojourner Truth, President Wilson, Marcus Garvey, Father Divine, as well as less prominent people, including Klansmen and their victims, laborers, black soldiers, and defiant runaway slaves. The presentation of this short play provided the students with ownership of their past and present; in a way it resembled a term project or commencement exercise. The speeches, with language from the eighteenth and nineteenth centuries, were not easily mastered; the performance was not polished, but the students who participated in it were emotionally committed to their roles and their naive, sincere presentation was very well received.

The next day, the students and adult activists of Palmer's Crossing flocked into Hattiesburg for the Fifth Congressional District convention at St. Paul Methodist Church. The momentum that had begun with the painful efforts to register voters was building, and people were becoming more and more involved in the parallel Democratic party political process that the MFDP leaders had been very conscientious in establishing and meticulous in following. The convention went smoothly as delegates to the state convention were elected and platform issues were discussed.

On the afternoon of August 4th, Pete Seeger, who had been expected in Hattiesburg on previous occasions, came at last to the Palmer's Crossing community center to perform. The hot sun beating down on the low, flat roof of the center turned the building into a sauna. It must have been well over 100 degrees inside, but the heat did not wilt our spirits. Pete Seeger sang, played his guitar, and talked to the students and adults about music and its importance in struggles for human rights and social justice. After the concert, two students from Mississippi Southern University approached a group of volunteers and spoke of their support for integration and sympathy for what we were doing to advance it. Because of the hostility of local white citizens to white civil rights volunteers, the MSU students' expression of support was received with polite disbelief, although it was entirely likely they were sincere.

On Wednesday, August 5th, SNCC president James Forman and Freedom School supervisor Staughton Lynd came to the weekly mandatory meeting. Forman told us that plans were under way for continuation of the Freedom School project after the summer. He said that some of the volunteer teachers had already agreed to staff schools throughout the state, while other volunteers, along with local people, would continue to staff the community centers to provide people with libraries, recreation, day care, health care, and literacy and basic education programs. Then Staughton Lynd, in an uncharacteristically stern voice, lectured the Freedom School teachers on the importance of following the Reeses' orders, concluding with the words. "If anyone has any objection, let's hear it now. Otherwise I'll assume everyone is agreed." I believe Staughton's harsh tone may have resulted from his discomfort at having expressed criticism to teachers of leaders he felt obliged to support.

The students at Priest Creek, meanwhile, had been preparing for a debate on August 7th with the students at St. John. The students knew that their rival team had been preparing intensely, and gathered for a long session the night before in order to save themselves from a humiliating defeat. This competition in and of itself was a milestone in their academic careers because their education before the summer had never included the experience of competing in an academic contest with their peers. In the morning session, Joe Harrison, a folk musician who had chosen to remain in Hattiesburg after touring with a group called the Roving Band, came to Priest Creek to tell the students what had happened at the MFDP's statewide convention at the Masonic Temple in Jackson. He explained the challenge process as it had been explained to delegates: at the convention in Atlantic City, the MFDP would first argue before the Democratic Party credentials committee that blacks had been excluded from the "regular" party and that the MFDP was the only state party loyal to the national ticket. If the committee refused to seat the MFDP delegation, then, with support of eleven of the one hundred-eight-member delegation, the issue could be brought to the floor. There, if eight state delegations requested it, a roll-call vote would be taken and, it was believed, chances for seating the MFDP delegation were excellent. In Jackson, Ella Baker, the convention keynote speaker, had told the delegates bluntly that instead of spending evenings with television and radio, they must spend time "reading some of the things that help us to understand this South we live in." Baker also warned the delegates against electing newly arrived opportunists, "who, for the first time, feel their sense of importance and will represent themselves before they represent you."[1]

Joe Harrison discussed the importance of music in a protest movement: music lifted our spirits; music brought us together; music made us strong; music led us to victory. He also led us in singing. Then at 9:45, we heard the group from St. John's coming down the road. They sang "Oh, Freedom," and we went out to greet them with our song, "Ain't Gonna Let Nobody Turn Me 'Round." COFO staff took photographs as we gathered under the trees, and the debate, "Violence is Necessary to Obtain Civil Rights," began with our side taking the affirmative position. Both teams debated on a level equal to the other's; however, the Priest Creek team had the advantage of more supporters and was declared the winner. We sang then to heal wounded feelings and restore the good mood. All mornings at Freedom School had been fine, but this one was especially memorable.

For some time, following a proposal from Staughton Lynd, plans had been underway for a Freedom School convention in Meridian, a site Staughton suggested because of "the large Freedom School structure and because of the symbolic association with Philadelphia."[2] At the convention, students from around the state would merge the programs they had developed in Freedom Schools to meet the needs of Mississippi youth. The statewide program that emerged from the convention would then be sent to candidates for statewide office for inclusion in their political platforms.

On August 4th, the bodies of the three missing civil rights workers— James Chaney, Andrew Goodman, and Mickey Schwerner—had been recovered from under an earthen dam at a farm in Neshoba County. On August 8th, Hattiesburg Freedom School student delegates and teachers accompanying them boarded buses for Meridian, arriving in time to march in a solemn procession to the First Union Baptist Church for a memorial service for James Chaney. As we walked in silence through the streets, we passed many black people standing on the sidelines or peering at us from the porches of their pleasant homes. Some of the marchers called out, "Join us" to the black spectators, but not one person that I could see entered the procession. The church was filled with mourners, as well as reporters and television camera operators. The service was conciliatory, with several local ministers delivering the message, "We must forgive." The shockingly tepid response to Chaney's murder was broken when CORE's David Dennis delivered an angry eulogy.

He told us he wanted to talk about "the living dead" in Mississippi and throughout the nation. These were the people who didn't care, from the President to the governor of Mississippi. He blamed the people in Washington, D.C. and the people of Mississippi "just as much as I blame those who pulled the trigger." He did not grieve for James Chaney, he said, for Chaney had his freedom "and we're still fighting for ours." "I'm sick and tired" he declared, "of going to funerals of black men who have been murdered by white men." He told us he had vengeance in his heart and asked everyone to feel angry along with him. He concluded by charging the congregation: "If you go back home and forget; if you don't register and demand your votes; if you don't fight, God damn your souls." James Chaney's mother, Fannie Chaney, and his younger brother Ben were sitting in a front pew. As Ben cried for his brother, the cameras turned to focus on his tears as a microphone was brought close to his face to catch the sound of his sobs.

Following the memorial, one hundred Freedom School delegates and their accompanying teachers went to the Meridian Baptist Seminary, a three-story brick structure built on a hill, where we were housed and the Freedom School convention was held. Prior to the convention, the Mississippi Student Union and fifteen Freedom School students, most of them from Meridian, had met in Jackson on July 25th to plan the conference. This executive group had elected as its chair sixteen-year-old Joyce Brown from McComb, where the Freedom House had been bombed out in July, just a few days before Bob Stone and Ira Landess arrived there. At first, Freedom School classes had been held in the bombed-out building, because after a decade of beatings, shootings and bombings—Klan violence financed by local oil millionaire Emmitt Thornhill—no leaders of any local institution offered their facilities. Then Joyce Brown wrote a poem, "The House of Liberty," which was distributed at the convention. Addressing the black leaders of McComb in the second stanza, Brown wrote:

> I asked for your churches, and you turned me down,
> But I'll do my work if I have to do it on the ground;
> You will not speak for fear of being heard,
> So you crawl in your shell and say, "Do not disturb."
> You think because you've turned me away,
> You've protected yourself for another day.

Brown reminded the elders of McComb in the third stanza that "your enemy will still be there with the rising sun," and rebuked them again in the fourth stanza that "To a bombed house your children must come, / Because of your fear of a bomb, / And because you've let your fear conquer your soul."[3] After her poem circulated in the community, conscience-stricken local people found their courage, and arranged for classes to be held at McComb's St. Paul Methodist Church.

Joyce Brown was a stellar chair, presiding over the plenary sessions with confidence, intelligence, and sound knowledge of parliamentary procedure. The convention delegates, having produced newsletters, and having been involved in and informed of MFDP activities in the previous weeks, were well prepared for serious work on their platform. Stanley Zibulsky had assigned his students at St. John to write their own Declaration of Independence. Linda Clark, Theresia's sister, wrote the Declaration that was adopted at the convention. The first section of it stated:

> In this course of human events, it has become necessary for the Negro people to break away from the customs which have made it very difficult for the Negro to get his God-given rights. We, as citizens of Mississippi, do hereby state that all people should have the right to petition, to assemble, and to use public places. We also have the right to life, liberty, and to seek happiness.

Maintaining a parallel relationship to Jefferson's document, Linda explained that the Negro was powerless to seek redress for grievances arising from lack of food, schools, libraries, recreation facilities, better roads in their communities, mental health care, Negro policemen, fair circuit clerks, integrated schools, and colleges. Because the state of Mississippi denied them such benefits and imposed injustices such as unfair trails, unjust laws, police brutality, lack of access to public places, and denial of voting rights, the students declared independence from the "unjust laws of Mississippi which conflict with the United States Constitution."[4]

In two days of workshops, the student delegates prepared an impressive and wide-ranging list of demands that reflected the political awareness they had gained from the Freedom School Citizenship Curriculum. Of the state they demanded access to public accommodations. They demanded a building code that provided each home with, as minimum requirements, a complete bathroom unit, a kitchen sink, insulated walls and ceilings, a basement and attic, an adequate wiring system, and at least a quarter of an acre of land per building lot. They demanded better schools, including air conditioning, heating, laboratories, textbooks, and lunch rooms. They demanded integrated schools and better-paid, qualified teachers who were free "to join any political organization to fight for Civil Rights without being fired." They demanded health care facilities with integrated staffs and qualified doctors who addressed patients "properly," chest x-rays, annual check-ups, and the abolition of sterilization used as punishment for any offense. They demanded a public works program and equal distribution of federal aid under Title VI of the Civil Rights Act, along with the enforcement of the Fair Employment provision of that same section. They demanded enforcement of Section Two of the Fourteenth Amendment in order to eliminate discriminatory voter registration practices and the poll tax. They demanded the appointment of "qualified Negroes" to the police force and police protection from hate groups such as the Klan. They demanded wider, well-lighted streets and regular garbage collection. And of the federal government they demanded abolition of the House Un-American Activities Committee, an end to support for dictators in other countries, and imposition of economic sanctions against South Africa because of its policy of apartheid.[5]

The Freedom School convention was not all work, however, because guest speakers appeared. In his sonorous voice tall, dignified A. Philip Randolph told the conventioneers on Saturday afternoon of his efforts to build the first successful black workers' union, the Brotherhood of Sleeping Car Porters. In a contrasting but equally effective style, the always self-effacing Bob Moses—bending forward with his palms held up before him—spoke of the present struggle for rights in a low voice that demanded and received attentive silence. On Saturday night, the Free Southern Theater (which John O'Neal had organized with Gilbert Moses and Doris Derby after he left the Hattiesburg project) presented a performance of *In White America*. Freedom School teachers got to know each other, as well as attend a meeting where Liz Fusco, a Freedom School teacher in Ruleville who would succeed Staughton Lynd as Freedom School Coordinator, explained how our students could gain access to scholarships in Northern colleges established by the National Scholarship Fund for Negro Students. She also told us that, through an arrangement with the College Entrance Examination Board in Princeton, our students could take the PSATs at Freedom Schools; the tests would be graded separately from the national SATs, and their scores would be sent directly to the colleges to which the students were applying.

On August 4th, the same day that the slain civil rights workers' bodies were recovered, the American government claimed that on two separate occasions Vietnamese patrol boats had fired on the U. S. destroyer Maddox in the Gulf of Tonkin. On August 5th, President Johnson asked for a Congressional resolution authorizing him to take "all necessary measures" to repel armed aggression against the United States. Reports of these attacks have since been exploded as myths, but on August 7th, Congress was persuaded by them to pass a joint resolution that provided Johnson with a blank check to expand the war. The Freedom Summer volunteers had not often read newspapers during the summer and did not know about the Gulf of Tonkin incident until we saw Staughton Lynd shake his head as he read a newspaper account of the Congressional action and say, "This is going to lead to big trouble." We could not have foreseen at the time how much trouble the incident would provoke, nor how much some of us would be moved to respond to the widening of the war.

Returning to Hattiesburg on Sunday evening, I found that I was too late for a mandatory meeting, one that for once I was really sorry to have missed. Joyce Brown (of the Hattiesburg COFO staff) had lectured the female volunteers because—and this news came as a shock to me—interracial sexual relationships had become common knowledge among a disapproving Hattiesburg community, and therefore abstinence was recommended. The male volunteers were scheduled to have their lecture on Monday evening, delivered by Doug Smith, the teenage assistant project director.

Interracial sex in Mississippi during Freedom Summer has reached mythic status. Whether the relationships were initiated by black males or white women, or through mutual attraction, interracial sex was problematic, for it offended and even endangered the black community, stirred resentment among black women staff and volunteers, and damaged the reputation and undermined the effectiveness of women who were known to "sleep around."[6]

Of course, interracial sexual relationships occurred in Hattiesburg, but Sheila Michaels believes that nothing more went on than could have been been expected among consenting adults. Moreover, as Hattiesburg was the largest project in the state and safety was of the greatest concern to Sandy Leigh, every volunteer had to check in with Sheila every night. As for the volunteers in Palmer's Crossing, we were working too hard in the high Mississippi heat to have enough energy for a sexual encounter of any kind. The Palmer's Crossing volunteers probably felt as I did: that even in possession of energy and desire, the horror of disappointing the people who sheltered us and the fear of putting them in danger from white men's anger kept our libidos in check.

During the week following the Freedom School convention, work began on the library in the community center. People donated lumber; boys began to build shelves and girls began to paint them. I worked on cataloging books with Carolyn and Diane Moncure and their grandmother Mrs. Carrie Bouchee, a trio of very hard workers. One has arrived at acceptance in a community if people gossip in one's presence, and I could not resist eavesdropping as Carrie Bouchee and Vergil Grady, two of the women who cooked our dinner (Mattie Henderson and Lucille "Big Sister" McDowell also cooked for the volunteers) gossiped about their neighbors. They complained about "the way some women promise to come to cook and then don't." Noting my interest, Mrs. B. explained to me that the people who live "up on the hill" really get together on a project, while those who live "in the flats" can't seem to get much done. Mrs. Bouchee would, she promised me, do all she could for the library.

In this, the next to the last week of Freedom School, the students were eager to do something to implement the Civil Rights Act of 1964. It was against SNCC policy to participate in confrontational actions testing the civil rights act, but my students, who had been arrested and jailed for picketing in support of voting rights, were not to be stayed. In late July, they began discussing possible actions among themselves. They thought of going to the drive-in, but students had been arrested earlier in the summer for that action. Going into a restaurant would probably lead to arrest also, and might even provoke a violent reaction from segregationists. Finally they made the best choice, the one most appropriate in light of the Freedom School experience. They would go to the Hattiesburg Library and ask for library cards. When they had made their plans, they asked me to accompany them downtown. Aware that these student veterans of protest were determined to carry out their mission with or without me (but were less likely to be arrested if I was with them), I agreed.

On Friday, August 14th, six students: Curtis Duckworth, Gwendolyn Merritt, Carolyn and Diane Moncure, Lavon Reed, Jimmella Stokes, and I—all of us by prearrangement wearing blue chambray shirts that were part of the SNCC uniform—got on the bus into Hattiesburg after classes and arrived around noon. As we went into the Hattiesburg Public Library—a medium size building with stacks, of course, and a pleasant area for sitting and reading— the young woman sitting and talking on the telephone at the information desk (ironically also wearing a blue chambray shirt) took one look at us and I saw what I had heard described but never seen before: her eyes nearly bolted from their sockets. She quickly ended her conversation, called another number and said, "Mrs. Tracy, I need some help down here," then asked us what we wanted. The girls asked for library cards. She mumbled something about cards not being issued and then her supervisor arrived. The students repeated their request. Mrs. Tracy began her reply by explaining, "I'm a Yankee and I'm sympathetic and not sympathetic." She spoke of "a custom that has been here since before you were born" and explained that the "Council" had decreed that the library not be integrated. The students listened patiently and then replied that they could not see why they should not have library cards. The librarian continued at some length as the students continued to listen patiently. When they did make a comment, she responded with comments such as "Look, close your mouths and open your minds," "Try to act intelligent," and "You don't really want to use the library." The woman concluded by telling us that she could not put us out, but if we stayed, she would have to call the police and close the library to everyone. Jimmella said, "If we can't use the library, then nobody else should." I was very impressed by the students' demeanor; throughout the encounter, they had been dignified and courteous but determined. I had said nothing during the entire exchange, but when police were to be summoned, I asked the students, "What do you want to do?" They said they wanted to stay.

We sat in soft chairs and read newspapers while the supervisor called the police; within twenty minutes the police chief, Hugh Herring, entered the library. He asked if I was the leader. I replied,

"I'm not the leader; I'm a friend of these students." He said, "All right, get out. We're closing the library." I learned later from an article in the *Hattiesburg American* that Chief Herring was acting under orders from the mayor, Claude F. Pittman, Jr., who explained that the sudden order to close the library was due to "a pre-school inventory" of all the books, which Mayor Pittman hoped would be finished by Monday.[7] We and the handful of other people in the library left. We decided to have lunch and walked down Main Street to Woolworth's, where the lunch counter was too crowded for us to eat together. Before we left the store, I stopped to drink water from one of two fountains, the one with the faded "Colored" sign over it. We walked further down Main Street to the Kress store and, as there were not seven empty seats together at the lunch counter, sat at two booths. A young woman came over and took the students' orders, but did not take mine. When I asked her to take my order, she said, "We're not going to serve you. We have to serve the colored, but we're not serving the whites who come in with them."

"That's against the law of the land," I replied.

"I know, but my manager told me not to serve you."

The students, who had been responding with succinct eloquence in our encounters, said, almost together, "If you're not going to serve Sandy, we're not going to eat, either."

We left the Kress store and turned south on Main Street as the police car that had been following us pulled up in front of us at an intersection. The policeman who was driving got out of the car and said to me, "You're under arrest."

"Under what charge?"

"Vagrancy."

He asked for my address. I gave him the COFO office address: 517 Mobile Street.

"Do you sleep there?"

"No."

I would not, as I am certain he knew, have given him Mrs. Jackson's address; therefore I was a vagrant.

"I have orders to pick you up. Don't resist."

He took my arm. Relieved that the students had not been arrested, I entered the back of the car and sat next to another policeman, who asked me repeatedly during the five-minute ride to the police station, "Are you a nigger?" When we reached the Hattiesburg jail, I got out and saw Lawrence Guyot climbing the steps to the entrance, surrendering himself to serve a sentence following a conviction on the charge of interfering with a policeman during a picketing incident the previous February. He had a thick book in his hand—I have the impression that his finger was on the page he had been reading—and I thought with regret that I had with me nothing to read. The arresting policeman led me into the station and a policeman at the desk booked me; I emptied the contents of my purse that included twenty dollars in cash, thirty dollars in traveler's checks, and a checkbook from the First National Bank of Hattiesburg showing a balance of forty-five dollars. I was asked my occupation and whether I was working in Hattiesburg. I replied that because of my teacher's salary ($7,200!), I did not need to work in the summer and was a volunteer. Then another policeman took me to a section of the jail reserved for black women arrested on prostitution charges. The two women being held there stared in disbelief as I was placed in another cell that had two metal mattress supports, one on top of the other, attached to the wall. The mattresses were filthy, and I decided that if I were detained for the night, I would sleep on the bare metal bands of the support. Ten minutes later, the officer who had escorted me to the cell returned to take me to be fingerprinted and photographed. Chief Herring, who had ordered the students and me out of the library and closed it, told me that COFO had called and asked the amount of my bond. In an hour lawyers from the National Lawyers' Guild came to the jail to post bail in the amount of $100.00 from a collection raised by the COFO staff, which I later repaid thanks to funds contributed by staff members of the UFT. After I was released, I went to the COFO office, and my students, who had been followed there by a police car, were waiting for me. I assured them that I had not been abused and answered questions about the incident from the staff and volunteers.

On Monday morning, the Hattiesburg Public Library reopened, but when teachers at True Light Freedom School—Bill Jones, Susan Patterson, Tom Edwards, and Ben Achtenberg—took their students there to get library cards, the library was shut down indefinitely and the four teachers were arrested. The next day, while I was sitting with my class on the Priest Creek Freedom School lawn, Eleanor Jackson Piel arrived in a car driven by her husband, Gerard Piel, the publisher of *Scientific American*. Mrs. Piel introduced herself as a volunteer lawyer who had come to Hattiesburg to represent all the arrested teachers and have our cases moved to federal court. She took a statement from me and then her husband drove her to take statements from the True Light teachers.

The adult evening program that had all but ended following the scare of an attack by night riders was in part replaced by a typing class, a subject many adults had requested, that I was able to set up in the last weeks of the summer session. I was asked to give a lesson on poetry at an evening class at St. John, and on the especially beautiful evening of August 19th, I walked there from Priest Creek with Carolyn and Diane Moncure, Danny Parker, and Nick Allis. Suddenly, we heard the crunch of tire wheels on the gravel road, and then the mud-colored car with Kitchens at the wheel and Cotton in the passenger seat came up behind us and stopped next to us; a rifle was upright between them in plain view. They signaled to me to come over to the car. Cotton asked my name, address, and if I had money. After I answered those questions, Kitchens was more direct: "Is that nigger your husband? Are you fucking them niggers?" Male civil rights volunteers had been known to make provocative, macho responses to challenges from police; my response was to assume a schoolmarm persona, and with exaggerated dignity I said, "I beg your pardon." As he started to repeat his question, I interrupted him to say, "No Negro has ever spoken to me the way you have just spoken to me."

"Well," he responded, "you shouldn't be living with niggers. Those nigger gals will tear your hair out."

"I've always conducted myself as a lady and everyone else around me has conducted herself or himself as a lady or gentleman. That is until now. You have a foul mouth and shouldn't talk to people that way."

After scolding him, I haughtily turned on my heel, rejoined the group and we went on to St. John for a classroom experience that dispelled the bad feeling of the encounter with the vulgar constable. I played the Folkways recording of black poets reading their own poems that I had brought with me from New York; these included Langston Hughes reading "The Negro Speaks of Rivers"; Claude McKay reading "If We Must Die"; Margaret Walker reading "For My People," and Sterling Brown reading "Ma Rainey." I spoke to the students about the tradition of black poetry in America; I told them about the Harlem Renaissance. The students clearly enjoyed the lesson, and I asked if they had ever wanted to write poetry. Some of the younger adults said that they had written poetry. One of the older women confided that she had written poetry when she was in school and had wanted to write poems since then, but she felt writing poems was not important enough "to set aside chores." I told her that her feelings were important and that she should write what she was thinking about, because she was living through an experience worthy of poetry. Danny reinforced this point by comparing the depth of the the black experience to the shallowness of the white experience. "Compare," he said, "the blues, for example, to Lawrence Welk; Bessie Smith to the Lennon Sisters."

I predicted a new Southern renaissance would be one outcome of the civil rights struggle, and hoped they would participate in it. When the lesson was over and we said goodbye, one of the students, Mr. Edwards, invited Danny, Nick, and me to his home. We went with him to the small wooden house he shared with his bedridden mother. A gracious host, Mr. Edwards went into the kitchen and brought out a pan of pork chops and ribs and a pan of corn, food he must have prepared in anticipation of our coming. Nick and I protested that we could not eat because we had had our dinner, but Danny made up for our lack of appetite—or grace—by eating heartily while Nick and I drank ice water and coffee. We learned that Mr. Edwards had worked for the Dixie Pine Lumber Company since 1939 and was earning $1.33 an hour.

Afterward, Danny, Nick, and I walked back to Mrs. Gray's house. A white car passed us near the school and later seemed to be waiting at the Grays' home. Three men, at least two in high sheriff hats, were inside the car, that which passed us several times. When we got to the house, Lorne Cress and Cornelia Mack were there. Lorne, who had been harassed by Kitchens at the beginning of the summer, became very angry that we had walked to the Grays' house because she felt we had invited danger. Later, we had a very long talk about the Movement and the future of the Mississippi Project. Lorne and I both regretted that Hattiesburg had been the way it was—that black and white volunteers had not entered into one another's lives more deeply. This heavy discussion melted when we considered Cornelia, who was spending her first night of the summer in company with people her own age, away from her host, Mrs. Robinson. She began to unwind, drink beer, and become giddy. Danny observed, "Here everybody else is tired from dissipation and Cornelia is just beginning." It had been a full day.

> *I did not learn the details of Lorne's encounter with Kitchens until 40 years later when I interviewed her for this book. Her ordeal occurred when she and four other volunteers were returning for from Hattiesburg to Palmer's Crossing. It was very dark and the driver, Morty Malvain, was driving very slowly. Then the car that had been following their car flashed its lights and sounded its siren. It was Kitchens, who got out of his car, came to the driver's side and told Morty to pull out his driver's license and read it to him. "If you say anything," he warned, "I'm going to kill you" He went to the passenger side and hit Stan Zibulsky, calling him a "beak-nosed motherfucker." Then he saw Lorne, the only female and the only black person in the group, sitting in the back between two white male volunteers. Her dress covered her knees in the conservative manner female volunteers were careful to observe. But that did not stop Kitchens from calling out to her, "What are you doing back there with your dress all over your head? What are you letting them do? Suck your pussy? Get out of that car." Lorne was terrified, but she refused to move Then, in a startling change from tormentor to protector, he said "I don't want to see you again in this car with them. If you need anything, you just come to me."[8]*

On August 20th, the next-to-last day of Freedom School, Mrs. Piel came out to Palmer's Crossing to take statements from Jimmella, Carolyn, Diane and me about the attempts to get library cards and eat together at the Kress store. Mrs. Piel told me that she had succeeded in removing the vagrancy charge to federal court. On this afternoon or another in that week, Doug Tuchman drove me into Hattiesburg and accompanied me as I went to a well-stocked housewares store to buy a gift for Mrs. Jackson in gratitude for her hospitality. I considered one thing and another, and then selected a blue enameled Le Creuset saucepan because I was certain that, as an accomplished cook, Mrs. Jackson would appreciate fine cookware. Indeed, I have seldom chosen a gift that pleased the recipient as much as that saucepan pleased Mrs. Jackson. When I went to the front of the store, I found the proprietor confronting Doug, scolding him for being one of the great number of Jewish civil rights workers in Mississippi.

"You don't know what they're like," he declared, before delivering a string of stereotypical slurs about black people.

A travel agent presented a more positive aspect of white Hattiesburg when I purchased an airplane ticket for my return to New York. The attractive young woman who arranged my flight clearly knew I was a civil rights volunteer, but she was so cordial to me that I allowed myself to believe that she was sympathetic to the Movement, as I had heard such people did live in Hattiesburg.

To provide continual "in-service education for project workers," Sandy Leigh established a research team to develop a profile of Forrest County's geographic, economic, and political structure, as well as its leadership, institutions, beliefs, and values. Much of the needed information was provided by allies in the white community, who met with the team in clandestine meetings. Some of these allies were known sympathizers to the the civil rights movement and suffered retaliation; others remained inconspicuous and were able to supply information regularly. A reporter for the *Hattiesburg American* was considered "an ally of sorts" and informed the team of the relationships and actions of adversarial whites. According to this reporter,

> the high sheriff and the local FBI director were high school buddies and were also card-playing partners; the manager of a large hardware store was a local official in the White Knights, a Ku Klux Klan organization; a popular radio disc jockey, although he denied KKK membership, was instrumental in directing much of the white brutality which occurred in the county and was associated with the death of Mack Parker in the early 1960's in neighboring Pearl River County.[9]

Not all assistance was given voluntarily. The parish priest in Hattiesburg was too afraid to give communion to Dick Kelly, a known civil rights worker, along with the other parishioners because "most of the local Catholics were racists just like most other white people." Dick "literally had to meet the priest at midnight, and enter the church from the rear."[10]

During the last week of the summer session Arthur Reese surprised me when he came out to the Priest Creek school and greeted me with a smile. He had misjudged me, he acknowledged, because he had thought I was a teacher who was rigid in her pedagogy, but he had come to understand that I was not like that at all, and that I was sincerely concerned for my students. I was glad we were able to part on good terms.

Friday, August 21st was the last day of classes. The Freedom School experience at Priest Creek had been far more successful than anyone could have been anticipated, yet the students were ambivalent. Their attempt to get library cards was a crowning moment— what was then known in pedagogical jargon as a "culminating outcome." They were sorry about the end of classes, sad to see us leave, but fired up with new energy and ideas they were eager to put into effect when Earl Travillion reopened for fall classes. I was pleased that the students were aware that the Freedom School experience had equipped them for what lay ahead of them. In the notes I had made over the summer, I wrote, "We were innovative and hard working; our school was by any definition a fine school: no attendance sheets, absentee postcards, truant officers or report cards—just perfect attendance."

Gerard and Eleanor Piel were returning to New York and took Nick Allis, Danny Parker and me in their rental car to New Orleans. We were all nervous driving south on the road, which in those days had only two lanes, because the deep pine woods on either side were reminders of the many deadly encounters others had had on such densely wooded roads. When we separated from the Piels in New Orleans, Danny, Nick, and I decided to have dinner together in the French quarter. As we walked toward a restaurant on Bourbon Street, I saw a man standing on the porch surveying us as we approached; his unfriendly, alert stare foretold what was coming: a refusal to admit us. With his usual suave composure, Danny suggested we go to a restaurant in a friendlier part of the city; we went there and had a good farewell dinner before going to the airport to fly to our separate destinations.

But Freedom Summer was not over when I returned to New York. The next day, I took a 4:30 bus (I know the precise time because I found in the files the FBI created about me—which I later obtained under the Freedom of Information Act—the copy of a note I had left on my mailbox for a friend) to Atlantic City to work for the seating of Mississippi Freedom Democratic Party delegation, a group that, from sharecropper Fannie Lou Hamer to pharmacist Aaron Henry, included representatives of all socioeconomic levels of Mississippi's black population. Having built their organization through years of painful, dangerous activity, having diligently adhered to regulations in all stages of the process of selecting delegates, the MFDP delegation had arrived in Atlantic City on Friday confident that their case would be heard and their grievance redressed, because Democratic conventions in other states—New York among them—had passed resolutions urging the seating of the MFDP delegations. They began energetically lobbying other delegates.

The MFDP delegates presented their case before the Democratic Party credentials committee on the the afternoon of Saturday August 22nd. Several witnesses—Ed King, Aaron Henry, Rita Schwerner, and Martin Luther King—testified at the televised hearing, but the testimony of former sharecropper Fannie Lou Hamer about her eviction from the plantation where she had worked for eighteen years when she registered to vote and her beating in the Winona jail was so compelling that President Lyndon Johnson, aware of the power of her story, immediately called a press conference, and the networks drew away to focus on the president before Hamer had completed her statement. However, that night the networks carried her statement, with its emotional conclusion, "Is this America, land of the free and home of the brave, where we have to sleep with our telephones off the hooks because our lives are threatened daily, because we want to live as decent human beings, in America?" Her testimony brought a flood of telegrams of support throughout the night.[11]

I did not hear Mrs. Hamer's words, for, along with other SNCC and CORE supporters, I was standing among banners bearing the faces of Goodman, Chaney, and Schwerner, keeping vigil on the boardwalk in front of the Convention Hall. Meanwhile, the messages and pledges of support both prior to the convention and following the broadcast of Mrs. Hamer's statement encouraged the MFDP delegates to believe that their petition to be seated might be successful. However, in my lobbying of the New York delegates, I found skepticism. In a team effort, Doug Tuchman and I spoke to delegates in their hotels; one encounter was particularly vivid. Sensing that a man would prefer to be approached by a man, I often deferred to Doug; however, one delegate he spoke to interrupted him and, nodding at me, said, "I want to hear from her; she's the brains in the team." I restated what Doug had already told him: that Mississippi's regular Democratic party had systematically excluded blacks from participation in the political process, whereas the MFDP had been inclusive, and moreover, had pledged to support the Democratic nominee as the regular Democrats had not. My argument weighed no more strongly with him than Doug's had, for the man's response was, "We have to support the regular party." Other delegates we encountered were less forthright; they listened politely but noncommittally, and I sensed their resistance to the MFDP position.

None of us—MFDP delegates and supporters—knew at the time of the array of forces operating against us. Confrontations with Southern law officers and ad hoc racists had not prepared us for the extent of the the espionage and surveillance used against us in Atlantic city: FBI agents or their informants infiltrating strategic meetings, wiretapping telephones, planting microphones in the SNCC storefront headquarters, and interviewing delegates while posing as network reporters. All of the intelligence they developed was sent to the White House.[12] While the MFDP supporters were lobbying and MFDP delegates were in meetings or caucusing, members of the Johnson administration were pressuring credentials committee delegates supportive of the MFDP, threatening, in some cases, loss of a job for a delegate or a delegate's spouse. In an action that effectively divided MFDP supporters among the credentials committee, the White House initiated a compromise proposal calling for the seating of Aaron Henry and Ed King as delegates, together with the members of the "regular" delegation who pledged to support the Democratic party nominees in the November election, and the welcoming of the MFDP delegates as "honored guests" of the convention. On Tuesday, August 25th, the compromise was presented to the credentials committee, dissenting voices were not allowed to be heard, and the compromise proposal was passed.[13]

When the proposal was presented to the delegates that evening, it brought to the surface class differences within the MFDP delegation that had been simmering in Mississippi since the precinct meetings. Delegates favoring the compromise were oriented toward the NAACP, described by Bob Moses as "more established people from the large cities," but described more vividly by Fannie Lou Hamer as folks "that will sell your mama, their mama, anybody else for a dollar."[14] The pressure was sharpened when long-time supporters of the civil rights movement—Robert Spike of the National Council of Churches, MFDP legal council Joseph Rauh, SCLC leader Bayard Rustin, and Senator Wayne Morse—urged acceptance on the grounds that it represented victory. When the delegates caucused, many were leaning toward accepting the compromise as a measure of progress. Ultimately, however, the MFDP delegation was persuaded by the passionate urging of Victoria Gray, Annie Devine, and Fannie Lou Hamer to reject the compromise. The "regular" Democratic Party delegates were seated. They had recessed their state convention before the national convention ended and reconvened after it, where they voted to endorse Barry Goldwater.

Pete Seeger sang, played his guitar, and talked to students and adults about music and its importance in struggles for human rights and justice.

5. Other Mississippi Freedom Schools ᔐ

According to Staughton Lynd's report of July 26th, thirty-eight Freedom Schools had been established in twenty communities across the five congressional districts of the state with an enrollment of 2,135 students, twice the number that been anticipated. Approximately 175 teachers were teaching full-time in the schools, and from 50 to 100 teachers were being recruited. Typically, the Freedom Schools had enrolled 25 to 100 students and a staff of 5 or 6 teachers; classes met in church basements, then later moved outdoors; junior high school students, elementary school students, and even adults attended classes: citizenship and African-American history in the morning, more specialized classes such as typing and French in the late morning or afternoon. Alternatively, students engaged in special projects such as creating a student newspaper. In the evening, adults and students who worked in the day came to classes. Freedom School schedules and curriculum needed to be adapted to community practices and needs. In Shaw, Holly Springs and Carthage, students' regular schools were in session, and they came to Freedom School after their regular classes for instruction in a subject otherwise not available, such as a foreign language, as well as an informal and flexible pedagogical style they did not otherwise experience.

Lynd described three typical school situations: (1) isolated rural; (2) urban or suburban, with strong previous civil rights activity; and (3) urban or semi-urban, with weak civil rights activity. The most successful schools were in categories (1) and (2). Thus, amidst the sparse alternatives of Holmes County in the northwestern delta region, "students traveled long distances over hot, dusty roads to

attend Freedom School." Students at the Mileston Freedom School
were rewarded for their efforts when "school adjourned each afternoon at 2 p.m. and moved down the road to the community center
for an all-ages football game." The "classic instance of a successful
school in an urban setting—indeed, the Mecca of the Freedom
School world—is Hattiesburg, with 600-odd students in five
schools." Lynd attributed Hattiesburg's schools' success to the
intense civil rights campaign during the previous winter and
spring.[1]

The reports that Freedom School coordinators and teachers sent
to Lynd throughout the summer provide more detailed evidence of
the schools' accomplishments and shortcomings, rewards and difficulties. In Mississippi's Second Congressional District in the Delta
region, volunteer Pam Parker wrote after her third week of teaching
in Holly Springs that she taught African-American history to a
group of fifteen girls, most of them juniors and seniors in a
Catholic high school, as well as a twenty-five-year-old married
woman with four children and a twenty-three-year old woman, a
"poorly educated" college graduate. Teaching this group provided
Parker with "what every teacher dreams about," for they were eager
to learn "anything and everything"; they were responsive to all they
were taught; they disagreed among themselves, and would soon,
she hoped, disagree with her. Her students "drained" her, but she
went home at night exhausted, but happy.[2]

From Greenwood in the Second District, coordinator Judy
Walborn wrote to Lynd on July 7th, explaining that African-
American history and the Citizenship Curriculum were taught in
general sessions, followed by English sessions—where, as with the
Citizenship Curriculum, teachers related poetry and prose to the
students' lives—while subjects such as biology and French were
taught on a rotating basis in a third session. Walborn invited Lynd
to visit, and asked for good beginning algebra texts, along with "1
top-flight math teacher, if and when possible."[3] Judy Walborn's
report of July 15th informed Lynd that 102 students were enrolled,
of whom about one-half came each day; the students' ages ranged
from twelve to twenty, and they were in grades seven through
twelve. Walborn reported that the teachers were finding discussion
of the Citizenship Curriculum and the Freedom Democratic Party

in small groups was much more successful than in general, large-group discussion because students were more willing to ask questions. The teachers' use of role-playing to measure students' comprehension of the history curriculum—with students taking the roles of a white northern Abolitionist, two white southern planters, a planter's wife, an "Uncle Tom Negro, and a rebellious slave"—"was one of the most successful things we have ever tried!"[4]

Norma Becker reported from Greenville in the Second District on July 25th that "attendance is still essentially unstable and erratic, though there is some visible growth among the small group of 'regulars' that attend daily." Becker also reported that although the Mississippi Student Union group was "going along rather well," "an impassioned power struggle" had split the group "straight down the middle."[5]

From Shaw in the Second District, Wally Roberts wrote Lynd on July 20th to say that the Freedom School opening had been delayed until July 13th, partly because the students' regular high school was in summer session, but chiefly because of "the fatal mistake of not making real, personal contact with the high school kids." The first week of school had not gone very well, in Roberts's view, because the students had said, when asked, that they were interested in academic courses, when they were really not interested, but "did not want to offend us." As a result, the first day's attendance of forty junior and senior high school students dropped to ten, and did not increase much by week's end. The staff then made an effort to establish contact with the students by "watching their football practice and just hanging around with them." Some teachers were organizing projects such as a clothing distribution drive, and teaching "classes in math, typing, chemistry, citizenship."[6]

On July 20th, Morris Rubin, a UFT volunteer teacher in Shaw, wrote to Lynd in terms that contrasted sharply with Wally Roberts' diffident report. Rubin claimed that the Shaw Freedom School had evolved into a "continuing seminar class with about twenty teenagers in the M.S.U., and who represent the real leadership in Shaw." Rubin described the students as having "a kind of uniform brightness," and were so involved in the Movement that "next to Football, one could say that the Movement is the most important thing in their lives." In order to improve living conditions, Rubin reported, the students wanted to picket, set up boycotts, and meet with the white power structure. They gave off, in Rubin's view "an almost pyrotechnic effect"; nevertheless, they realized their need for training, "and are eager for whatever guidance we can give them."[7]

Rubin believed that encouraging the students to take advantage of the National Scholarship Fund for Negro Students program would liberate them from "the educational mud of Mississippi," but at the same time he was concerned that the educational opportunities in the North would deprive Mississippi of the students' leadership. Rubin was enthusiastic about the progress students had made in Freedom School and the broadening experience they had gained through the artistic and musical activities at the community center, and therefore believed what he saw as the "sacrifice of all programs to the Freedom Registration Drive . . . a real and ominous error." Rubin ended his letter with the acknowledgement that he had "learned more from the people of Shaw than I will be able to apprehend and systematize for many months.[8]

In the Second District's Clarksdale, coordinator Sandy (Sanford) Siegel, wrote to Lynd on July 9th explaining that the use of a church for a youth convention had delayed the start of classes in one of the four freedom schools planned for that community, that another school had not yet opened, and that the two schools that had opened were "quite successful, the main difficulty being recruiting and retaining students."[9] On July 17th, Siegel wrote Lynd that the Clarksdale Freedom School project was underway with four different schools" that were having "various successes, but all seem to be having the problem of attracting and retaining students." Siegel reported the attendance at all four schools as between forty and fifty students a week: "the average for the first week was 15; for the second week it has been about 8." The sessions were shorter, with morning classes devoted to informal discussions on current events, the Movement, and African-American history, and essays on these subjects were being written in all four schools. Classes in music, art, and typing were held in the afternoon. Some discussion of math and science had occurred, "but this has been spotty." Siegel found that making the classes interesting and stimulating for students and teachers was "a constant struggle." No two schools operated the same way, although there had been "good days and bad days for individual schools." The Freedom School convention in Meridian had aroused great interest, however, and students elected delegates based on the quality of the speeches in which they presented ideas for a statewide student platform; all the candidates, in Siegel's opinion, were capable leaders.[10]

Sandy Siegel wrote again to Lynd on August 20th, enclosing applications from Clarksdale students interested in the NSSFNS program and providing an analysis of the impact of class differences within the black community. According to Siegel, the NAACP had concentrated on voter registration, with the result that Clarksdale had approximately 1,200 registered voters, but that little had been done "for the poorer people of the community." In Siegel's analysis, this latter group, alienated from the NAACP, had also been alienated from COFO by the efforts of the COFO project director to cooperate with the NAACP leadership. Because many of the students in Clarksdale had not participated in the Freedom School, Siegel believed that more "manpower" should have gone into the community center, in order to organize "the community by blocks to have daycare nurseries, home improvement projects, vocational training, literacy education, Freedom School classes and tutoring sessions, libraries, etc." Siegel reported that he had met and admired a group of young people, some of them no longer in school, who had organized themselves into a Youth Action Group because of their interest in community activism. Previous efforts to organize a Mississippi Student Union in Clarksdale had failed because COFO worked from the top down, but the Youth Action Group, had "grown from the bottom up." Siegel wrote that he was trying to convince these young people to join MSU because they would have better results and opportunities through COFO, and that he hoped to get this accomplished before the group fell apart for lack of support. Siegel, who expressed the hope that he would return to Clarksdale in February, 1965, described the complexity of his situation:

> It has been difficult working in Clarksdale. We have not had steady COFO leadership here and the problems are perhaps more subtle than those in other areas. There has been a freedom movement here for 12 years, and consequently, many people have become upset

about it. The town is relatively free from harassment and violence, and the emphasis has to be changed from fighting somebody to developing the Negro community by themselves. It also appears that Higgins High School here is one of the better high schools in the state (many students do not feel there is a need to boycott it).[11]

In the Second District's Holmes County—an "isolated rural" community, which Lynd identified as a location of successful Freedom Schools—coordinator Anne Marie Williams reported to Lynd on July 31st about the situation in the Pilgrim's Rest Freedom School. It had opened on July 13th with fifteen students, but after the first week, enrollment remained steady with twenty-five to thirty students—most from high school, but a small number of elementary school students—each day. Williams reported that the students had "a great deal of creative talent," which the teachers were drawing out into the creation of poetry, a play to be presented, freedom songs and a newspaper. The staff were in the process of "working on a softball team that will play against other Freedom Schools." Delegates to the Freedom School convention had been chosen and one delegate had been sent to Jackson to plan the convention. The older students were active in voter registration work. Williams looked forward to the completion of the community center, to which the Freedom School, "one of the best assets to the community," would then move.[12]

Kirsty Powell, who became coordinator of the Second District's Ruleville school when Liz Fusco went to Indianola to set up a Freedom School, submitted an analytical and detailed session-end report that began with criticism of the Oxford orientation. Powell wrote that too much emphasis had been placed on preparing for the dangers, and not enough on preparing to teach; with better preparation for teaching in Freedom School, the volunteers could have left Oxford with "a much more positive understanding . . . of what we were setting out to do." While Powell thought the core curriculum of Citizenship and African-American history was excellent, the volunteers did not have enough time at Oxford to explore it, and it was late at arriving at the projects.[13]

After setting up the school, which was located in the back of an old house with a yard and "trees for sitting under; porch, with bathroom at one end; a wide hallway which was to become office; an incredible attic . . . and two small rooms about 12 x 12 which were to be library and everything else," the teachers opened it for sessions. As "regular" school was in session in the mornings, adults came to school then, and students came in the afternoons; evenings were left clear for individual tutoring or special classes. The adults were offered "baby minding," an invitation that Powell acknowledged was "repented of" because "looking after anything up to 15 kids ranging between 15 months and 5 years was a far more formidable task than any of us realized." The morning schedule remained constant through the summer; classes ran from 8:30 to 11:00 or 11:30. The first hour was devoted to the Citizenship Curriculum on Monday, Wednesday, and Friday; Tuesday and Thursday, the first hour was devoted to Health, which covered first aid and recipe sharing that "ended in the production of a collection of Freedom School recipes," and would have been improved, in Powell's view, by the addition of basic physiology "with plenty of pictures" and a discussion of buying and housekeeping. The second hour was devoted to writing and sometimes math, and the third hour was spent on reading. Powell reports that all the students—twelve to fifteen—remained in one class for writing , with three to six teachers circulating to help answer questions and correct errors. The students were encouraged to write as freely as possible about a topic discussed in citizenship class, a method that produced some "very interesting (albeit weirdly spelled and punctuated), genuine writing, most revealing of thoughts, feelings and experience." The adults were all tested for their reading level, with those testing below third grade going to a basic literacy class. There success was related to regular attendance and high concentration, which, Powell reports, discouraged the students, with the result that "the less literate students attended least faithfully." The students who tested at a third or fourth grade level were taught by an instructor who used a newspaper similar to *Junior Scholastic*, which the students enjoyed. Powell taught students who tested at fifth grade and above using materials on African-American history, most of which were written especially for such readers. Powell pronounced the group "a delight to teach," and the readings always produced "very pertinent and often moving comments relating to the thing read to situations in Miss. today."[14]

Powell described her own method for teaching reading to a group with some reading skill. She first introduced the piece to be read—usually three or four paragraphs long—supplying background, explaining new concepts, and introducing new or difficult words. Second, she would then have the class read silently, section by section, asking questions and discussing answers briefly at the end of each section read. Third, the class, each one in turn, would read the whole passage. Fourth, the class would discuss the meaning of the passage as a whole.[15]

As Ruleville Central High School held classes from 7:30 to 1:30, classes for high school students met from 2:00 to 5: p.m. At the beginning of the session, the school had six teachers, so students were divided into six different classes: ten- to twelve-year-olds; thirteen- and fourteen-year-olds; fifteen and sixteen-year-old boys; fifteen- and sixteen-year-old girls (Powell does not explain why students in this age group were separated by gender); seventeen-year-olds; eighteen-year-olds and older. Powell estimated that daily attendance was between fifty and sixty students. At the end of the first week, three teachers were transferred, and the teachers developed three different schedules to accommodate the staff changes.[16]

Under Schedule 1, the students met in age groups for Citizenship, Reading and Writing in the first hour. Electives, taught by community people and teachers, were offered in the second hour on a one- or two-day-basis; typing, French, music, reading, African culture, health, art, and biology. In the third hour, students were offered recreation, other electives, and canvassing "when needed." Powell thought this schedule worked well in terms of the good relationships that developed between teachers and students. That the whole school never met together she considered a weakness. The younger students, in Powell's opinion, came to school more faithfully than the older students, although some teachers built good relationships with the older ones.[17]

The departure of three teachers, and their replacement after the third week led to the design of Schedule 2, which included a general session during the first hour that began with freedom songs, announcements, comments from students, and followed by a talk by a teacher, community center worker, or community member—a local rabbi, for example—who spoke on the Freedom Rides.

One of these first hour classes was a book review session, in which teachers and community center volunteers reviewed various kinds of books—from beginning readers to books of biographies, travel, and adventure, to *Huckleberry Finn*. After this session—which Powell thought was very successful—the library was open for students to take out books. Third hour classes in this schedule were electives, recreation, and canvassing. However, second hour was the most consequential, for students broke into three groups for "expression": art, in which students made posters, writing, in which students wrote about the ideas expressed in the presentation of the first hour, and role-playing—the most popular of the "expressions"—in which students improvised the organization of a picket line. Powell explained that the week when the school began functioning under this schedule was the week that students began working to picket the high school to urge the teachers to vote, with the result that role-playing consisted almost entirely of role-playing the picketing, which ultimately led to real confrontation between the students and the administration of Ruleville Central High School that had serious consequences for the student leader.[18]

Schedule Three was similar to Schedule Two, except that during second hour the students were divided into age groups. At this point in the Freedom School experience, the value of the general session was questioned, because of the difficulty of talking to the ten-to-twelve-year-olds and the eighteen-year-olds at the same time. In the next-to-last week of the session, the staff decided to hold a general session once a week and divide the students into age groups. As a result of the switch of teachers mid-session, only "the 10–12's and the 13 and 14's continued as separate class groups with the one teacher." The tens and twelves were very enthusiastic and grew so much that by the beginning of Schedule 3, Powell reports the group had to be split. Because of the switch in teachers at mid-session, the older students, in reaction to the disruption, did not do as much reading and writing as the other age groups. Powell acknowledged that "we didn't do as good a job with the older students as we might have." With respect to electives, Powell reported these were popular but difficult to organize, and things improved "when we submitted to the inevitable and started banging a gong to induce people to change over on time." Typing was the most popular elective; six typewriters were "mustered" for two classes of six students each afternoon. A "small but faithful group" continued the course, which included physiology, First Aid, and "even some dissection—frog!" In French, students with great interest in learning a foreign language had "simple conversation," but unfortunately the school lost the French teacher at the end of three weeks. Music and African Culture "began and fizzled out" Reading was not a great success as an elective, and Art lost the interest it had held for students after Schedule 2. Dancing was very popular with girls, who taught teachers "the monkey" and other dances. Role-playing, which became an elective in the last three weeks of the session, involved improvising a play that was presented with great success on the last day of school. Powell acknowledged that "we were perhaps too ambitious in the number of electives."[19]

Powell taught African-American history to the thirteen- and fourteen-year-olds by modifying the curriculum to exclude "the more sociological topics," and introducing Harriet Tubman as a topic by "telling the story, talking about it, looking at pictures, reading about it." Then she supplied the students with books, magazines, mimeographed material and pictures, and encouraged them to do historical or creative writing, draw pictures, copy poems or historical documents, like runaway slave notices. At the end of the each unit, the students' work was displayed on the back porch; at the end of the summer, the work on all the units was displayed in a chronological arrangement to present an overview of African-American history.[20]

In her evaluation of the Ruleville Freedom School, Powell cited the establishment of a library of 4,000 shelved, easily checked-out volumes that included "everything from Nancy Drew to Thomas Mann." While conceding that Mann would be more appropriate for a college library, Powell preferred to "cling to the thought that a Richard Wright might come out of Ruleville." She thought the school was "extraordinarily lucky in the high quality of its teachers"; for even though the staff had "problems of personal relations," on the whole they worked well as a team. Powell's belief was that the more a Freedom School coordinator could "act 'as mere coordinator' and not as head, the better." She reported that Ruleville was free of the tension that existed between voter registration and freedom school volunteers in some projects.[21]

The report coordinator Connie Lee Claywell sent Lynd on July 9th from Carthage in the east-central Fourth District began with an apology for not writing sooner, but explained "we're all so exhausted at night after classes and ball playing and meeting the people and lesson plans, we just fall out." The students she described as being "really thirsty for knowledge and just soak up our classes." Despite losing the building they had anticipated using for Freedom School, the illness of volunteers (including Claywell), as well as the departure of skillful teachers, Claywell wrote that except for being "a little out of touch with the rest of the world" (because of the lack of telephones), things were fine; the "people are wonderful, my teachers are exceptional, and freedom school is swinging."[22] In a letter Claywell wrote on July 27th, she again apologized for not having written sooner, explaining that since her last letter, police had stopped a carload of students and workers, taken them to the police station, fined them twenty dollars for speeding and sent them home. Claywell also reported that they had "reluctantly" left the Harveys, the family they had been staying with, because their hosts had been pressured by the family from whom they leased their house and land. "We are now split up—and still functioning—" Claywell reported, "but it's not the same."[23]

In an undated report (probably mid-July), Dan Wood and Gloria Bishop wrote from the Fourth District's rural Madison County that two schools had been established: one at St. John Church in Valley View with an initial enrollment of 25 students that grew to between 40 and 50 students and one at Pleasant Green Church in Sharon with an enrollment that grew from 19 students to between 30 and 35. The age of the students in each school ranged from children under twelve to adults in their sixties. Much to the surprise of the staff, "the students begged (and we do mean begged) for a foreign language—any foreign language," and the staff then adapted the schedule to one-hour blocks from 8:30 to 2:30 with an hour from 11:30 to 12:30 for lunch. In the morning, the students studied Citizenship and Black History and English and Reading; they had an hour from 10:30 to 11:30 to select books from the library to read "because living conditions in the rurals make reading difficult in many homes." In the afternoon they studied Math, then French, German or Spanish, and spent the last hour in singing freedom songs or enjoying student presentations. Wood and Bishop acknowledged that they were "spending more time on 'hard-core' subjects than the suggested curriculum emphasizes" because the reading and writing skills of the students were very low. These students had a "profound interest in learning to read and write and work simple math problems," for their skills were far below the level of the math in the curriculum.[24]

Wood and Bishop reported a number of unexpected problems. Some host families were fearful that the presence of whites in their homes might result in attacks; therefore the teachers had to be moved to families that accepted the living arrangements "for the length of the project." The lack of telephones forced the coordinators to waste time traveling to Canton for small matters that could have been quickly settled by telephone. However, Wood and Bishop cited as the greatest concern "the lack of interest on the part of older boys in the Freedom School," most of whom were dropouts and "the word 'school' falls deafly on their ears." Bishop and Wood hoped to "pull" the older boys into the program through emphasizing sports, community action, and social seminars. Despite the frustration arising from the difference between "what we want to do and what we know we can do," the coordinators expressed great satisfaction with what they were accomplishing:

> We are fortunate to be living and working in rural Madison County, because the people are wonderful and the country is beautiful. The success of our program can be seen on the faces of the children as they begin their four mile walk to school at seven and seven thirty in the morning, be the morning clear or cloudy. The success of our program can also be heard in the singing of Freedom Songs. The students add verses to the songs and make requests for favorite Freedom Songs. You can hear groups of students singing songs and speaking foreign languages as they walk down the dusty country roads. But our success is unquestionable and sure, because the students and the adults in the community say to us repeatedly, "Don't leave. Stay here with us." Perhaps we should, and some of us will.[25]

Virginia Chute's report of the week of July 20th from the Gluckstadt Freedom School in Madison County begins with the information that the school's scheduled July 13th opening had been postponed because of threats and harassment from the local Constable, "Bruno" Holley. On Sunday, July 19th, the congregation of the Mt. Pleasant Church voted to allow the Freedom School teachers the use of the social hall; the vote was close, and Chute believed the vote would not have carried if "Reverend Taylor had not spoken strongly in favor of the school."[26]

The school opened the next day, with fourteen students ranging in age from twelve to forty-seven. Chute established a schedule for her students: 9:00 to 9:30 was given over to announcements, reports and Freedom Songs, followed by two hours of classes. The class beginning at 9:30 was devoted to the Citizenship Curriculum and/or the Guide to Negro History. The 10:30 class broke up into groups for "special subjects" There was a half hour break at eleven for badminton and a food treat, and the last hour was devoted to reading aloud and discussion of the aspect of the Citizenship Curriculum or the Guide to Negro History covered earlier. Chute began the Citizenship class by asking the students what they thought freedom meant. "Equality for all was as far as the discussion got," so Chute shifted the discussion to asking the students for what things were necessary for a person to be "really free." The students cited education, the right to vote, adequate housing, and equal employment opportunities.[27]

Next, Chute and the students "exchanged information on what conditions are like in each of these areas in the South and in the North." Chute reported that "the discussion proceeded very well—much information being volunteered." Chute assigned the students to write three reports based on articles from copies of *Ebony* magazine on a Harlem rent strike, the origin of Jim Crow, and Frederick Douglass. After recess, Chute divided the class into three groups, providing one group with a Spanish record and an accompanying text, directing eight students to practice typing using one typewriter and three written keyboards, and assigning other students to read or help unpack books for a community library. The class came together again to sit on benches under the trees and read aloud from excerpts of a speech by Frederick Douglass, as well as selections from a book of poems by Langston Hughes, which one student asked to take with him over night. Mrs. Chute concluded the session, as she concluded each session, by asking the students to write summaries of the morning's activities.[28]

The next day, two more students came to class, bringing attendance up to sixteen students, including three women. Mrs. Chute engaged the students in a discussion of the disadvantages to African Americans in the North, then went into a discussion of African history, for which Mrs. Chute drew a map "indicating approximate locations of early African countries and universities," adding parenthetically that all Freedom Schools could use such a map. Chute then divided the students into three groups and followed the plan of the previous day.[29]

On Wednesday, July 22nd, another teacher joined Mrs. Chute and took half the class. Mrs. Chute's lesson on African-American history dealt with slavery's ancient origins, its arrival in America, the conditions of slaves, and slave revolts and the Amistad mutiny. The new teacher, Peggy Gunn, took over the Spanish class and gave a math class; Chute worked with the typing class. Students again read poems by Langston Hughes, wrote summaries, and signed out books.[30]

On Thursday, Chute again dealt with issues connected with slavery and read descriptions of conditions under slavery by Harriet Tubman, Frederick Douglas and Booker T. Washington. Arlene Bock from the Canton Community Center came to teach math and Spanish, for Peggy Gunn was absent. A student read his report on *Ebony*'s account of a Harlem rent strike; another student read aloud the "Famous Bondsmen" section from *A Pictorial History of the Negro*, and another student read aloud abolitionist Elijah Lovejoy's last speech. Students studied math or typing and wrote summaries.[31]

On Friday, July 24th, Chute, once again without assistance, assigned reports based on *Ebony* articles for the following week. A student read her report on "The Birth of Jim Crow." In the 9:30 to 10:30 class, Chute reviewed the week's work by questioning students about topics covered. She read the Emancipation Proclamation, "lectured" about Reconstruction, and the class discussed the Civil Rights Bill of 1875 and the reasons for the failure of Reconstruction. During the 10:30 class, the Spanish class "studied on their own"; the typing class worked on "Freedom Now" phrases, while Chute "had quite a few 'artists' working in a short time" with a supply of paper, crayons, magic markers, and paint. At 11:30, the students enjoyed a break for cake supplied by "the Mother of several of the students." In the 12:00 to 1:00 class, one student read aloud a portion of a speech made by Frederick Douglass; then several students read aloud from a book on Negro folklore, and "seemed to find the exaggerated Negro dialect quite difficult." Chute reviewed the week's work by asking students to refute myths about Negroes and was pleased that they "did quite well—some were very good—in content and expression." In Chute's opinion, the "biggest hit of the week" was the Langston Hughes poetry, for there was "hardly a time during the week when some one wasn't reading our one copy of his Selected Poems."[32]

The week's work in the Gluckstadt Freedom School must have pleased the once reluctant Mt. Pleasant congregation, for on Sunday, July 26th, they agreed to open the church social hall for a library, "because of course there is no library available to Negroes in the area."[33]

Marcia Hall, the Canton Freedom School coordinator, submitted a daily progress report from July 3rd through July 10th for three schools in Canton, also in the Fourth Congressional District. The staff had arrived in Canton on June 29th and had spent the following days dividing the staff among the three churches, attending mass meetings, becoming acquainted with local citizens, and cleaning and arranging supplies in the three schools. On Sunday, July 5th, they held a picnic at the home of a Canton resident for interested students and their families.[34]

Thirty-six students came to Canton's Asbury Church on the first day of classes, which began at 9:30 on July 6th. The session began with a "general discussion" of the Movement and the purpose of the Freedom Schools. The students were divided into four groups of nine, each headed by a teacher who led small group discussions in separate classrooms. After the students were dismissed at noon, the staff met to plan the organization of the the school. They decided that four homerooms with approximately nine students would spend an hour and a half studying African-American history and the Movement. Then students would go to teacher-led "special interest classes": math and literature were offered on Tuesday,

Thursday and Saturday; science and "art-drama" were offered on Monday, Wednesday, and Friday. In the afternoon from noon until 2 p.m., students could work on "special projects," a newspaper or a play; typing and French lessons were also offered at this time. The schedule had to be adapted because fourteen new students came the next day, but the day after that, attendance dropped to thirty-five, and a teacher was transferred to another school. Moreover, the students found the ambitious curriculum and schedule the staff had planned too demanding, so both had to be adjusted. More role-playing was introduced into the study of the Movement and African-American history, and school ended at 1:00 p.m.; however, the building would remain open for students who wanted to pursue special projects or studies with teachers. The week ended with Asbury students planning a dance on July 18th for which a group of Asbury student musicians would supply the music.[35]

The Pleasant Green School in Canton opened at 9:00 a.m. on Monday, July 6th, with nine older students and ten elementary-age children. The session began with the singing of freedom songs; then the older students discussed the problems facing black people in Mississippi while one teacher played games with the younger children. Later, the teachers decided to have the younger children come at 2 p.m. and to recruit more older children. Tuesday, seven older students joined the group, and the group discussed early African-American history which led to a discussion of the modern civil rights organizations and "their leaders and their beliefs." The students then worked on a lesson about the meaning of chemistry and chemical structure. Their session closed with a discussion on citizenship and student life in Mississippi. An afternoon session for younger children involved them in games and drawing pictures. On subsequent days, the older students wrote essays about what they disliked in their regular schools, listened to lectures, held general and small group discussions about African-American history and the Movement and wrote letters to imagined Northern friends about their homes, families and living conditions in Canton. Hall noted that even these older students were only around fourteen, "and therefore the teachers have to make up many of the activities and questions since the curriculum is often too advanced for them." The school was nevertheless making progress, Hall noted, and the students were interested. The Friday session ended with the singing of freedom songs, "the best singing our group has had so far."[36]

Twenty-two students arrived at 9:45 a.m. on July 6th at the New Bethel School in Canton. After songs, a prayer, and the introduction of teachers, the students had a general discussion of the Citizenship Curriculum. Then they broke into groups for classes in history, math, science, English, and journalism. One teacher offered them an hour-long dancing class three days a week. On Tuesday, the lesson on African-American history was followed by four student-led discussion groups. The groups reassembled to report on the individual group discussion. At 12:15, students went to special-interest sessions. When school ended at 1:00 p.m., some students stayed to take a dancing lesson. On Wednesday, special projects were established: acting out important events in African-American history and writing essays for the school newspaper. The teachers also used question-and-answer games to test how successful the history discussion had been. In the afternoon, a local white man, Jake Vinson, came to the church to tell the teachers to leave because, he claimed, the church was on land he owned. Hall describes Thursday as "a very bad day," because the students drifted in and out after the break. Reading tests, given on Tuesday, had been completed and students were divided into three groups—remedial, average, and "the good ones to really concentrate on reading." Another teacher worked with one student, "a very fine boy who has very poor eyes." On Friday, one teacher completed his lecture on African-American history by "speaking on the Movement itself." Hall noted that while lectures could give out more information at a faster rate, discussion made the students more interested, and she hoped more group discussion would replace lecture. An hour was spent reading in small groups, and then the students held a debate and presented a short play in the last hour. Jake Vinson returned to threaten them with being forced out of the church. One student said he had threatened to bomb the church and the homes of Freedom School students, and for this reason some of the students had stayed away.[37]

In her closing comments, Hall claimed the Canton Freedom Schools were proceeding well. She reported that more of the teachers were adapting to the conditions and worrying less about their teaching abilities; students at all three schools were enthusiastic and becoming less shy; teachers and students were becoming closer. Hall acknowledged that Asbury school had the largest enrollment and organization was difficult at times, but the mostly older students in attendance adapted well to the curriculum; they had undertaken and were sustaining such projects as writing a newspaper and taking French or typing. Hall wrote that Pleasant Green was "coming along much better as time passes." She reported that the youth of the students taxed the teachers's imaginations, and because of the students' shorter attention span, activities had to be varied. Their participation improved if the topic "affects them directly." Hall described the New Bethel students as "very enthusiastic"; they carried on good discussions and had a very good relationship with their teachers. They had formed a singing group that promised to be very good. Jake Vinson remained the only problem. However, while his threats had driven some students away, they had made "most of the students even more anxious to come to school."[38]

In the Fifth District in Southeast Mississippi, Moss Point coordinator Tony O'Brien reported to Lynd that in the period from July 1st to July 21st, the average attendance was thirty students. Mornings were spent on citizenship: "lectures, analyses of local evils, pupils' reports on same (in particular, the evils of Magnolia High), role-playing occasionally." In the afternoons they were offered an ambitious array of courses: French, Spanish, English, Drama, Algebra, Advanced Math, Science, Art, Music, Negro History, Mississippi History, History of Religions, and History of Revolutions. Of these, O'Brien reported, Drama, Mississippi History, Advanced math, History of Religions, and History of Revolutions were dropped due to lack of interest. As a result of paring down, English, science, Spanish, algebra and French were in place for the afternoons; African-American history was transferred to the mornings so that all the students could take it. An art class and a music class, "plus some baseball and (if we could only keep a stable class!) a nursing class that meets occasionally" made up the recreational curriculum for Tuesday and Thursday afternoons. Classes for adults in literacy, basic English, and arithmetic met in the evenings.[39]

However, by the second week, the school began losing students until on the "worst morning [it] had only six." Badly discouraged, the teachers "began preferring to do office work when, after their brilliant course in the History of Revolutions had been thrown out, they found themselves without pupils even for algebra." The staff split up; some teachers taught while others canvassed. Through canvassing, teachers discovered that the students were too busy with other matters to come to school; "the best students were eager to be out canvassing for voter registration and had formed attachments to the VR staff," who were, in O'Brien's opinion, "one of the best local youth VR groups in the state." Moreover, some parents had kept their children away from school after being frightened by a shooting at one of the mass meetings. Attempts to get students to return or to recruit new students were unsuccessful, so the staff took the students on a trip to the segregated beach in Pass Christian, and were planning visits to "the other coast projects and perhaps Hattiesburg. The pattern of morning classes had settled into "a combination of lecturing, writing reports of stories, and role-playing." O'Brien wrote that for the following two weeks the students would be drafting a platform to take to the Freedom School convention. One problem, O'Brien acknowledged, was that the students were "hopelessly unaccustomed to thinking about long-range plans," and he hoped that they could be introduced to the practice.[40]

Florence Jones, Coordinator for three Freedom School sites in the Fifth District's Gulfport, submitted a report to Lynd on July 16th in which she expressed satisfaction that the staff was providing classes for "over 80 people: 30 children, 35 teenagers, and perhaps 18 adults." The subjects ranged from African-American history to typing and French, "but all of them turning on the issue of Civil Rights and citizenship." The Gulfport Freedom School had three sites, "two of them (Shiloh Baptist Church and the New Evening Star Church) in North Gulfport, . . . and one (the Longshoremen's Hall) in Central Gulfport." Jones did not provide details about the curriculum and scheduling, but explained that each school had a "core of regular attenders," who had enough confidence in their teachers to make classes "something like a progress in self discovery," for the more teachers and student got used to "talking about

Freedom with one another, the more often remarks are made by the students that show the vein of bitterness and skepticism that exists even in the youngest." Nevertheless, Jones wrote, the students had enough enthusiasm for their role in the struggle for Freedom "that they have suggested of their own accord that this is the most important thing they've ever learned, and they have decided to call their school newspaper 'The Press of Freedom.'" Jones hoped that the students would go "the next stage" and start a Gulfport branch of the Mississippi Student Union.[41]

As for the adults, Jones reported that those who attend classes regularly were using the opportunity to improve their reading and writing enough to pass the voter registration test, or having passed the test, to study government, especially the Constitution, "in order to understand the bigger part they could play in the political struggle." However, "the numbers are too few." Every time the staff "preach in church about the Freedom classes—say 6 churches each Sunday—a dozen people shake us by the hand and promise to come along, who never actually turn up"; the younger adults of nineteen and twenty "turn up once or twice, but never for a third time."[42]

Jones wrote that the staff used two or three voter registration workers teach in the evenings, "and, by way of payment," some teachers went canvassing from time to time on Saturdays and in the afternoon. The arrangement worked well, according to Jones, because the teachers could teach more effectively in the morning and the evening when they had spent time doing something different, and in the process became "better informed on the scope of the whole project when . . . talking to the people in the town about what they might do to help us. Besides, hardly any students were interested in afternoon classes, except those who want to learn typing, and a class had been provided for them."[43]

Jones's report provided insight into community tensions. The president and vice-president of the local NAACP, a doctor and the local president of the Longshoremen's Union, had "gone out of their way" to give support to the project; they had arranged for the Longshoremen's Hall to serve as a site for the Freedom School in Central Gulfport when the original site was being used for a choir festival and had also arranged for the staff to meet with the

Ministers' Alliance, "who were at first very suspicious of us and had to be talked round." The ministers arranged a meeting for the staff with the Mayor of Gulfport, who agreed to let them have use of a local school, "but—alas!—was obliged to inform us subsequently that it is not part of the Board's policy to let any but its own teachers into the school." In the following week, the staff

> took ten persons down to the Courthouse all together, some of the ministers have gone back to entertaining their old suspicions about us. But we still preach in their churches, and take the opportunity to explain how God's work is never popular with the well-positioned. It amounts to a form of blackmail. (In fairness, I must say that there are two or three ministers in more lowly positions who are prepared to go with us all the way.)[44]

Jones was disappointed that no local teacher had come forward to offer services so that more students could be taught, and that when the summer was over, "somebody in educational circles here will be prepared to say that we were not such a bad institution after all."[45]

In his late July report, Staughton Lynd had observed that in a black community where canvassing for voter registration was too dangerous, a Freedom School was possible "as an instrument for building confidence" in the black community.[46] He cited McComb as a case in point. McComb, in Southwestern Mississippi's Third District, had been under Klan violence for more than a decade; during the summer, six bombings had destroyed the Freedom House, as well as several homes and businesses, with the result that McComb became known as "the bombing capital of the world." Hellen O'Neal, a volunteer teacher from Tougaloo described her first sight of the McComb Freedom School:

> I arrived in McComb on a a Sunday afternoon. The house and garage had been bombed. The garage, which was detached, seemed to be leaning to one side with papers, bits of building, and branches scattered around the front lawn and in the driveway. Ralph Featherstone [the director of the McComb Freedom School] came out of the back door and introduced himself. I said I was from the Jackson COFO office and I had come to teach Freedom School.

I said, "Where is the Freedom School?" He pointed to the bombed-out garage.[47]

However, the Freedom School flourished, and by late July had an enrollment of 100 students.[48] The McComb Freedom School students were militant, following an example that had been set for them in 1961, when students walked out of school because the principal had expelled a student, Brenda Travis, for her civil rights activities. During the summer the McComb produced several issues of "Freedom's Journal," with students taking turns as editors. The July 24th issue contained a poem by one of that issue's editors, Edith Moore, "Isn't It Awful?" that dealt with their situation:

Isn't it awful not to be able to eat
in a public place
Without being arrested or snarled at
right in your face?
Isn't it awful not to be able to go to
a public library and get an interesting book
Without being put out and given
a hateful look?
Isn't it awful not to be able to sleep
peacefully nights
For fear you may get bombed because
you want your rights?
Isn't it awful not to be able to get
your schooling where you please?
Just because of our race, color and
creed we cannot feel at ease.[49]

In the August 11th issue, the editors, Sue Sephus, Marilyn Carter, and Viola Williams, praised their fellow students for attending school and canvassing for voter registration, but declared many of the adults in McComb "a great disappointment to their race" for not sending their children to Freedom School and for not trying to register to vote. They reminded their elders of Frederick Douglass's statement, "If there is no struggle, there is no progress."[50]

Ira Landess sent Lynd an end-of-summer evaluation of the McComb Freedom School, claiming as its major achievement the establishment of an academic program—French, Spanish, remedial reading, chemistry, biology, math, typing, and art—that was important to the students because they were offered "in a friendly and encouraging environment, some practical, solid, traditional subject areas, some of which had not been open to them at all." Landess believed that the African-American history curriculum, "while not a failure," could be "a rather artificial curriculum," because it reminded students of their history of deprivation and ostracism. Landess suggested that African-American history should not be "a freak study," but the classes "ought to be integrated, made a single part of a broad curriculum." Landess believed that African-American history could be made more "incisive" if studied through literature. After realizing that four days of teaching Reconstruction had left no impression on the students, he assigned *Freedom Road*, which brought the period to life. He was certain that the students would never forget reading a single chapter of *Black Boy* and that perhaps the most valuable experience of all for the students was reading "Two Men and a Bargain" from Lillian Smith's book, *Killers of the Dream*.[51]

Ira Landess's reservations about the African-American history curriculum were echoed in a letter from Judy Walborn to Liz Fusco in November, 1964. Reflecting on the Greenwood Freedom School while drafting a curriculum for a Freedom School program planned for the summer of 1965, Walborn acknowledged that the teachers had been doing "a great deal of propagandizing," and that the black history curriculum emphasized the Movement too heavily because the Freedom School students had been activists for two and three years, and "knew a great deal about the realities of their situation." Walborn reported that Freedom School teachers had helped the students to "conceptualize that understanding on a more sophisticated basis," but after six weeks, everyone was "satiated with the topic"; however, when the teachers switched to "a more academic, content-filled curriculum—specifically to a college-prep math and English and literature curriculum," many of the students, "especially the brighter ones," responded favorably.[52]

These reports reveal some of the problems Freedom School faculty had to overcome: community tensions in Clarksdale and Gulfport; a lack of match between course offerings and student interest that resulted in sharp drops in attendance in Greenville and Clarksdale; threats against the schools in Canton resulting in an attendance drop; harassment of host families resulting in displacement of volunteers in Gluckstadt. However, the reports are more striking in their revelation of the resourcefulness and dedication of the volunteers. Kirsty Powell in Ruleville, Virginia Chute in Gluckstadt, and Marcia Hall in Canton created strong structures in their schools and adapted curriculum to student needs. The reported instances of male students' resistance to Freedom School, perhaps resulting from their attraction to the masculine appeal of voter registration, or aversion to the large numbers of women teaching Freedom School, or from the impression that Freedom School was as emasculating as "regular" school, was countered in Shaw and Holmes County by the support for football. An important factor in the success of the Freedom Schools was the willingness of teachers to set aside a curriculum that was not suitable for students who were already Movement veterans, or not satisfying to students who recognized how much their own schools had cheated them, and supply instead traditional academic subjects.

In a number of Freedom Schools, innovative teachers led students in the creation of plays, some of which were performed before sizable audiences. In Holly Springs, UFT teacher Deborah Flynn led her students to improvise *Seeds of Freedom*, a play based on the life and death of Medgar Evers. With Flynn supplying background, the students researched Evers' life and death, then developed the play through discussion and improvisation until they were ready to create a script for a 50-minute play, which was performed in late July before an audience of two hundred. *Seeds of Freedom* was performed in other Freedom Schools and toured with the Free Southern Theatre. In McComb, *McComb, USA*, a long and complex play, was presented in a living newspaper format, probably with the assistance of teachers, based on the actual violent acts against the African-American community. In Mileston Freedom School, students presented *The American Negro* in seven short scenes depicting the experiences of African Americans in a historical context. Students at the Gulfport Freedom School created a short play, *Memories of Freedom School*, providing the history of COFO's arrival in Mississippi and presenting the memorable events of

Freedom School.[53] The disciplined collective work involved in creating and performing these plays undoubtedly led to a significant expansion of the students' language and social skills.

Charles M. Payne has observed that, within the civil rights movement, "Freedom School work had relatively low status value" because women did much of the work and voter registration was "the prestige assignment." Payne cites the report of one male volunteer as evidence of the frustration arising from the discouraging work of following the "long, slow road" of Freedom School work:

> Running a freedom school is an absurd waste of time. I don't want to sit around in a classroom; I want to go out and throw a few office buildings, not to injure people but to shake them up, destroy stolen property, convince them we mean business . . . . I really can't stand it here.[54]

That young man's despair is in contrast to the commitment and pride in their work revealed in the majority of reports, mostly from women, retained in the SNCC archives. If Freedom School teaching was not considered prestigious, I do not believe the majority of women who taught felt that way. The assessment of Holly Springs volunteer Gloria Clark is, I believe, representative of our views:

> I was always made to feel that what everyone was doing was equally important. There was much project support for the Freedom schools and we had male teachers as well . . . . In fact we were encouraged to develop our potential . . . and skills to assist the communities we served.[55]

Freedom Schools varied in effectiveness; however, in the opinion of Clayborne Carson "many youngsters were deeply and permanently affected by the unique educational experience."[56] That the Freedom Schools were profoundly successful, despite shortcomings and failures here and there, was the substance of an evaluation by Liz Fusco, a Smith College graduate and former Peace Corps volunteer with high school and college teaching experience, who succeeded Staughton Lynd as the Freedom School coordinator at summer's end. In Fusco's opinion, what made the Mississippi Summer Project different from other civil rights activities in the South was the asking and answering of the questions posed by the Citizenship Curriculum, and "the continual raising of them in many contexts." The curriculum, in her opinion, was at the heart of the schools' success, for in the beginning of the summer, the ambition of the students was to escape the intolerable conditions in Mississippi, but through the Citizenship Curriculum, they learned of the actual condition of the the situation of African Americans in the North, and the truth shattered "their dream of it as a paradise." In Freedom School, the students discovered that "they themselves could take action against the injustices—the specific injustices and the condition of injustice which kept them unhappy and impotent." They became "articulate about what was wrong, and the way things should be instead." Questioning "why there were no art classes, no language classes, why there is no equipment in the science labs, why the library is inadequate and inaccessible, why the classes are overcrowded" led to the main question: "Why are we not taken seriously?"[57]

The students were taken seriously in Freedom Schools, Fusco claimed; they were encouraged to talk and were listened to; they were "assigned to write and their writing was read with attention to idea and style as well as to grammar." Students were encouraged to think, "and this was painful as well as releasing" because, in her view, to be taken seriously requires taking one's self seriously and it requires confrontation. From being able only "to whine, or to accept passively, or to lash out by dropping our of school or getting themselves expelled," the students learned to discipline their thinking so that their responses to their situation would be meaningful. Fusco cited the resolutions students drew up mid-summer as evidence of the transformation they had undergone at Freedom School, for at Meridian their resolutions said "with terrible clarity what they felt about their world: what a house should be, what a school should be, what a job should be, what a city should be—even what the federal government should be."[58]

It was Fusco's view that Northern volunteer teachers had been transformed by what they had learned from their students, and even the veteran project directors, who had "first thought of the Freedom Schools as a frill," or at best, "a convenient source of canvassers," were transformed by witnessing young people emerge "as discussion leaders, as teachers, as organizers, as speakers, as friends, as people." Because the project had been so successful, Fusco predicted, aspects of the Freedom Schools would continue "into the regular academic year in the form of tutorials and independent study, as well as . . . longer range work with art, music, and drama." Fusco believed that the progress of students, whose educational experience had been dull at best and at worst "tragically crippling," was evidence "that a total transformation of the young people in an underdeveloped country can take place, and . . . that it can happen all over the South."[59]

On August 31st, Liz Fusco sent a memo "to the field," informing people of preparations for the program to be established for the 1964–5 school year. These included the renovation of buildings and libraries in Cleveland, Greenville, Hattiesburg, Holly Springs, and Greenwood; the "underground" circulation of petitions by the Mississippi Student Union designed to culminate in a state-wide school boycott; and the beginning or resuming of classes in a number of communities. Her immediate recommendation was to organize high school students and their parents to register at white schools. According to Fusco, the registrations may be accepted, as in Clarksdale, but if students were refused admission, the parents must get a registrar "to say an unequivocal 'no' in order to supply an affidavit for the Justice Department." Fusco's second assignment to Freedom School volunteers was to prepare for the boycott by getting the kids "to start making their demands and grievances coherent, and put them in the form of a petition, and start the slow underground work of person-to-person talk among the kids who do not come to Freedom School."[60]

Without the benefit of the exhaustive preparations for the summer Freedom Schools, without the power to confer diplomas, and without the support exhausted communities could not provide beyond the summer, the post-summer Freedom School programs were not as well organized as the summer schools had been. Some teachers had stayed behind, but the Freedom School students returned to their segregated schools, and after school they were often involved with community activism. Liz Fusco wrote Judy Walborn in late October that "the kids" were helping to canvass for the Freedom Vote in support of the candidacies of Fannie Lou

Hamer, Aaron Henry, Annie Devine, and Victoria Gray to lay the basis for an MFDP challenge of the Mississippi delegation when Congress reconvened in January. After that, Fusco reported, they would work "toward a realistic decision at Thanksgiving time about whether or not to boycott the schools, and what kind of alternative action to take if not that." The students' activism meant, Fusco acknowledged, that "the real academic concentration . . . is not realistic in the light of what's really happening." Tutorials and seminars would have to be better developed, and "as to the teaching staff—what can we know about what we can count on?" Fusco, who had advocated for the Negro Scholarship Program to bring Mississippi students to schools in the North, reexamined the impact of sending students North, either with teachers who had taken the students with them or had sent for them later, or by the families who, "in the vague old idea of setting them free," had sent their children off, "often to ghettos, often to be lonely." Fusco now declared herself "absolutely opposed to getting the kids North just because it's North."[61]

The fall 1964 Freedom School program began tentatively, with volunteer teachers often uncertain of the time they would commit to remaining in Mississippi. In Greenwood, Judy Walborn planned to return to California, and Rich Miller assumed leadership, at least until December. On September 3rd, he wrote Liz that the program being prepared included a college preparatory course focusing on "reading comprehension and vocabulary questions likely to appear on college entrance exams and college boards" in the hope that "decent SAT and ACT scores will attract scholarship money" so that the students would have an option other than "going to Mississippi Valley State, which is really just a continuation of high school and where the penalty for being involved in civil rights activity is expulsion." Miller reported that the staff remaining in Greenwood was too small to do more than set up a large study hall where the students could come for help. Miller also reported that a local high school English teacher had provided them with a reading list and told them of problems she had encountered in getting the students interested in applying to out-of-state colleges. When asked if she would "talk up" the program the Greenwood staff was starting, she smiled and said, "Well, I promise you one thing. I won't talk it down." Miller concluded his report with the announcement, "we're broke," and asked that fifty dollars be sent immediately.[62]

In response to a request in August from Liz Fusco about plans for establishing a Freedom School Community Center in Columbus after the summer, Mike Higson responded that, although there was interest to get school going again, he doubted that a place would be available, for Columbus was a "long way yet from being community minded—too many people, for example, openly state they do not want to be involved at all to make a Center an easy proposition."[63]

However, a newsletter published by COFO in November revealed that MSU students were active in Columbus, expressing demands for improvements at Hunt High School. They complained that they were not offered a foreign language; they did not have qualified teachers; they were not enabled to express themselves in writing; they were reprimanded for asking questions; they were provided with out-of-date texts in poor condition; there was only one biology teacher and physics and chemistry classes were overcrowded. The newsletter also reported that thirteen Columbus MSU students had met in Jackson to discuss the possibility of a statewide school boycott, and would return to Jackson around Thanksgiving after learning whether or not other students would support a boycott.[64]

Dave Edmonston wrote Liz Fusco in mid-October that at the first Freedom School session in the Gulfport Freedom School, only three high school students showed up, but that the response of the class to the discussion of Negro history nevertheless pleased him. When one girl came late, Edmonston had, as Fusco had previously suggested, asked the other students to fill her in, "which was helpful as a review to them, and was successful in drawing the new girl in."[65]

The disappointing conditions in Moss Point that Tony O'Brien had reported to Staughton Lynd during the summer deteriorated even further by early December, as evidenced in two letters to Liz Fusco. Mary Larsen began her letter with the statement, "Moss Point is a discouraging place to be." Larsen acknowledged that she realized "the importance of consciousness of injustice"; "that the job of the Freedom School is to foster this kind of awareness, & so the Freedom Schools are the best weapon against apathy," but, she concluded,

> Things seem so futile here. Last Sun. we had perhaps 12 kids at F.S., where loud irrelevancies were shouted at each other. Harry is a problem, with so much to prove to everyone. And so many are like that, tho less extreme. I am, I fear, a poor catalyst for clear thought.[66]

Nancy Sours began her letter to Liz Fusco with a similarly morose declaration: "Morale here is abysmal." She wrote that complaints about the project director had led to a "palace revolution" during a Fifth District COFO meeting in Hattiesburg in late November. There the Moss Point volunteers had aired their complaints against their director, and Sours came from the meeting with the clear impression that the Moss Point project was "in serious trouble unless some form of internal structure can be forged in the near future" that included "the rudiments of internal democracy, at least giving projects the right of veto over their director." Another matter that distressed Sours was "the perennial chaos" due to the continual presence of a group of truant teenage boys, who, not having been put to good use by the project director, behaved in a way to "alienate or even intimidate anyone who ventures into the office." They turned a Freedom School class "into a screaming contest"; attempts by Sours and fellow volunteer Mary Larsen to conduct an orderly discussion were continually shouted down. The pleas of the white female volunteers were ineffectual against the teenagers, as well as the male staff, who failed to clean up the mess they made cooking, with the result that Sours and volunteer Mary Ellickson cleaned up and washed dishes. What compensated Sours for these and other distresses were "the expected ones—the children, Mrs. Scott, and the family with whom I stay, the Gadneys." Mr. and Mrs. Gadney had become "very dear friends," and Sours found theirs was "a really wonderful home to return to after a depressing day. Somehow the small group of really dedicated community people keep faith in us long after we've begun to lose faith in ourselves."[67]

Meanwhile, Liz Fusco was very busy with implementing a Freedom School structure under far more hectic conditions than those Staughton Lynd had faced. She had to resolve staffing problems, such as the one that arose when two women volunteers were sent by Fusco to Indianola to start a program for children under fourteen. One volunteer found herself burdened with adult and high school evening classes and received no cooperation "from the voter registration people"; the other volunteer telephoned Fusco complaining that she was lonely and unable to function in Indianola. Fusco solved the problem by transferring the unhappy volunteer to Jackson to do research for a federal program and sent a nineteen-year-old volunteer to Indianola to set up the children's program. The overburdened volunteer was able to report to Liz that, without this young woman, "there could have been no Freedom School; there is now new life, new energy, new directions since she came. There is now a program, and it is being carried out: geography, reading and writing, and dancing (African and folk) for the children 5 to 14."[68]

Raising funds and gathering resources were also Fusco's responsibilities. An Adopt-a-Freedom School campaign that had begun before the summer continued beyond it. Appeals sent out to New York schools resulted in the adoption of a school in Shaw and a school in Greenville. One Manhattan junior high school embarked on "a massive food collection," and the UFT continued to contribute funds on a regular basis to support Freedom Schools in Holly Springs and Hattiesburg.[69] Of course, many individuals and organizations continued to support the ongoing Freedom School project. Liz Fusco typically acknowledged these contributions in gracious notes, such as the one she wrote to one contributor:

> What $25.00 can buy towards Hope, Justice, and Freedom is more than what that same amount could buy toward anything else: James Baldwin's *Go Tell It on the Mountain* in multiple copies. and Richard Wright's *Native Son* in the same number, and then a week's worth of primary colors and paper cups to mix them in and brushes an paper, and a few children's books so there can be quiet for discussion inside, and them some envelopes and stamps for the writing to be sent somewhere, and the paper and pencils themselves—a Freedom School week can be bought for one class.[70]

Fusco's requests for books from publishers, organizations, and individuals produced enough books to fill warehouses in Jackson and Atlanta that could be distributed to the Freedom School libraries. The problem, however, was that not enough of them met the need for books on black history, on Africa, on American politics; for good novels and children's books. Fusco became impatient with the quantities of books donated in the spirit of "give all your old books to the Mississippi book drive."[71] "Please, no more second-hand textbooks," she wrote to one donor. "That's the only kind of books these kids have ever seen. Raggedy, used, discarded, and therefore worthless—in these they see the image of themselves as the white man sees them."[72]

However, on December 25th, 1964, the same day she wrote the letter scolding the donor of second-hand textbooks, Fusco addressed a joyful letter to another donor who had sent the right stuff:

> Boxes and boxes of books of poetry have arrived, and if you could have heard the shrieks in the Jackson (mostly mine, but not only mine!) you would have been most gratified. it was a really heartbreaking thing to have to keep the staff's hands off the books until I could get them distributed equitably—and people in the office have checked them out of the Jackson Freedom Library already. All over the state, in fact, staff if [sic] reading poetry—that is the first step, of course, because if staff doesn't there will be no incentive for kids to, in fact, in Starkville, which is a Negro ghetto just like the name suggests (the white folks live fine), Bill Light and Ron Carver and Ron Bridgeforth and Jimmy Jones read poetry aloud to each other to music, and lately the local kids have taken to reading aloud and not just listening. And they're writing it there, too. So we win![73]

Another letter Fusco wrote to a donor on December 25th apologized for not acknowledging each package of books that had been sent and went on to explain why she did not have time to acknowledge each delivery:

> If we had a full-time person doing nothing but books for the Freedom Libraries it would be a full-time job; and if we had another doing correspondence for the Freedom Schools and Freedom Libraries, that would be a full-time administrative job; and if we had another reading and reviewing and recommending books, that

would be full-time; and if we had another traveling around to Freedom Schools and helping out, that would be much more than full-time. I am doing all these jobs myself, in addition to helping coordinate opportunities for Freedom School kids.[74]

Liz Fusco's Christmas mood swing from the joy of poetry to the stress of many responsibilities is not surprising in light of the uncertain and disorganized situation of the post-summer Freedom School project. A more daunting obstacle to maintaining the project resulted when disillusionment following the rejection of the MFDP delegation at the Democratic convention bred racial tension. In November, the SNCC staff assembled for a retreat at a Methodist church center in Waveland, near the Gulf Coast, for the purpose of determining SNCC's future: either a centralized, hierarchical political organization that James Forman favored, or the loosely connected structure Bob Moses wanted to continue. Other issues surfaced, including Mary King and Casey Hayden's early second-wave feminist paper on the role of women in SNCC, but the issue dominating the meeting in increasingly strident and hostile discussions was race and the role of whites in SNCC.[75]

The issue of race emerged again in the meeting—about which Nancy Sours had written Liz Fusco—in Hattiesburg one week later. Moss Point was one of three projects experiencing a "palace revolution," for the volunteers of Gulfport and Biloxi, along with the volunteers of Moss Point brought complaints to Jesse Morris of the Jackson COFO office about their project directors' drinking, sleeping with female volunteers and taking project cars for personal use. In the day-long meeting, comments were often rancorous on both sides ("There are a lot of bullshitting Negroes in the Movement"; "I won't take orders from white folks in the Movement"). The meeting ended without resolution, and the volunteers from Biloxi and Gulfport probably returned to their projects with morale as "abysmal" as that of the Moss Point volunteers.[76]

Black separatism emerged at a second Waveland retreat in May, 1965; it resounded with increasing heat at other SNCC meetings as the faction supporting it gained adherents and ultimately white workers were purged from SNCC in 1967. Bob Zellner, the first white staff member hired by SNCC, has observed of this struggle,

"It is ironic that SNCC sought its soul by becoming all black at the same time that Malcolm X was moving to a more inclusive, and I think a more revolutionary stance of working with revolutionary whites."[77]

Liz Fusco left Mississippi in the spring of 1966, and shortly afterward wrote a long letter—"Letter to to Kathy (Whom I Don't Know) Who Wants to Know (From Me) Whether she Can Learn More About Sociology in School or in the South"—in which she revealed the strain of struggling to maintain in this atmosphere a coherent statewide Freedom School program. Fusco acknowledged that

> the entire Freedom School experience must have changed the students' attitude toward what learning can be, because in Freedom School, summer, 1964, here was a teacher who was interested in what they said and what they thought and what they felt, and who did not grade (usually), or beat, or humiliate them. Here was a teacher who in most Freedom Schools, encouraged them to talk out of themselves , and to laugh, and sing, and play sports, and did all that with them, and taught them some French or Spanish or German, and talked to them about Negroes. And all of that was something Mississippi kids had never known school could be.[78]

However, what followed that wonderful summer, according to Fusco, was disappointment. The Freedom School students who went North after the summer in search of Freedom found instead loneliness and despair. The students who remained in Mississippi remembered learning French, but the teacher who had taught them French had left and the voter registration people in the project did not know French, so they returned to "what they now saw much more clearly to be an inadequate school, but against which they had no program, and to which they were tied for sports and the diploma."[79] Therefore, Fusco concluded, "until people from the North who want to teach are ready to come down for a 9-month term, and until the FDP has its revolutionary school board ready to hire, and revolutionary taxes ready to pay teachers, there can be no academic instruction that will mean anything in the Movement."[80]

6. The Aftermath of Freedom Summer ✍

When I returned to New York and resumed teaching at Benjamin Franklin High School, the Vietnam War was underway and teachers soon became aware that former students had been transformed into soldiers. At union meetings, teachers from around the city shared their grief for those former students that had already been killed or wounded, as well as their fear for other teenage warriors in harm's way. The impact of thrusting such young men into a conflict for which they had not been prepared was made clear to me when a student came to tell me of his brother, who had been a student in my class only the previous year. After serving a tour in Vietnam, he had come home shattered by his experience, but his family discouraged him from talking about it. Only to his brother could he confide his despair, expressed repeatedly through the simile, "It was just like in a movie." Opposition to the war grew, and in the spring of 1965, at a demonstration in Washington, D.C., Norma Becker and I ran into Staughton Lynd, who charged us, "You two have got to do something about this," and we did. We wrote a statement opposing the war, and by compiling a mailing list in a not very organized way, we secured 2,700 names to a statement opposing the war that appeared in the *New York Times* of 30 May 1965: "To Our President, A Former Teacher." When a number of teachers expressed a desire to "do more," the ad hoc committee we had formed took on a more permanent status as the Teachers Committee for Peace in Vietnam. Eventually twenty to thirty people worked on a more or less steady basis in a tiny office at 5 Beekman Street, a kind of anti-Pentagon, that they shared with other anti-war organizations. Here they sent out newsletters, contacted teachers in other cities and encouraged them to form similar protest groups; they took out ads, both in the *Times* and the American Federation of Teachers newspaper; they sponsored meetings and discussions, prepared and distributed literature, sent delegates to the AFT convention and sponsored demonstrations along with other organizations. My anti-war activism caught the attention of the F. B. I. and the file the agency had established about me during the summer of 1964 was reactivated.

In September, 1965, I was appointed to teach at Erasmus Hall High School in Flatbush, Brooklyn. The school population was around 6,000, and the school operated on double session. Most of the students were from middle-class Jewish families, but increasing numbers of students from the primarily African-American community of Bedford-Stuyvesant were entering the school, to the undisguised dismay of the administration and many teachers.

Erasmus Hall is the oldest public high school in the country, and was a private academy even before our nation was independent. Alexander Hamilton had been a student, and the school took pride in the large number of Merit Scholars, academic prizewinners, Ph.D.s and other distinguished citizens, such as Barbra Streisand and Bernard Malamud, numbered among its graduates. I had heard much of the high academic achievement of the students, so I was surprised by the generally low quality of the literature—mostly short story anthologies—being taught in the English classes. The newly appointed chair worked to upgrade the level of the material, and she succeeded in requiring the inclusion of Shakespeare's plays and other classic works in the English curriculum. It is not easy to ask teachers to change their routines, especially when they have been teaching the same material and following the same lesson plans for decades, but the chair made her job even more difficult by her lack of confidence and insight. She regarded any questioning of her ideas as a hostile act. Her department was very large—fifty-five teachers—and she succeeded in undermining the morale of many of them. Her attempt to extend her control even to the most personal matters was revealed in a memo to the women of the department instructing them on the dress code she wanted followed and included the warning, "No matter how thin you are, you must always, always wear a girdle." To their great amusement, the memo reached some men of the department, who then teased their female colleagues with the charge that they were "not following the dress code."

The first characteristic I noted about the students at Erasmus Hall was their parrot-like behavior. They spouted cliches about "the Free World," "the Communist conspiracy," and how "things down South were bad." They had been trained to repeat by rote what was taught them and generally the formula worked. When I challenged them or invited them to challenge me, they remained mute, suspicious of a trap. Like students in the segregated Mississippi schools, they had learned that "silence is safest."

The second thing I noticed about these students was their dishonesty. Students at Benjamin Franklin cheated during tests; they held their notes in front of them or in their laps, but their efforts were clumsy and easily detected, and could be stopped by a good-humored request for the cheat sheet. It was not until I gave my first test to an honor class at Erasmus Hall that I knew what cheating was. Everyone was involved, and I knew I would need a thousand eyes to see it all. I tried to circumvent cheating by asking students questions demanding analysis from an individual point of view rather than a formula response. While some of the students were opportunists, a significant number of others were oppressed by the stifling atmosphere of the school and the pressure of competition to get into good colleges. One boy began a composition with the sentence, "People stink," and followed that with a list of betrayals and disappointments. Another extremely intelligent, genuinely interested student said, almost in despair, "It doesn't matter what I do or how well I do it; there's always someone who can do it better. I don't expect to get into the college I would like to go to because so many are ahead of me."

Only the most tepid adolescent writing was allowed publication in the school literary magazine. The principal refused to let the staff of the school newspaper publish anything dealing with non-school affairs; no mention was to be made of the Vietnam war or the civil rights movement. When the school's representatives on a TV high school quiz game lost to those of another high school, he tried to have the newspaper omit the score from publication.

So much dishonesty on the part of adults probably contributed to an active quasi-criminal underground at the high school. I became friendly with a very attractive, bright, and hip member of the resistance who told me, "You can get anything you want here— a fake hall pass, a phony report card, anything." She worked in the student government organization store, where she and her friends managed to steal several thousands of dollars each year. She claimed to believe that one of the reasons the practice had continued so long was that the faculty advisor also had his hand in the till. I have no idea of this was so, but this suspicion about the faculty advisor was shared by another colleague, and it is difficult to believe the thefts could have continued so long without his knowledge.

If there was drug use at Benjamin Franklin High School, I was not aware of it, but I knew involvement with drugs was significant at Erasmus Hall. My student friend described a bust. About fifteen students were rounded up one day. The Dean of Boys entered classrooms, and ostentatiously searched the students' desks in the presence of their classmates. They were taken to the principal's office, where a police detective was waiting to question them. They were not informed of their rights, for it was understood that they did not have any. Some students had drugs of one kind or another in their possession. All of them were searched, except my friend, who refused to surrender her pocketbook even though she had managed to get rid of the pills she had been carrying. The students believed that a student informer had been used against them.

During this period I learned from friends of the worsening conditions at Benjamin Franklin High School. A group of teachers at the school began a campaign in 1965 to halt the deterioration. Unfortunately, the teachers found few parents with will or time enough to join the campaign for improvements. New York State Senator Jerome Wilson and United States Senator Robert Kennedy visited the school and met with higher-ups at the Board of Education, but nothing was accomplished. Rather than fix the problem, the Board made tentative plans to close the school in five years.

Formerly a three-year school, Franklin had opened in September 1965 as a four-year school with 3,100 students, an increase of 600 over the previous year. However, the New York City Board of

Education had failed to assign enough teachers to cover the classes, which were taught by a series of per diem substitutes. Burned out, many of the old hands at Franklin retired or took advantage of the seniority system to transfer to high schools with a less demanding environment. As a result, one-third of the faculty were completely inexperienced, but like the rest of the teachers, they were expected to teach the standard syllabus of the academic curriculum. However, extensive tests administered the previous year revealed that the average sophomore at Franklin was reading at a fifth grade elementary school level, making it impossible for even a talented and dedicated teacher to teach the standard academic curriculum. Aware of their deficiency, students lost motivation and became bored and restless. Violence increased: a stabbing in the halls in November, a lunchroom riot in December. The students cut classes, strolled through the halls in an exaggerated hipster gait and smoked on the stairwells. When challenged, they responded, "I'm going to fail anyway." Their contempt for themselves extended to everything in their environment, and that included the teachers. "If she were really any good," one student remarked, "she'd be teaching somewhere else." But even in this malaise, some teachers refused to yield to despair. Due to the determined efforts of a guidance counselor, Irwin Goldberg, 150 Franklin graduates went on to some form of higher education in 1965.

Meanwhile, overwhelmed by the rigid atmosphere at Erasmus Hall High School, I had migraine headaches every week. After one year, I transferred to what was then known as a "600 school" (I have no idea of the significance of the number, but such schools have long been out of existence), a school for emotionally disturbed adolescent girls in Greenwich Village. Under the leadership of a talented principal, a dedicated staff of 22 teachers taught approximately 80 students typing, cooking, beauty culture, and a couple of briefly covered academic subjects. Class sizes were small—never more than 10 and usually 6 or 7—and the emphasis was on establishing an affective relationship with a student rather than on building skill in a subject area. The students received a great deal of attention and care. Many students made progress, but not all could be helped. Some students had been forced into sexual relations with a father or male relative. Most were sexually active, and although the principal had been able to establish a connection with the birth control clinic at a local hospital, a number became pregnant. These were not the assertive, high energy students, but passive adolescents, born to a single mother and carelessly parented, who sought motherhood in a desperate and unreasonable longing to "have someone of my very own to love."

However, the teachers' dedicated effort at the Livingston School could yield at best minimal results; graduating from high school and getting a service job was the highest expectation for students. I missed contact with students whom one could assist to achieve more substantial results. I transferred yet again to what was then an all girls' academic high school: Washington Irving High School near Union Square. The students were working-class white, Hispanic, and black, as well as middle-class white and Chinese. Teachers in long service at Washington Irving remembered ruefully that once a finishing school atmosphere had prevailed at the school and time was reserved for the weekly serving of tea. Once again, I found a group of enlightened and talented teachers, but the prevailing atmosphere during the time I taught there was as oppressive as that of Erasmus Hall High School. The male leadership was heavy-handed; expression of opposition to the Vietnam war was repressed, and a dress code decreed that students could not wear pants. During a particularly cold January, the students decided to wear pants to school one day. As they entered the school, they were met by a phalanx of male administrators and faculty who ordered the girls to change into skirts or go back home. One of these men was quoted as justifying the no-pants dress code on the grounds that walking in jeans brought the students' genitals into friction against the crotch, causing them to become too sexually aroused to concentrate in class. I realized that I did not want to spend more years struggling within the school system against that kind of thinking. I was an early participant in the women's movement, and had gained enough confidence to begin work on a doctorate. In January 1970, I got a position to teach at New York City Technical College, and in subsequent years taught there and at other branches of the City University of New York.

During this time, I maintained contact with Mrs. Jackson, remembering her at Christmas and calling her on July 4th, the anniversary of my entry into Mississippi. I also kept in touch with my Priest Creek Freedom School students, who had returned to Earl Travillion Attendance Center energized by their experience, especially having encountered for the first time books by black authors, and in this way acquiring a lasting love of reading. Another and unexpected benefit of their Freedom School experience was "a better understanding" of "why their teachers did some of the things they did in order to keep their jobs." For their part, their teachers, all of whom were black and supportive of their students, became more forthcoming with them. Some of the teachers had received graduate degrees from Northern universities and were familiar with the works of black authors, but because of the limitations imposed by the segregated system, were unable to teach these books in their classrooms. However, after the summer, students were able to discuss Freedom School and the Movement; in government class, especially, students were able to talk about current events. Shirley Anderson remembers that teachers were tolerant of students who joined in COFO activism, but encouraged them to keep up with their studies.[1]

Freedom School students in Palmer's Crossing did not let the summer experience fade from memory or lapse into nostalgia; it remained a source of inspiration. Freedom School had served as a rite of passage, enabling them to assume an adult role in the Movement. After the summer, Shirley, Gwen and Jimmella were active in voter registration. Under the leadership of Mrs. Gray and Mrs. Anderson, they became "literacy teachers," going to people's houses and helping them to understand the Mississippi constitution in order to register to vote.[2] Jimmella and I corresponded, and in a letter of May 16, 1965, she wrote that she and others had gone with Dick Kelly to Tougaloo College to form a Young Democrats Party, to be "made up of both Negro and white college and high school [students] of the state," and run on a county rather than a school basis to avoid being segregated. Of the white students from Ole Miss at the meeting, the chapter president "really impressed" Jimmella, but a woman from that chapter seemed to Jimmella "like Ross Barnett."[3] In a letter later that year, Jimmella boasted that her class of eighty seniors, the only class of that size to graduate, "was a rough class," and had already achieved a victory. At their insistence, they were buying their class rings from a company headed by a former president of the Mississippi NAACP, who had tried and failed for sixteen years to be permitted to come to their school. On the day he finally was able to come to the school, the students, according to Jimmella, "had the whole faculty 'shook up'."[4] Shirley, Gwen, and Jimmella graduated from Earl Travillion in 1966. Shirley and Gwen, who had been friends since kindergarten, went to Jackson State College for two years. However, when Shirley's parents reminded her that she had always said as a child when she passed the University, "That is the place where I'm going to college," she decided to transfer to USM and persuaded Gwen to transfer with her.[5] Jimmella went to Bishop College in Texas, but was never comfortable in its conservative atmosphere.

In February, 1967, when the case Eleanor Piel had brought suit against Kress for denying me my civil rights in refusing to serve me was to be argued before a jury in New York, Jimmella came up from Hattiesburg and the Moncure sisters came up from New Orleans to give testimony at the trial. However, the trial was short; lawyers representing Kress requested a directed verdict of dismissal which Judge Charles Tenney granted. We were all disappointed, but Jimmella, Carolyn, Diane—who were staying in my apartment— and I were nevertheless able to have a good time together in New York.

In Hattiesburg, meanwhile, younger students became activists. One cold Saturday morning, in January, 1965, when an ordinance forbidding anyone under eighteen from picketing had been passed in Hattiesburg, Anthony Harris, who had attended Mt. Zion Freedom School (where Pete Seeger had tried but failed to teach him to play the guitar), his older brother and a friend, all of them under eighteen, put signs around their necks and went marching around the courthouse. Suddenly a passing squad car made a u-turn to come alongside, and two police officers got out, tore off the signs, threw the boys into the car and drove them to police headquarters. The policemen took the boys down a long hallway to an interrogation room, where they ordered the boys to sit on a cold, wet cement floor and threatened them with a beating. The door to the room then opened and in rushed a "small, petite black woman, yelling and screaming, 'You have no right to hold these kids.

I demand that you let them go.' " The officers, Harris recalled, responded just as he and his brother did when Daisy Harris, their mother, raised her voice: they followed her orders.[6]

Between 1966 and 1970, Mississippi began a stair-step approach to integrating its schools. Josie Brown and her best friend Glenda Funchess, who had gained confidence from their experience at the Mt. Zion Freedom School in Hattiesburg, were among the first wave of black students to attend an all-white elementary school in 1966. In 1969, Clarence Clark entered Hattiesburg High School, where his classmates included a boy well known to him, for, as he said, "I've been reading your name in your used textbooks for years."[7]

Along with other COFO projects in Mississippi, the Hattiesburg project was reduced, as summer volunteers returned to college or jobs. Veteran SNCC staffers resumed their education—Hollis Watkins, for example, enrolled at Tougaloo—or moved into other areas of civil rights activity—Lawrence Guyot became chairman of the Freedom Democratic Party—or withdrew from activism to consider new directions. Sandy Leigh left the Hattiesburg COFO office, designating Doug Smith to assume his roles director of the Hattiesburg project and director of the Fifth Congressional COFO projects.

The volunteers who remained after the summer included Dick Kelly, who worked in voter registration and tutored students after school; Barbara Schwartzbaum, who taught in a Freedom School; and Cornelia Mack, who was in charge of an adult literacy program.[8] Reverend Beech remained for a time with the Ministry Project, providing assistance such as raising funds or helping Mount Zion Freedom School student Betty Dwight get a scholarship to Tougaloo College.[9]

In the fall of 1964, Phyllis Cunningham became an employee of the Medical Committee for Human Rights to form, with the assistance of black community leaders and civil rights workers, community health and welfare organizations in the Fifth Congressional District. While the Health and Welfare Committee in Hattiesburg was strong, two groups on the Gulf Coast were dissolved after pressure from the white communities; in one case, because of threats that welfare allotments would be cut, and in the other—a group formed by black Baptist ministers—because of threats by white Baptist clergy to end financial aid to black churches and to fire maids employed by white Baptist families. Cunningham and her colleagues also tried to introduce sex education classes into the black high school curriculum to counter the high rate of attrition because students were not allowed to continue their education after bearing children. This proposal was regarded as too controversial by black principals.[10]

At this time, local activists in Hattiesburg and other communities began to turn from COFO to a home-grown organization, the Mississippi Freedom Democratic Party, and to work to build the party through a challenge to the seating of the five Democratic Congressmen, an effort launched when attorneys for the FDP filed a brief claiming that the Mississippi congressional delegation had systematically excluded blacks from the electoral process.[11]

When the U. S. House of Representatives opened its session in January, 1965, it passed a resolution, with 149 representatives dissenting, to administer the oath of office to the Mississippi delegation; however, the resolution allowed the challengers to pursue their case further. The FDP launched an intense campaign; throughout February and March, more than 150 lawyers recruited by the FDP came to Mississippi at their own expense and traveled through the state to record testimony from black citizens who had suffered violence and economic reprisals in their efforts to register and vote, while in Washington FDP supporters continued to lobby in support of the challenge.[12]

However, in mid-June, Governor Paul Johnson summoned the state legislature into special session to repeal Mississippi's discriminatory voting laws; Congress had meanwhile enacted much of President Johnson's Great Society program, including the Voting Rights Act. The act, which President Johnson signed into law on August 6th, authorized the Attorney General to send examiners into counties where blacks had been prevented from voting, suspended literacy tests, authorized the monitoring of elections by Justice Department observers, and required Mississippi and similar states to submit any new voting requirements to the attorney general for prior approval. In September, the House Subcommittee on Elections met to consider the challenge. The voluminous recorded testimony of discrimination against black voters was not discussed, nor did the testimony of black Mississippians have any impact on the subcommittee's action which was to dismiss the challenge, a recommendation that was ratified by the House Administration Committee and upheld by the full House membership.[13]

The defeat of the challenge was a setback for the FDP, but in the Fifth Congressional District, efforts were made to build membership. The business of an FDP meeting in Biloxi on February 28, 1965, as stated by Victoria Gray, was to "bring in the other twelve counties of the district to go into this FDP." the group voted to form a committee to organize the other twelve counties; a call for volunteers drew responses from, among others, Helen Anderson and Peggy Connor. Under the rules of the organization, a county would not be considered organized unless three people from each of the five districts within the county were elected to form a county executive committee; only then would FDP members be issued membership cards. Further evidence of the FDP's struggle was that only Forrest, Jackson, and Harrison counties within the Fifth District had offices.[14]

At the same time, the Hattiesburg COFO staff was reported to be "very active in all phases of civil rights work," which included operating a community center (one had been closed by the city because of faulty wiring), running a literacy program for adults, setting up neighborhood meetings concerned with federal programs for health and welfare, and working with the Freedom Democratic Party and the Mississippi Student Union. Voter registration workers were trying to organize maids and gardeners into unions; efforts were being made to set up meetings between USM students and COFO staff with the aim of establishing a dialogue between the white and black communities; four full-time voter registration workers were responsible for organizing an area of the black community to persuade citizens to register to vote and to report on family needs of assistance.[15] Some changes in personnel had occurred since the November meeting, resulting in a reduction in staff and volunteers. Reverend Beech and Barbara Schwartzbaum were no longer in Hattiesburg. Phyllis Cunningham moved to the MCHR office in Jackson to help coordinate "a statewide crash program concerning discrimination in hospitals and local health and welfare organizations which were receiving federal aid."[16] Douglas Smith remained as director of the Hattiesburg project. Other summer volunteers continued their work in Hattiesburg. Cornelia Mack was in charge of a "very intensive" adult literacy program. Dick Kelly continued to mentor members of the Mississippi Student Union. He remained on the voter registration team, providing protection to people going to register. He drove people in his car and was arrested five or six times. On one occasion, Kitchens stopped him and said, "You need to trim that beard," and put a knife against his throat. He took him to jail and put him in a cell with three big white men, telling them Kelly was a "nigger lover" as an incentive to beat him. But the three men hated Kitchens more than they hated white "nigger lovers," and they spent the night cursing Kitchens.[17]

However, Kitchens' reign of terror ended on the night of March 26, 1965, when Constable F. L. Humphrey (Cotton) assisted Constable Kitchens in patrolling Palmer's Crossing. Driving Kitchens's car, Humphrey pursued a speeding car. When the speeding car came to a halt on the front lawn of a home, Humphrey also stopped, got out and approached the car in preparation for making an arrest. He was shot once in the throat and twice in the back of the head. Kitchens was among the first to arrive at the scene after the shooting; when reporters arrived, they found "Kitchens was staring down at the body. Tears streamed down his cheeks. He kept shaking his head, as if to awaken from a bad dream. Did the man who killed Humphrey think he was pumping the bullets into Kitchens?"[18]

Indeed he did think he was killing Kitchens, or so the man who was arrested and charged with murdering Humphrey, Clodies (Clyde) Shinall, claimed when he was arrested and brought to trial. Testifying in his own defense, he stated that he triggered a long-barreled .22 revolver against the man he thought was Kitchens because Kitchens had beaten him and threatened to kill him on a prior occasion. The jury took an hour to find Shinall guilty, a verdict that carried an automatic death sentence.[19]

The widely held belief is that the actual reason Shinall wanted to kill Kitchens was to avenge Kitchens' forcing the woman Shinall loved into a sexual relationship, because access to black women in

Palmer's Crossing seems to have been, in Kitchens's mind, one of the perks of his position. In any event, Shinall was never executed. Perhaps the fear of turning Shinall—who was represented by NAACP lawyers and whose trial brought throngs of supporters from Palmer's Crossing—into a martyr in the year following the murders of Chaney, Goodman, and Schwerner was a factor in that result. Court records are unavailable, but what I have learned from Mrs. Clementine Benton of Palmer's Crossing, is that the Hattiesburg NAACP, under the leadership of Dr. C. E. Smith, interceded on Shinall's behalf when he was on death row. The Hattiesburg branch was also successful in persuading the national NAACP to take up Shinall's case, with the result that his sentence was commuted to life in prison. After serving a long term in Parchman Penitentiary, Shinall was released into the custody of his sister, who was employed by the Indiana prison system, with the condition that he never return to Mississippi. Clyde Shinall died in 2003. As for Constable Kitchens, he resigned his position after the murder of Constable Humphrey, and was never seen again in Palmer's Crossing.[20]

From its inception, COFO had been beset by tensions. The NAACP, resentful of SNCC's cutting-edge activism, casual lifestyle and dominant influence on the young, withdrew from the coalition in the spring of 1965. After the NAACP's withdrawal, SNCC staff reassessed their relationship to COFO, and, responding to their own loss of initiative and morale, decided the coalition was no longer relevant. At a statewide meeting of Mississippi activists at Tougaloo in July, 1965, a resolution was ratified that mandated that COFO projects turn over resources to the FDP executive committee in each county, in which workers who so wished could become part of the FDP structure.[21]

In September, 1965, The University of Southern Mississippi, still under the administration of William D. McCain, admitted two African-American students: Gwendolyn Elaine Armstrong and Raylawni Branch, who had been active with COFO in Hattiesburg.

However, Klan violence had not ended. On January 10, 1966, the prophecy Hattiesburg's leading activist, Vernon Dahmer, had made to Doug Tuchman became reality when Klansmen drove in two carloads to the property where Dahmer lived with his wife and the three of his children. According to Dahmer's son, Vernon Dahmer, Jr.:

> One carload pulled up in front of the grocery store, which was very near the house, like a hundred yards away, on the same property. Another car pulled up in front of the house, with Klansmen in it. They all dismounted. Began shooting. Shot the picture window out of the house and the display window in the grocery store. Then they tossed gallons of gasoline into the structures and set them afire.

Shouting to his wife to take their children and flee, Dahmer grabbed his shotgun and continued to fire back at his attackers to allow his wife and children to escape. He saved his family, but fire and smoke so damaged his respiratory tract that Dahmer died the next day.[22] Among the last statements he made was, "If you don't vote, you don't count."[23] Pinkey Hall spoke for everyone in the Hattiesburg movement when she said the murder "really put a scare on us to know that they went there and ambushed him the way they did."[24]

In 1968, James K. Dukes, the Forrest County District Attorney, prosecuted members of the Ku Klux Klan for the murder of Vernon Dahmer. Dukes is emphatic on two points: "None of the men who were responsible for Dahmer's death were from Forrest County," and "they were indicted by an all-white grand jury." The Klansmen were tried, again by an all-white male jury, and four of them were convicted. "The people of Forrest County," Dukes claimed, "put a hole in the Klan." However, although Dukes brought Sam Bowers, the Klan's Imperial Wizard, to trial four times for planning Dahmer's murder, he failed to get a conviction. "People became fearful," Dukes explained, "of being ostracized, of being harmed." After that, according to Dukes, "the prosecution ran out of gas."[25]

Under the direction of other activists, the movement that Dahmer had built continued in Hattiesburg, which was notable for the emergence of women leaders. Peggy Jean Connor, who had taught literacy classes and had been one of the founders of the Mississippi Freedom Democratic Party, served as FDP executive secretary. Her name is the first among the litigants in *Peggy Jean Connor v. Paul B. Johnson, Jr.*, a suit for reapportionment of the

Mississippi State Legislature. Pinkey Hall served as a member of the FDP executive committee. Daisy Harris, whose first action had been an attempt to register to vote on Freedom Day in January 1964, became Secretary of the Hattiesburg NAACP. Victoria Gray continued in her leadership of the FDP, and in 1966, represented the Party in Washington, D.C.

In the summer of 1965, the Child Development Guild of Mississippi, a pioneer Headstart Program, opened in Hattiesburg with Helen Anderson as director of the project. CDGM was established through the efforts of a New York psychoanalyst, Tom Levin, who with other activists, submitted a proposal for a six-week summer preschool program to the Office of Educational Opportunity which granted nearly 1.5 million dollars to serve six thousand children through eighty-four centers in twenty-four counties. CDGM centers were staffed by women and a few men who had strong identification with the Freedom Democratic Party. In Hattiesburg, the successful Freedom School project in 1964 encouraged parents, many of whom had avoided political activism, to become eager participants in the CDGM program. Five centers— including one in Palmer's Crossing—were established in the summer of 1965, and three more the following summer.

The Hattiesburg CDGM program was highly regarded for its work with preschoolers. Helen Anderson did not have a high school diploma, and some the teachers in the program resented people with less education who earned more than they did. An important benefit to women who had with dedication voluntarily cooked and served hearty meals to Freedom Summer was that they were now being paid for their labor. I visited Hattiesburg for a few days during the summer of 1965, and learned of the enthusiasm about the program because of the benefit to the children, but also because of the significant benefit of income to adults. Local people, working as cooks and teacher's assistants, earned from fifty to sixty dollars a week. Of course, the Headstart program drew opposition from whites, especially among the Delta plantation class, who harassed CDGM workers and attacked Head Start centers, but with the benefit of their Movement experience, community activists resisted intimidation and all the centers opened on schedule.[26]

Although the first CDGM program was very successful in terms of student achievement and community satisfaction, the state's political leaders were determined to destroy an independent, federally-funded organization dedicated to racial equality. In the first year, they succeeded in getting Tom Levin removed as director and replaced him with a moderate twenty-six-year-old white man, John Mudd. State leaders, including Governor Paul Johnson, Senator John Stennis, Representative William Colmer, and Representative John Bell Williams then put pressure on Sargent Shriver to withhold the program's funding from the Office of Economic Opportunity. The CDGM opponents also succeeded in getting funding for rival centers through OEO's Community Action Program. When CDGM centers were threatened with closing in the second year, supporters from the National Council of Churches and organized labor rallied to their support, and a campaign to save CDGM was launched by the Citizen's Crusade Against Poverty. Funds for a reduced number of CDGM centers were allocated for a second and third year; however, when the grant ended in December, 1967, CDGM ended its existence as an independent organization.[27] Some workers in the five Hattiesburg CDGM centers were able to get employment in the OEO Head Start programs that replaced them. Helen Anderson became a driver for Forrest County's school bus system. In August, 1973, Mrs. Anderson was diagnosed with cancer, and, to the sorrow of her family and friends, died in December of that year.[28]

In the spring of 1967, Hattiesburg activists, who included Daisy Harris, J. C. Fairley, Reverend J. C. Killingsworth of Bentley Methodist Chapel, Alice Fluker and a white supporter, Father Peter Quinn, became impatient with the long-standing refusal of white business owners and the Hattiesburg bus company to hire black workers. These leaders, officers of the Hattiesburg NAACP chapter, formed themselves into the Forrest County Action Committee and launched a boycott. Enforcing the boycott through harassment of people who continued to shop would lead to arrests, but in a discussion one night with Reverend Killingsworth, James Nix, an army veteran and musician, developed a plan modeled after one originated by the Deacons for Defense and Justice, an anti-Klan defense group in Louisiana , to recruit twelve people—"guys that wouldn't rat on me or wouldn't back off"—into a group who called themselves The Spirit ("because a spirit is invisible"). The young men slept during the day and worked at night; they "pulled guard" at churches where meetings were held; they visited the homes of people who were not supporting the boycott and "chastised" them so that they knew The Spirit "meant business." The Spirit broke windows and committed "a lot of misdemeanors," but James Nix claims he made sure "that no felonies were committed."[29] The boycott continued through the summer and ended in September when all the targeted businesses but one (which later closed) agreed to hire black workers. The banks hired black tellers; grocery stores hired black clerks.[30] The bus company hired three black drivers; Doug Smith was the first to be hired, and then was promptly drafted. Smith served in Vietnam from 1968 to 1971.[31]

After the success of the boycott, the Action Committee turned its attention to bringing equal education to Hattiesburg schools. At the Committee's invitation, a representatives from the Department of Health, Education and Welfare came to Hattiesburg to visit the schools, and, according to Daisy Harris, "in *one* day, Rowan [High School] set up a clinic, . . . they got a nurse, in *one day*, to prove to the government that they're doing what's to be done."[32]

Daisy Harris continued to work after the successful boycott with the Hattiesburg NAACP—"organizing voter registration and mass meetings; we kept busy every day"—as secretary until 1969. She attended business classes at Pearl River Junior College and then worked at the local Hattiesburg TV station, WDAM, from 1975 until 1978. Then, having divorced her first husband in 1972, she remarried and, as Mrs. Daisy Harris Wade, moved to Cleveland, where she remained until 1985 when she moved back to Hattiesburg. Reflecting on the changes in Hattiesburg since the 1970s that she helped to bring about, Mrs. Wade says they include "seeing the homes going up."

> We're moving into the neighborhoods wherever we want to live. And I can go into a bank, and there's a black girl and a white one, and there's one sitting over here as vice president of the bank. . . . I can just walk out of this building and walk out front and feel like a lady. . . . And when I refer to myself, . . . I mean to *black women,*

it made us feel like we were somebody. . . . The job market has increased. Blacks are in management jobs. We don't have to go to windows anymore. We can walk through the front door to be served. We can sit in a restaurant wherever we feel we want to sit. And there's a black waiter or white waitress or whatever. . . . "Separate but equal" was the thing in the South. . . . There's no two things alike as long as it's separated. . . . But now . . . whatever the white kid gets sitting up in that classroom, the black kids are getting the same thing.[33]

7. Freedom Summer As a Life-Shaping Event ᶜ⌒

In the seventies and eighties, many Freedom School students of 1964 completed their high school education, took jobs, went on to college, began careers, married and had children whose school experience would be very different from what their own experience had been. In June, 1970, the Supreme Court ruled on the petition for *certiorari* Eleanor Piel had argued before the Court the previous October in my case against Kress. The Court ruled in my favor, declaring that the summary judgment of the lower court had been in error, and my case should have had a hearing. I agreed to Kress's offer of a settlement rather than renew litigation, and turned my share, after expenses, over to the Southern Conference Educational Fund, which, under the direction of Ella Baker, arranged for the money to be used for the education of Vernon Dahmer's son and daughter.

In 1973, when I was an assistant professor of English at the College of Staten Island, I adopted a six-year-old African-American girl, Delores. When I returned to Hattiesburg in 1980, I brought her with me. Word went out that we were staying with Mrs. Jackson, and my hard-to-impress-daughter was amazed by the many people who came to visit me ("like you were a TV celebrity") and to report on their own and the community's improved fortunes. Most people, like Mrs. Jackson, had new homes. The roads that had once burned my feet through the soles of my shoes were now paved. Priest Creek Baptist Church was in a new building, but Kress, Woolworth and most of the downtown shops were closed, supplanted, of course, by a highway mall. Employment opportunities and wages had improved significantly, because Hattiesburg's position as the seat of Forrest County, where federal programs mandated affirmative action, benefited workers of both races; however, whites continued to be more prosperous than blacks. I was almost disappointed that I could not show my daughter the jail where I had been detained, as it had been torn down, but I was pleased to show her the library, for it had become a full-service, fully integrated community resource.

Through our telephone calls and in her letters, Mrs. Jackson kept me informed of the improvements in Hattiesburg. "Used to be," she said one time, "that the white man got the job; now, if you got the skills, you got the job." She reported that so much progress had been made in Hattiesburg, "not even Reagan could take it away from us." During our last telephone conversation, Christmas 1988, she told me that Hattiesburg now had a fully integrated high school. Mrs. Jackson died in the spring of 1989, when I was teaching in the English Department of Winona State University in Winona, Minnesota. In 1990, I gave a prize in honor of Mrs. Jackson to the winner of a contest I sponsored at Winona State University for the best essay written by a first-year student. I wrote of the tribute to the *Hattiesburg American*, explaining that Mrs. Jackson had been proud of the progress her community was making toward economic and social justice, and I thought the people of Hattiesburg would be happy with my tribute to her. Some weeks later, I received a letter from Mrs. Jackson's granddaughter Mary, who thanked me for an honor that would have pleased her grandmother. Mary informed me that she was a social studies teacher in the previously all-white Hattiesburg High School; that she had married a man who had a Master's degree in criminal justice from Ole Miss and who was one of two black parole board members for the state of Mississippi. Her seventeen-year-old son, who was about to graduate with honors from the high school where she taught, had scored 24 on the ACT, and had been awarded a scholarship for the premed program at Xavier University in New Orleans.

Civil rights veterans have held a number of reunions since since 1964. Project volunteers attended a reunion in California in 1989, while at the same time volunteers assembled at Queens College in New York for a twenty-fifth anniversary reunion honoring James Chaney, Andrew Goodman and Mickey Schwerner.

The Queens College reunion journal records responses from the volunteers to the premise, "I'd like others to know that twenty-five years later, . . ." Of the Hattiesburg volunteers, Nick Allis wrote from Marina del Rey, California that "I am trying to represent the little guy as a lawyer."[1] Terri Shaw wrote from Washington, D.C. that "I have been an editor at the Washington Post since 1970, most of that time specializing in news of Latin America." Umoja Kwanguvu, who had been William D. Jones when he taught at the True Light Baptist Church Freedom School, wrote, "I am coordinator of Special Events, Student Activities of LaGuardia Community College." Douglas Tuchman wrote from New York that "I am an Entertainment Booking Agent" for an agency that represents Mercer Ellington and Don McLean, and "I produce concerts and festivals, also."[2]

Of the SNCC activists, Dorie Ladner wrote from Washington, D.C. that "I am doing emergency room social work at District of Columbia Hospital providing services to the poor. I am continuing the struggle 25 years later in active protest with Anti-apartheid Committee, Coalition for Homeless, Tenant Rights, El Salvador, and Nicaraguan Coalitions." Hollis Watkins wrote "I am still here in Mississippi (my home state) trying to survive and make Mississippi a better place to live." Lois Chaffee wrote, "I am alive and well and living in New York City. I work for the NYC Department of Employment as a grant writer and developer of employment programs. After Mississippi, I went to graduate school and joined the women's movement as soon as I heard of it."[3]

Teachers who had served elsewhere in Mississippi also responded. Gloria Xifaras Clark, who had taught in Holly Springs, wrote from Massachusetts, "I am still the same. Politically active in urban politics, health care, AIDS, and human services." Heather Tobis Booth, who had taught in Ruleville, Shaw and Cleveland, wrote that "I am President of Citizen Action, a federation of 26 statewide organizations with 1.75 million dues paying member working on health care, toxic waste, . . . and keeping on keeping on as Fannie Lou Hamer used to say we should."[4]

Many of the respondents had continued their education after the summer, and had flourished as doctors, lawyers, social workers, teachers and academics, and writers and journalists, a large number of whom revealed in their comments that their experience in the civil rights movement had shaped their professional goals. "I am still as concerned about the development of this society as I was 25 years ago. As such, I have treated my profession (teacher) as a revolutionary activity and will probably never cease to cease to be involved in inner-city schools," Linda Wetmore, a Californian and former volunteer in Greenwood County, wrote. A former volunteer in Holmes County, Chicagoan and Cook County Hospital physician Peter Orris wrote, "I am still passionately and actively involved in struggles against racism and other oppressions prevalent in our country." John H. Strand, a former volunteer in Panola County wrote, "I am continuing my work for social and economic justice through my efforts as Superintendent of Schools to build a public school system in Peoria, Illinois which provides truly equal educational opportunities and holds high expectations for all children regardless of their ethnic or socioeconomic background." Joel Aber, a former Holmes County volunteer, wrote from Columbia, Maryland, "I am an activist in . . . the National Education Association, fighting for better teaching and working conditions and teacher empowerment represent my county's teacher on the state NEA's Human and Civil Rights Committee."[5]

Former Coahama Country volunteer Stan Boyd wrote from Silver Spring, Maryland, "I am a teacher of . . . U.S. History . . . at Beneker High School in Washington, D.C. (public 98% Black, 99% graduate and go on to college). . . . I have been active in educational reform, the peace movement and the Washington Teachers Union." Patricia Barbanell, a former volunteer in Columbus County, wrote from Albany, New York, "I am district-wide coordinator for Arts-in-Education, bring artists into public school classes to raise consciousness and facilitate positive social and political change. I work with a wide range for students and educators in an inner city District, activating for greater opportunities for minorities and for non-Eurocentric visions in America."[6]

Martha Davis, a New Yorker and former volunteer in Clarksdale, wrote, "I am a clinical psychologist who teaches, does research and has a private practice. . . . After 25 years the Mississippi experience is still vivid, I still feel I received more than I gave." Ruth Gallo, a New Yorker who had volunteered in Meridian, wrote "I am a labor attorney and still struggling for peace and justice." Mark Levy, a New Yorker and UFT volunteer teacher in Meridian, wrote, "For ten years I worked as a teacher of social studies and Third World Studies on the Jr. Hi and then college levels in NYC. For almost 15 years now I've worked on the staffs of several unions. . . . Union work for me means being part of the same struggle for economic and social justice in this country." Reverend Gilbert S. Avery, a volunteer Freedom School teacher in Sunflower County, wrote from Philadelphia, "I am Director of a church social agency providing service to poor people and organizing communities. I am still committed to the struggle for justice, peace, civil rights and human rights. I am still shaped and formed with the values, experience and gifts I received from the good and brave people of Mississippi."[7]

Some of the respondents became well known after Freedom Summer. One of these was Congressman Barney Frank, a volunteer in Hinds County, who wrote, "I am prouder of being there than of anything else in my life." Susan Brownmiller, who had been a volunteer in Lauderdale County and later published the feminist classic *Against Our Will*, wrote, "I am very proud to have been there." Kathie Amatniek Sarachild, a volunteer in Panola County who also became a noted feminist author, wrote, "I've still got my eyes on the prize and will never turn back."[8]

In 1994, the Mississippi Community Foundation issued invitations to former Freedom Summer volunteers to return for a "homecoming," and I was one of the more than four hundred volunteers who returned to Jackson in late June. When I arrived in the Jackson airport from Minneapolis at 9:30, I saw that it was not the one Norma Becker and I had landed in over thirty years before when we came down to inspect Freedom School sites with the COFO staff. Banners in the airport announced the international ballet competition that had been a proud feature of Jackson's cultural life for several years, and a wall poster advertised a Degas exhibit at the Mississippi Art Museum. Another banner welcomed the returning civil rights volunteers.

I took a taxi to the Holiday Inn, and spent the rest of the evening catching up with an old friend, Jan Goodman, who had been a volunteer in Greenwood and had worked for a time in the FDP's

Washington office. Jan eventually went on to law school and has become prominent in the area of workers' rights. The next day we went to the plenary session at Tougaloo College presided over by Chuck McDew, who became a sit-in leader when he attended South Carolina State University; he was one of the founders of SNCC, and was elected chair in 1961. McDew had worked primarily in McComb, Mississippi, and narrowly escaped death several times. He had gone on to teach African-American History and the history of the Civil Rights Movement at Metropolitan State University in Minneapolis. McDew explained that the Mississippi Community Foundation had been established to correct the distortions of the film *Mississippi Burning*, which presented the murder of the three civil rights workers from the point of view of "two FBI guys bonding." The reunion was designed as part of the MCF's effort to "tell the story," and rebuild the history of the civil rights movement.

The keynote speaker, Beatrice Branch, state president of the Mississippi NAACP, acknowledged that she had benefited from the struggle, but had much bad news to report. Although Mississippi had more elected black officials than any other state, white businessmen still controlled the economy. Eighty per cent of Mississippians still lived below the poverty line, and employment practices excluded blacks from decision-making positions. Studies had shown, Branch claimed, "that Generation X hates us more than their parents did." Branch urged that the problems facing African Americans—the loss of black business, unemployment, youth violence, teen pregnancy, and school drop-outs—must be part of the agenda of the continuing struggle.

The panel sessions that followed were described in the report of the reunion by Freedom Summer veteran Elizabeth Martinez in the September 1994 issue of *Z Magazine*. Martinez observed that although "the panels were generally excellent, with presenters who spoke strongly and relevantly, all but two of them had a three-to-one, four-to-one, or even a six-to-one ratio of male to female participants. And one of those two exceptions addressed parenting skills."[9] More bluntly, Phyllis Cunningham observed that the panel sessions were led "by men in suits calling on other men in suits by their first names." As Susan Brownmiller noted in her July 19th

Village Voice article about the reunion, a number of the women present—Pam Allen, Kathie Amatniek Sarachild, Marion Davidson, Jan Goodman, Sheila Michaels, Brownmiller and I— had begun organizing for the women's movement within a few years of Freedom Summer, but at the "Homecoming," "Feminism was another subject too fraught for discussion."[10] The only session reflecting feminist influence was the "Workshop for Children," during which Bob Moses did not speak as scheduled, but invited everyone born after 1964 to move to the center of the group and speak what was on their minds. Many of the respondents were confident young women. The daughter of two SNCC volunteers spoke of her pride in and gratitude for what her parents had done. An African-American daughter of two other SNCC volunteers announced that she was a lesbian and had been torn between the civil rights reunion and the 25th reunion in New York of the Stonewall uprising. "I want to deal with sexism and homophobia," she declared. One young African-American male said of himself, "I'm not a thug; I'm not angry all the time; I cannot jump high; I cannot sing; I do not hate white people, and I do not think black women have a problem. I'm a college graduate, now a graduate student, who sees there is a problem and wants to do something about it." These and other speakers at the workshop were enthusiastically applauded by the young people, who included a group of savvy, street-wise high school students from Washington, D.C., and I became hopeful that their response signaled the distance young Movement-identified people had moved from the homophobia and sexism of their parents' generation.

I did not attend any panel sessions at Tougaloo College on Saturday, June 25th because tours had been scheduled to go to the principal communities where volunteers had served, and I got on the bus destined for Hattiesburg. I had witnessed progress during my visits in 1965 and 1980, and had learned of more progress from Mrs. Jackson, but knowing good news about Hattiesburg did not prepare me for the exultation that gripped me when our bus load of volunteers arrived at St. John United Methodist Church. People from the community that had sheltered us—including former Freedom School students—and volunteers rushed toward each other, calling out greetings and falling into each other's arms. I was standing alone for a minute, searching for a familiar face, when a green Lincoln Town Car pulled up and Jimmella Stokes jumped out and rushed toward me, saying "I knew you'd be here." Before we went into the church for a welcoming ceremony, I learned that my former student was a counselor for the homeless in Hattiesburg, was the mother of a twenty-year-old son at the University of Southern Mississippi and was as full of spirit and community concern as she had been as a teenager.

Eleven women, alumnae of the Mount Zion Freedom School, went to the front of the small church. Their spokesperson, Glenda Funchess, who had become an attorney and an instructor in USM's criminal justice department, told of the inspiration Freedom School had given her and her peers, the majority of whom "went on to postsecondary institutions to pursue their dreams and are now professionals working to make Mississippi a better place for its citizens." Glenda Funchess said that the students who had attended Freedom Schools in Hattiesburg never had an opportunity to thank the volunteers for "coming South in 1964 in an effort to instill in young economically disadvantaged boys and girls a true sense of self-worthiness." The group singled out for special recognition Dick Kelly, who had remained after the summer to encourage them in their studies. His former students gave Kelly a key to the city and a proclamation from the mayor of Hattiesburg recognizing the volunteers' contribution.

Then the returning volunteers addressed our hosts: all of us expressed our gratitude to them for their courage in welcoming us during that turbulent summer, for sharing their homes and food with us, for protecting us, and for shaping our lives. Lawrence Guyot, who had become a youth counselor in Washington, D.C., told the group that of all the Mississippi communities he had served, he "had come to Hattiesburg because it was special." Victoria Gray Adams presented certificates honoring "Freedom Fighters" to Hattiesburg's early pioneers in the civil rights struggle, or in a number of cases, to their survivors. One of the deceased pioneers was Curtis Duckworth, Jr., who was among the six students I had accompanied to the Hattiesburg Public Library. Jimmella told me that Curtis, who was gay, had moved to Chicago when he was older and there he contracted AIDS. His parents had long been dead; the grandmother who had raised him was dead, and his remaining aunt was too old and poor to care for him. Curtis is believed to have died in Virginia, but who, if anyone, was with him when he died is not known.

After the ceremony, our hosts served another wonderful dinner. We parted from our friends, reentered the bus and went on a tour of the city, our way led by a police car. I commented that the last time I had seen one of those, I had been inside it. This time, however, the policeman driving the car was black. We went past the empty Kress store; the courthouse where people had faced arrest in order to register remained, but the old jail had been replaced by a large four-storied prison with walls topped by rolls of razor wire. However, signs of progress prevailed. The city had grown and looked prosperous. One could not discern, from the appearance of a home, the race of the family that owned it. Only the downtown area of formerly black-owned shops and businesses seemed shabby—the small office that had been Hattiesburg's civil rights headquarters was boarded up and seemed to my eyes to have shrunk in size. We passed the library to which I had taken my daughter in 1980, but a newer, larger library, I learned, would soon replace it.

When we returned to Jackson, I discovered that the positive experience of Hattiesburg was not the norm elsewhere in Mississippi. One of the chartered buses had gone to Neshoba County for a gathering at the county courthouse in Philadelphia, ten miles from the site where James Chaney, Andrew Goodman, and Mickey Schwerner had been killed. On the courthouse steps, Benjamin Chaney called out, "How many people here are from Philadelphia, Mississippi?" But he received no answer. Later, the bus stopped outside Meridian, and the volunteers descended from the bus to visit James Chaney's grave site, rebuilt after an attack by vandals in 1989. In his address, Chaney told the group, "There has not been meaningful change in Mississippi."[11] However, in Hattiesburg, there had been meaningful change. The June 26th edition of the *Hattiesburg American*, which thirty years earlier had reflected the white community's intense hostility to the civil rights volunteers, ran a front-page account of our reunion, together with photos and an editorial acknowledging past error and thanking us for our "selfless contribution."[12]

Moreover, justice in Mississippi was advancing through a combination of integrated juries and a generation of district attorneys committed to redress past wrongs. Byron de la Beckwith had been tried twice in 1964 for the June 1963 murder of NAACP leader Medgar Evers. Two all-white juries had acquitted him, but, with prodding from Jackson's *Clarion-Ledger* reporter Jerry Mitchell, Hinds County Assistant District Attorney Bobby DeLaughter reopened the case in 1998, and with new evidence and new witnesses, obtained a conviction from a jury consisting of four whites and eight blacks. De la Beckwith was sentenced to life in prison, where he died in June, 2001.[13]

Another important trial took place in 1998, after Bob Helfrich had become Forrest County Assistant District Attorney. Prompted by Jerry Mitchell's reexamination of the Dahmer murder in the *Clarion-Ledger*, Helfrich became convinced that the prosecution of Sam Bowers must begin again for the crime, on the grounds that "it was a sore on our past that needed to be cleansed." In his prosecution of Bowers, Helfrich had the benefit of access to FBI files and the testimony of four FBI agents who returned to Hattiesburg to testify. The jurors—male and female, black and white—convicted Bowers, who was sentenced to life in Parchman Prison. Until De la Beckwith's death, Bowers was one cell away from him, with a black prisoner in between.[14]

Further change in the racial climate of Hattiesburg was revealed in Ellie Dahmer's decision in 1992 to run for the office of election commissioner in District 2 of North Hattiesburg. She won and was very successful in the office, thereby, according to her son, Vernon Dahmer, Jr., "carrying on my Dad's dream."[15]

In 1997, the University of Southern Mississippi began a major collecting effort to document Freedom Summer in Hattiesburg. The project director, University Archivist Dr. Bobs Tusa, sought donations to the collection of curriculum guides, students' work, photographs, newspaper clippings, letters and diaries that would be preserved in the USM Archives, lodged in the McCain building, named for the former president of the University who had refused admission to Clyde Kennard. However, some form of reckoning has been achieved in the naming of another building on campus: Kennard-Washington Hall, where the registrar's and admissions offices are lodged; the Washington half is named for Dr. Walter Washington, the first African American to earn a doctorate at MSU.

Along with many others—local activists and summer '64 volunteers—I sent papers, letters, and photographs. In addition to building the "Freedom Summer" archive in the library's civil rights collection, Bobs Tusa organized a "Freedom Summer Symposium" that was held in June 1999—the 35th anniversary of Freedom Summer—in conjunction with the opening of an exhibit at the USM Museum of Art: "Faces of Freedom Summer: The Photographs of Herbert Randall." Bobs Tusa brought together Hattiesburg activists of that summer: Victoria Jackson Gray Adams, J. C. Fairley, Peggy Jean Connor, and Daisy Harris Wade; SNCC workers Curtis Hayes Muhammad, Hollis Watkins, Sheila Michaels and Doug Smith; and Delta Ministry leader, and Rev. Bob Beech. Dr. John Dittmer, author of *Local People: The Struggle for Civil Rights in Mississippi*, served as moderator.

A significant number of former volunteers returned to Hattiesburg for the events: Joe and Nancy Ellin; Umoja Kwanguvu, Doug Tuchman, who stayed with the W. B. McFarland family, his hosts during Freedom Summer; Dorie Ladner and Joyce Ladner; Terri Shaw and Paula Pace. Anthony Harris—now Dr. Anthony Harris, Vice President of Texas A&M-Commerce, attended the symposium, and was shown in a Randall exhibit photograph receiving guitar instruction from Pete Seeger. Dr. Cecil Gray, well remembered as Victoria Gray Adams's young son Ceecee, came in his adult identity as Chair of the African-American Studies Department at Gettysburg College. The talented Sandy Leigh became an amnesia victim as a result of a beating inflicted on him in New York in the seventies. Now known as Guy Wilson and living in Alabama, he attended with his care-giver, Sarah Taylor.

In 1996, I had adopted two teenaged Chinese-born daughters, Cynthia and Lily. I was scheduled to participate in the events, but having decided to retire from Winona State University and return to the east with my two younger daughters (my oldest daughter was living on her own in New York), I was too involved in the process of moving to attend. However, Bobs Tusa created an opportunity for me to revisit Hattiesburg in order to address the Mississippi

Librarians Association in October, an opportunity that was expanded to include a visit to Dr. Neil McMillen's African-American Studies class. Bobs Tusa had tracked down former students and graciously arranged for us to have lunch together before my visit to Dr. McMillen's class. These were: Jimmella Stokes Jackson, Dianne Moncure Sutton, Lavon Reed Trotter, Carolyn Moncure Mojgani, Theresia Clark Banks, and Shirley Anderson. As lecturing has never been my pedagogic style, I assigned the former students to become teachers of the African-American history they had lived through by saying something about "the bad old days." Joining us in the class were students from other Palmer's Crossing and Hattiesburg Freedom Schools: Lillie Jackson Easton, Theresia's brothers Clarence and Chester and her sister, Linda—now Julia—Clark Ward; Dr. Anthony Harris, who had moved from Texas A&M to be an assistant to USM president Horace Welding Fleming, Jr.; and local activists Linda Wilson Galloway, who had been a SNCC field secretary; MFDP Secretary-Treasurer Peggy Jean Connor, former Forrest County NAACP President J. C. Fairley, and former Forrest County NAACP Secretary Daisy Harris Wade. The class—evenly divided between black and white students—was clearly impressed by the oppression that was consistently inflicted on black people in Hattiesburg before the civil rights movement. Together, the students and I told of our "class trip" to the Hattiesburg library, our failed attempt to have lunch together at the Kress store, my subsequent arrest, and its coda in the Supreme Court decision, *Adickes v. Kress.* Anthony Harris spoke of his encounter with the police because of underage picketing and his subsequent rescue by his mother. Mrs. Wade exclaimed, "Things didn't end in 1964," and proceeded to describe the progress that had been made since then. Her son amplified her account of the successful boycott of 1967 with a description of The Spirit, telling the class that people who defied the boycott knew "a visit from The Spirit was something to fear." A lively question-and-comment session followed the presentation; the comment I remember was offered by a young African-American woman: "I thought I got to college all by myself, but now I realize I have been climbing on your backs."

The next day, October 22nd, the Mississippi Library Association met in the university museum, where we were surrounded by

Herbert Randall's photographs. The format was the same as on the previous day; but the most memorable part of the meeting with the librarians occurred when one of the white librarians, a Hattiesburg native about the same age as the former Freedom School students, responded that she had not known of the conditions inflicted on black people when she was young, but if she had known of their struggles, she would have joined in them. The students and I were aware that such an action would not have been possible at the time, but we appreciated her empathy. Great-hearted Jimmella graced the moment by responding, "It's all right. You didn't understand. We knew that you didn't understand."

Later that day, I went downtown to the Hattiesburg Public Library, accompanied by Peggy Jean Connor. When we came in sight of it, I was struck by its grandeur and commented on how splendid the library was. Peggy Jean said dryly that it remained to be seen if the voters would think the library was worth its cost. When I entered the library and approached the reception desk, the librarians seemed to know who I was and greeted me warmly, which of course brought to mind the very different response I had received in the old library. I explored the sections of the library, studied the art, and was introduced to a young black librarian, Alisa St. Amant, who told me how much she enjoyed the work and the friendliness of her colleagues.

The people of Hattiesburg who were in the forefront of the struggle in 1964 are the city's wise elders now and remain ready to speak of the Hattiesburg movement to those who do not know its history. Peggy Jean Connor lives in her home on Mobile Street, a street that once vibrated with small black-owned businesses and purposeful civil rights activity. At her leisure, she enjoys visiting relatives, but responds when called upon to speak to young people, as happened in February, 2004 when a play, adapted from *Voices of Freedom Summer* by Frank Kuhn, was performed by students at Hattiesburg High School. She was one of the eighteen members of the Mississippi Freedom Democratic Party honored at the Democratic National Convention in July, 2004.

J. C. Fairley can well be described as having been at the center of the Hattiesburg movement since its beginning. He continued his radio and tv repair business until 2001, when he suffered a stroke and retired. However, he continues to serve his community by addressing classes on African-American history and groups at the university during Black History Month. Mr. Fairley was also one of the MFDP members honored at the 2004 Democratic National Convention.

After Daisy Harris Wade returned to Hattiesburg in 1985, she began working with the Mississippi Extension Services. For the past fourteen years she has been involved in nutrition education through a program administered by Mississippi State University, in which she instructs young mothers in healthy eating practices. She also serves as a substitute teacher at the Earl Travillion Attendance Center, but it is her work with young mothers that provides her with the greatest satisfaction.

Although she now lives in Petersburg, Virginia, Victoria Jackson Gray Adams frequently returns to her friends and family in Hattiesburg. However, her activism did not end when she left Hattiesburg. After her marriage to Tony Gray ended, Victoria married a career military man, Reuben Ernest Adams, Jr., and went with him in 1968 to Bangkok, Thailand. She had in care a young son, Reuben Ernest Adams, III, and her youngest child from her first marriage, Cecil, who was responsible for another stage in his mother's activism. Concerned by the absence of African-American parents at PTA meetings at the school Cecil attended, Victoria began to organize other mothers around issues of self-interest. When Victoria left Thailand in 1972, the organization African-American Women in Bangkok was "still going strong." While in school in Thailand, Cecil was given an assignment to write about a hero; he chose to write about his mother. His teacher, somewhat skeptical, explained to Cecil what a hero's actions were; Cecil responded, "That's my momma," and when he finished his description, his teacher was convinced he was right.[16]

Victoria's activism continued when Reuben was assigned to Fort Myers, Virginia. There she became aware of the plight of young wives of enlisted men who lived in private housing and could not afford to go out to dinner or a movie. Again, Victoria "got very busy organizing the women," sharing information about the Army Community Service as a source of support, as well as resources for support in the larger community. As a result, many junior wives began to feel a part of things and changed the way they lived. Victoria "left a group of very dynamic women" in Fort Myers when she moved in 1976 after Reuben was appointed to Fort Lee near Petersburg, Virginia. Once again, she became active in a wives' club, and led the successful effort to change the club's constitution that limited membership to wives whose husbands were non-commissioned officers (and were members of the NCO club) and opened it to all women who wished to join. In 1980, Victoria and her husband settled in Petersburg. She received a gubernatorial appointment to the Virginia Fire Services Board in 1985, and served as Campus Minister at Virginia State University from 1989 to 1997. Victoria continues an active life and her connection with Hattiesburg. In 2000, she and her son Dr. Cecil Gray taught a "Studies in Civil Rights" history class at USM.[17] Victoria was also one of the MFDP members honored at the 2004 Democratic National Convention. When she was recently asked how long she would be an activist, she replied, "As long as I can walk."

Raylawni Branch was secretary of the Forrest County NAACP in 1965 when the organization offered to pay her tuition to the University of Southern Mississippi. After attending USM for one year, she left and continued her studies at a nursing school in Brooklyn, New York. She is a retired Lieutenant Colonel from the Nurse Corps of the United States Air Force Reserve with twenty-five years of service. Raylawni Branch served in the Desert Shield-Desert Storm campaign. She returned to Hattiesburg in late 1987 and has recently retired from her teaching position at USM's College of Nursing.

Many of the northern volunteers who came to Hattiesburg in Freedom Summer pursued careers shaped by the Freedom Summer experience. After he left Hattiesburg in 1965, Reverend Beech went to Moss Point, working in Movement-related activities and serving as faculty member at Mary Holmes Junior College. He remained in Mississippi until 1969, when he won a fellowship to attend Harvard; there he explored an independent course of study on social conflict and social change. In 1970, Rev. Beech went to Kansas City as director of a branch of the Midwest Academy, a network of training centers for urban activists across the U.S. and Canada; the Kansas City center served the state of Missouri and neighboring states. In 1972 he went to Minnesota, directing various community organizations, working for several of Minnesota's community-based foundations and "pastoring little country churches." Since 1996, he has been involved in programs dealing with alcohol and chemical abuse. He lives now in Grand Rapids. Of his Mississippi experience, he remembers that often Mississippi volunteers were able, after their experience in that state, to see problems in their home towns that needed to be addressed.[18]

Sheila Michaels is currently an oral historian of people who have practiced nonviolent direct action. She has lately also returned to volunteer tutoring of reading. Sheila also claims responsibility for a significant language change. When she found that "Ms." was actually a rarely used stenography title, she made known that "Ms." might replace the mandatory distinction between married and unmarried women. After Gloria Steinem named her new magazine "Ms.," eventually the title became the accepted usage.

From 1966 to 1967, Phyllis Cunningham worked in a MCHR office in Selma Alabama, where she was responsible for providing health care for civil rights workers and the communities in which she worked. Then she moved to New York where she has been involved for more thirty-four years in efforts for affordable housing, community development, improved health care, and quality public education.[19]

After Dick Kelly returned to Chicago, he worked as a teacher and union organizer, and has remained an activist for social justice in Chicago and for the reform movement of the Catholic Church.

Lorne Cress remained in Mississippi for three years to work in voter registration. Eventually she returned to Chicago, where she helped to start a public school, the Woodlawn Community School, which she considers "all part of the same thing" she began in the civil rights movement.[20]

Barbara Schwartzbaum went to Howard Law School after leaving Mississippi in 1965. She became a member of the bar in 1969 and received a Masters in Law degree from Harvard University Law School in 1970. Since that time she has been a constitutional lawyer in several venues, including, as a Nixon appointee, Acting General Counsel and Deputy Regional Counsel for the New England Office of Economic Opportunity. She has been a professor at the Suffolk Law School and New York Law School.

Terri Shaw earned a Master's degree in journalism from Columbia University Graduate School of Journalism in 1965. She worked for the Associated Press in New York, and later became an assistant foreign editor at the Washington Post. Terri has embarked on a second career as a translator of Spanish, French, and Portuguese to English.

After leaving Mississippi, Paula Pace taught junior high school in New York for four years, then went to New York University Law School. She is now a mediator, involved in transformational mediation, the practice of helping people make agreements. Her career was inspired by the belief that emerged from Freedom Summer that there is basic good in the world and people can work out their differences.

Some time after Umoja Kwanguvu attended the 1999 reunion in Hattiesburg, he became ill, and in May, 2001, he died. Although he had retired from his administrative position at LaGuardia Community College, a large number of students came to his memorial and many of them spoke about the ways Umoja had helped them by mentoring them, getting them jobs, teaching them to speak well and defend their arguments; arranging trips to Brazil, Mexico, and the Caribbean; and helping them in the early stage of the AIDS crisis. A former colleague said that Umoja's devotion to LaGuardia Community College and its student body made it acceptable among faculty and staff to be proud of working there and to be devoted to the work they did.[21]

After the summer, Nancy and Joe Ellin returned to Kalamazoo, where Joe resumed his position as professor of philosophy at the University of Western Michigan, a position he still holds. Joe was active with the ACLU for a while and did draft counseling during the Vietnam war, but now his work at the university and his service as chair of his synagogue's religious affairs committee are his principal activities.[22] Nancy worked at voter registration; her efforts drew the attention of the Kalamazoo ACLU, and she soon became a board member, "as Secretary, of course." She was active in Democratic politics, and became an office of the Kalamazoo County Democratic Executive Committee. She also had a son, and her subsequent involvement with school matters led to her feminist awakening. Dismayed by the books the school system was planning to buy to replace Dick and Jane readers, she led a study which revealed that "one third grade book had more stories about male animals than about human females." The results of this study were published by the Michigan Women's Commission in a booklet called "Sex Discrimination in an Elementary Reading Program." Although the Kalamazoo school system bought the flawed books, the publishers later put out improved editions. Nancy produced a study, *Notable Black Women*, for Michigan's Office of Sex Equity. She served on the boards of Kalamazoo and Michigan Planned Parenthood organizations and has also been active with the Jewish Federation. Reflecting on her experience, Nancy Ellin has concluded: "I guess the moral of all this is, once an activist, always an activist."[23]

Doug Tuchman does not fit that premise, for his revelatory experience of Freedom Summer did not lead him to more activism, but to a career promoting bluegrass music, which he had loved since listening to it on the radio as a child. He was the first to bring bluegrass to New York, and had booked concerts in the area since 1970. He had also conducted a weekly radio show, "Honky Tonkin' " on WKCR-FM in New York since 1978. Those of us in Mississippi and the New York area who had known Doug were saddened by his death by heart attack on October 6, 2003, while he was on his way to a concert.

Stanley Zibulsky returned to Hattiesburg in the summer of 1965 and directed a Headstart program at St. John Church. After 35 years of teaching in the New York City public schools, he retired in 1996. He now is a volunteer reading tutor in an elementary school two days each week. He has become a runner, and most recently completed the 2004 New York City Marathon.

Ira Landess became a psychoanalyst and is in private practice in New York City.

Nick Allis and Danny Parker became lawyers, the field they had decided upon in their undergraduate days. Danny, now known as Barrington Parker, Jr., is a federal appeals court judge in the Second District.

COFO workers who had built the Mississippi movement pursued careers inspired by their activism. After serving as chair for the Mississippi Freedom Democratic Party, Lawrence Guyot went to Rutgers Law School in Newark, New Jersey and upon graduating settled in Washington, D.C. For more than thirty years, Guyot has been involved in community politics, serving as an Advisory Neighborhood Commissioner for his neighborhood. He has been very active in the struggles for racial justice, immigrant rights, income equality and statehood for the District of Columbia.

Hollis Watkins went on to become co-founder and president of Southern Echo, a Jackson-based leadership education, training and development organization committed to building new grassroots leadership and organizations through providing technical and legal assistance to African-American and working class communities lead throughout rural Mississippi and the Southern region.

John O'Neal brought the Free Southern Theater to New Orleans. The FST closed in 1980, and in the same year, O'Neal organized Junebug Productions, an arts organization based in New Orleans for which he serves as Artistic Director. Curtis Hayes, now Curtis Muhammad, is also in New Orleans, working as an organizer involved with urban education with the Louisiana Research Institute for Community Empowerment.[24]

Charles Cobb, Jr. became a journalist, best known for his work with All Africa Media Group. David Dennis became a lawyer. Both of these men maintain the spirit of the civil rights movement through working with Bob Moses, who from 1969 until 1975 had taught mathematics in Tanzania, where he also worked in the Ministry of Education. He returned to Cambridge in 1976 and began working for a doctorate at Harvard. Moses recognized the importance of mathematics when he assisted his children with their homework. Supported by a MacArthur Fellowship, he also taught math on the seventh and eighth grade levels and developed the concept of the Algebra Project. Moses applied the principles he had learned in the voter registration struggle: "A small dedicated band—even one person—could dig in, establish a beachhead, survive and perhaps get some kind of breakthrough . . . by linking every day issues to political participation."[25]

Beginning in Cambridge, Moses launched the Algebra Project, involving interested math teachers in working with students to build their math skills by linking mathematics with everyday situations. The Algebra Project gained supporters and sites were developed throughout the North. Hollis Watkins's work with the

Southern Echo proved helpful in 1995; the Echo had developed a math games league in Indianola, Mississippi that had drawn great student participation for the tournaments, as well as parent support. When permission to use a middle school for the competitions was withdrawn by a school superintendent, pressure from parents caused him to back down. Recognizing their power, the parents demanded science labs at the school. Moses had come to understood that "math is a tool for organizing around the issue of access in the economic arena." He also recognized the need for developing the Algebra Project in the South, but could not take on that work in addition to his work in the North. The solution came in the form of a renewed friendship. A "historical moment" had brought Bob Moses and David Dennis together in the sixties, and now that they were again in touch, it seemed to Moses that "some force larger than the two of us seemed determined that we should stay connected." Moses asked Dennis to lead the organizing of the Southern program and Dennis "picked up that entire burden," moving to Jackson as the Project's Southern Field Director. Charles Cobb also became involved with the Project and is co-author with Moses of the book that traces the Algebra Project back to its roots in the civil rights movement.[26]

The Ladner sisters were both SNCC field secretaries and Tougaloo graduates. Dorie Ladner is a social worker at Washington, D.C. General Hospital's unit, working with duo-diagnosed (dealing with substance abuse and mental illness) patients. She declares herself "a human rights activist."[27] Joyce Ladner earned a doctorate in sociology at Washington University in St. Louis, and then taught at a number of colleges before going to Howard University, where she served as vice-president for academic affairs from 1990 to 1994. She is the author of a number of books, including *Tomorrow's Tomorrow: The Black Woman* (Doubleday, 1971) and *The Ties that Bind: Timeless Values for African American Families* (Wiley, 1999). From 1994 to 1995, Ladner was interim president of Howard University. In 1995, President Bill Clinton appointed her to the District of Columbia Financial Control Board. She was also a senior fellow in the Governmental Studies Program at the Brookings Institution. She is now retired and living in Sarasota, Florida.[28]

A number of the former Mt. Zion Freedom School students who assembled in 1994 at St. John Church continue to live in Hattiesburg and have assumed leadership positions in the community. Glenda Funchess continues to practice law, and has been instrumental in getting the Mississippi Department of Archives and History to designate a marker for its significance in the Hattiesburg civil rights struggle Mount Zion Baptist Church. She also holds a ceremony each year to honor local heroes, including J. C. Fairley and Doug Smith. Glenda Funchess has also organized a program to educate high school students about the Movement through field trips to important institutions such as the Civil Rights Museum in Memphis.

Victoria Easterling was a fourth grade student in Mt. Zion in the summer of 1964. She has since earned a B.A. in Speech Communication and Theater from William Carey College, a Master's degree in Education and a Master's as an English language specialist from Argosy University in Sarasota, Florida and has completed her doctoral studies at Nova University. Mrs. Easterling is presently a language arts teacher at Mary McLeod Bethune Alternative High School in Hattiesburg.

Josie Brown, who was nine when she attended Mt. Zion Freedom School, graduated from Alcorn State University in 1977 with a B.S. in Sociology and Social Services. Mrs. Brown is a social worker with the Department of Human Services in Hattiesburg.

Stephanie Hoze graduated from Rowan High School in Hattiesburg in 1970 and then went to Alcorn University, graduating with a B.S. degree in Home Economics. Mrs. Hoze earned a Master's degree in Home Economics and a Specialist degree in Education Administration. She taught for seventeen years in Florida and Mississippi before becoming Food Service Director for the Hattiesburg schools, a position she has held for ten years.

A significant number of former Palmer's Crossing Freedom School students have, as they promised, remained in Mississippi in order to change it. Most have married and some of them are divorced, or divorced and remarried. Most have grown children; some have grandchildren. All of them remain friends, Shirley Anderson is case manager at the Ellisville State School, a facility for individuals challenged by disabilities in Ellisville, MS. What she remembers most about Freedom School is being exposed to books by black authors. About the changes that have taken place since 1964, Shirley appreciates "being able to go where you want to go if you have the money." However, she "enjoyed and misses the close-knit community and misses the concern for each other." She lived in Palmer's Crossing until six years ago and now resides in the city of Hattiesburg. "We moved away and others who were not bred there moved in. The community is not the same. Our generation was so busy and involved with the well being of the community. We believed that people can make a difference because people matter."[29]

Gwen Merritt Robinson is Chief Clinical Dietitian at River Region Medical Center in Vicksburg. Like Shirley, Gwen remembers Palmer's Crossing as a sheltered community. But when the Freedom Riders came, "they opened up a whole new world that we knew nothing about. . . . I was just amazed at the books that they brought." Gwen "never thought in a million years" that when we wore denim shirts and went to the library, we would be making history. Gwen wants her daughter "to know her history" because she "doesn't know what it means not to go to the same restroom, or eat in a restaurant—we had to go in the back. Even going to a movie theater—we couldn't sit in the same area that the white people did." Gwen remembers standing across the street from the Saenger Theater waiting to see a movie starring James Brown until the white people had seen it. A bunch of Klansmen came as they were waiting and threw pins at them.[30]

Gwen cites as an example of the progress made since then that "this generation can go to any college or university they want to," but when she and Shirley went to USM, "those were pretty perilous times, especially in the department that I decided to go in, . . . Home Economics." Gwen's goal was to be a dietitian; Institution Management was in that department, where there was not another black student at the time. Gwen remembers

> going to a night class—economics—and I was the only black person in there . . . and the teacher started talking about "the Negroes come down from Chicago in a big Cadillac. . . . I guess the point he was making was that black people leave the South, they make a little

money, and the first thing they do is buy a Cadillac and come home to show off. And I thought I've got to go through this because I want to graduate . . . but I was terribly humiliated at that time. . . . A few years later, I was working as a dietitian at Forrest General; here comes this student interning and she came over and needed some help. And guess what; she had married that man . . . and she was working under me. I was training her to get her ready to take the national exam that we have to take to become a registered dietitian. So one night her husband calls me and thanks me for helping his wife pass the test. I should have said, "Do you remember that class long ago and there was only one black girl in that room a and you humiliated me?" But I just said, "You're quite welcome."

I know if it had not been for the Freedom Schools, I wonder where my future—I know I had the drive, but having those Freedom Schools, as I said, it opened up a whole new world.[31]

Lavon Reed Trotter remembers being "raised up in Palmer's Crossing with a lot of unity because everybody in the community raised us."[32]

When SNCC came down, we embraced it. Our minds were open; . . . we wanted to prosper, so when the school came down and taught us a lot of things, it was mesmerizing. . . . The people came together and we sang freedom songs, and it raised my spirits. . . . A big eighteen wheeler came down to the community center, and when they opened the doors, there were books and books and books . . . that's when I was exposed to black writers. I read Richard Wright and W. B. Dubois. . . . From all that I knew that I could be somebody and that I was somebody and that I could excel.[33]

Lavon graduated from Jackson State in 1972 with a major in sociology. She applied for a job as a social worker in the in Gulfport Welfare Department, but she was turned down. Lavon then took a got a job as a social worker in Gulfport at the Gulf Coast Community Action Center. She later learned that she was a member of a class action suit against the state of Mississippi because her score on an exit exam at Jackson State was high enough for her to have been hired by the Gulfport Welfare Department. "The fact was . . . that they had discriminated from 1973 to 1976 to not hire black social service workers in the state of Mississippi. . . . Out of eighty-two counties they did not hire one black person." As a result of the settlement Lavon was awarded thirteen hundred dollars. Lavon remained at the Community Action Center in Gulfport, "and I ended up getting married there to Otis Trotter." Lavon has two grown daughters, Rosslyn and Lalya, who have learned from her "not to be competitive, but to excel." Lavon reflects with satisfaction that "things are really better."[34]

Jimmella Stokes Jackson received a B. A. from Bishop College in 1970. She moved to New York and became a caseworker in the New York Department of Social Services. Jimmella then worked for the Agency for Child Development and an alternative school program in Brownsville, Brooklyn before returning to Hattiesburg, where she ran a day care center for ten years. She returned to New York to work for the New York City Health and Hospital Corporation as a supervisor "for the implementation of the newly formed Managed Care Department." She retired in 1993 and returned to Hattiesburg, where she is a leading community activist. Jimmella keeps track of her high school peers and reports that Sam Williams lives in California and has become wealthy due to "a lot of upward mobility on his job" and that Charles Bester is retired and living in Jackson.[35]

My oldest daughter and I met Jimmella's son Akim when they were living in New York in 1980. At the time, Jimmella was going through a "horrific divorce" from Akim's father, and, as she says, "as big as New York was, it was not big enough for the two of us." She left New York abruptly to return to Hattiesburg, and with the help of her extended family, "raised a very strong, healthy, striking, intelligent young man," who is now thirty-one, living in Albany, Georgia and working for Verizon as an account executive.[36]

Now happily married to Charley Jackson, Jimmella has a another "light" of her life, Trey—short for Treveon—her grandnephew, who has lived with her since he was fifteen months old. The son of Jimmella's deceased older sister's daughter who became heavily involved in drugs, Trey is now eleven, and Jimmella says she "could not love him more if I had given birth to him. I'm also very proud of him. He is very, very bright; he plays all kind of sports, and has played strings in a city-wide concert."[37]

Jimmella currently has two major concerns: one is that "the AIDS-related deaths of African-American women—between 25 and 40, now it's dropped to 23 to 35—are not being addressed." She is troubled by the silence of "the ministers of Hattiesburg, of the state, of the country. Hattiesburg has a church on every street corner, and I'm very disappointed that the ministers . . . are not addressing [the problem]. It's not going away."[38]

Her second concern is that "there is no cooperative economics in Hattiesburg. There are people in Hattiesburg who have money—who have gone to college, gone away, come back to retire. They have money, but they're not investing it in Hattiesburg." Jimmella believes that there is enough wealth in the black community to create is own economic base, but the collective will is absent. The downtown historical district is being developed "—but that's with federal money, . . . and when the federal government gives you money, they control you."[39]

Carolyn Moncure Mojgani, who was fifteen years old in the summer or 1964, went to McDonough 35, "which was the best black school in New Orleans. Still, we'd had nothing like what we had that summer." As it had been for other students who had never read black writers or studied black history, the experience was "a revelation." After graduating from high school, Carolyn went to Newcomb College for two years, and then interrupted her college education when she married Parviz Mojgani, with whom she has a daughter and a son. However, twenty years later she resumed her education and earned her bachelor's degree from the University of New Orleans in 1998. She has been librarian of the lower school at Country Day School for eight years, and prior to that she was managing director for a children's book store for ten years. Carolyn has said, "Books have been my life," and she is currently enrolled in a Master's program for library information systems. However, she has taken time away from her studies to spend two years teaching English in China, thus following in the footsteps of her daughter, who taught there for a year after graduating from college in 1995.[40]

Dianne Moncure Sutton took nurses' training at Pearl River Community College, passed Mississippi state board exams and has been a Licensed Practical Nurse for 31 years. She worked at Forrest General Hospital and the Wesley Medical Center in Hattiesburg and the Children's Hospital of New Orleans, where she became interested in working in a respite program for parents of mentally and physically disabled children, which is the work she does now. Like Gwen and Julia, Dianne has experienced racism; in her case, the experience was recent. Three times she has sought a position at the Hattiesburg Clinic, which is on Highway 49 across from Forrest General Hospital. On the third occasion, she told the receptionist that she was interested in any position available. The receptionist told her of an opening in the urology clinic. "Are you sure it's open?" she asked; the receptionist assured Dianne the position was open and took her to see the office manager. The man began the interview by telling her how difficult the position was and ended the interview by telling her the position was taken.[41]

Like Jimmella, Dianne is concerned with the lack of an economic base in the black community in Hattiesburg and in Palmer's Crossing, which she remembers as "a thriving community" when she was young. She remembers that her teachers at Earl Travillion were "down-to-earth people who cared about [the students] getting an education. They were teaching about life and also took pride in what they were doing" Now, in her opinion, the school is "in the lower rung in education in Forrest County." Along with Jimmella, she is critical of black people who do not use their resources to advance the economic power of their community: "Once they became successful, they forgot where they came from." Dianne claimed that the white population of Hattiesburg had declined in recent years, while the white population—and the affluence—of neighboring Lamar County has grown. Her observation about population growth is correct, for Lamar County grew by 28 per cent from 30,424 to 39,070 between 1990 and 2000 and the number of school age children grew from 7,210 to 8,648.[42] "The simplest way I can put it," she says, "is that white people are running westward and black people are following them." Dianne, like all the former Freedom School students I have spoken to, is "proud to have been a part of history, a part that had an important influence on my life. Freedom Summer had a whole lot to do with the way I feel about myself."[43]

Dianne is proud of her family of four adult children; her oldest, a son, Maurice, has been in the army for sixteen years and is now stationed in Germany, where Carol hopes to visit him in 2005. Two of her three daughters, Tanya and Bianca, are homemakers who also work as salespersons, and her middle daughter, Kimberly, is majoring in education at USM. Carol is also proud of her ten grandchildren.[44]

Linda—now Julia—Clark Ward, who went to St. John Freedom School, recalls that the summer of '64 "started me to reading, and to this day I read an average of four books a week." She also gained a pride she had never known. "During that time people were treated different—even among black people—because of the color of their skin. I grew up with a sister that was light complected, and I was the darker one. In the summer of 64, . . . I got a chance to really express myself; I didn't know I was as articulate as I was." After graduating from high school, Julia went for two years to a business college in Jacksonville, Florida, and then worked for Bell South in Miami. In 1971 she transferred to Bell South in Hattiesburg; where two light-complexioned black people had been hired before her, but Julia "was the first real sister." She was also one of two black women trained for supervisors' positions in Hattiesburg because she called the Equal Employment Opportunity Commission in to do an investigation. She believes that everything she got, she had to fight for, "but because of the experience that I had and the fire that I had in me from that, I stood up for myself. Even in relationships.[45]

Married at eighteen and divorced at twenty-three, Julia brought up two sons by herself: an older son who lives in Jackson and manages a clothing store and a younger son with a master's degree in psychology who lives in the Dallas area of Texas. She remembers the summer of '64 as "to some degree the highlight of my young adult life. When my boys got old enough to understand the difference in black and white, I started teaching them this is what we had to do: when you turn eighteen, you go to register to vote. . . . It hasn't been the best life, but it's been a good life."[46]

Julia's sister Theresia Clark Banks has retired from work as a salesperson, but has remained an activist in Hattiesburg politics. The campaign she is most proud of resulted in the election of Johnny DuPree as Hattiesburg's first black mayor in June, 2001. In 1964, Theresia had written a poem for the Freedom School newsletter that included these words: "I pray and hope for a better America and a better Mississippi in which to live. Deep down I know that we shall overcome." In the celebration following DuPree's election, Theresia echoed the words of that poem. Black residents knew there would be changes, she told the *Hattiesburg American* reporters, but they didn't know how far reaching those changes would be. "We hoped and we prayed," she said. "We kept on praying and this is where it got us."[47]

8. Hattiesburg in the Present ⌒

When I drove north from the New Orleans International Airport in the spring of 2004, I was mindful of the great contrast between the smooth, four-lane highway and the fear-inducing, densely wooded, two-lane road of 1964. I left Highway 59 to enter Hattiesburg on the crest of a hill dividing Lamar County from Forrest County and descended into a Hattiesburg I did not recognize; it had become a mid-sized city of 43 square miles with a population of close to 45,000 people, of whom 49.3 per cent were white, 47.3 per cent were black (significantly above the state average); and 1.4 per cent were Hispanic. In the year 2000, the median age of residents was 27.1 years; the median income was $24,409 and the median house value was $66,100, all below the state average. Seventy-nine and one tenth per cent had high school educations or higher; 28.9 per cent had bachelor's degrees and 11.5 per cent had graduate or professional degrees.[1]

In the late nineties, the city had gone through a period of growth, as evidenced by the expansion of new business and the building of new homes. Job opportunities were made available because new businesses opened, existing businesses expanded, and industries relocated to Hattiesburg. The city was recognized in 1999 as one of America's hottest 150 cities for business relocation and expansion, a top retirement community, and a top-thirty finalist for the All America City Award.[2]

Four-lane interstate highways transect the city: I-49 running East and West and I-98 running North and South. The section of town I first saw in 1964 is now a pocket in the southeast section of the city that is designated "Historic Downtown" and signs are posted that read "Downtown: It's What Hattiesburg is Coming To." The Kress Building still stands on Main Street, but now serves as offices for a mortgage company, and an art gallery is across the alley where I was arrested. The bank where I had an account no longer stands across Main Street opposite the Kress Building, but the Saenger Theatre, which forced black patrons to watch films in the balcony—and where some of the Freedom School students sat in forty years ago— is now a legitimate theater, offering seasons of plays and live performances. Hattiesburg had seemed to me a dusty place in 1964, but small tree and flower-filled parks are now found throughout the city. Some of the large older homes I remember remain, and one or two have been converted into professional office buildings; however, numerous neighborhoods of pleasant homes, both modest and ambitious, now spread across the city. The mayor's office is located in the downtown area, along with other civic buildings, such as the courthouse and the Jackie Dole Sherrill Community Center, which is named for a female officer slain in the line of duty.

Glenda Funchess had invited me to speak there to a gathering of high school students and their parents who were attending Lift Every Voice: Freedom Institute 2004, a program she, with the help of USM librarian Karolyn Thompson, had created to make young people aware of the civil rights struggle. In previous weeks, Glenda and Karolyn had taken students on a field trip to the Civil Rights Museum in Memphis. In the community center, Glenda and Karolyn had set up a display of photographs of civil rights activists and news accounts of events in that struggle. However, the day was glorious, and most of the students for whom this event had been planned pursued other interests. Only two high school students— both girls—came, but a significant number of adult women who had been involved with the Hattiesburg movement were present. The announcement handed out to the students referred to the effort to get library cards, so I spoke of that event, but spoke more about the brave leaders who had been responsible for launching the campaign that brought so much progress in Hattiesburg. I asked the group for their evaluation of the progress, and their responses began with the refrain, "we've come a long way," but went on to cite continuing difficulties in getting jobs, which often required more persistence than was required of white applicants. Their comments were also self-critical: "One of the biggest problems we're facing among ourselves is that we don't help each other"; "We settle for half the pie instead of going for the whole pie"; "We're separating ourselves." However, they acknowledged that meeting all goals was difficult: "We have hard lives." And the rueful conclusion was that "You're damned if you do, and damned if you don't."

Former Mount Zion Freedom School student Victoria Easterling attended the presentation and invited me to speak to students at the Bethune Alternative School where she is a language arts teacher. I had difficulty finding the school, and was late in arriving on the day I had agreed to go there. The students, whom I judged to be in their early teens, had grown restless while they waited, and although they remained polite, they were not responsive to my remarks or questions. One of the few questions asked was "How old are you?"

Stephanie Hoze was present in the classroom and afterward took me on a tour of the "Mobile Street Historic District," which I never would have found on my own. In its heyday, Mobile Street was full of cars and people flitting in and out of shops owned by African Americans.[3] Peggy Jean Connor, who owned a beauty shop on Mobile Street, recalls a time when people "would get off from work, go home, dress up just to walk up and down Mobile Street."[4] While plans for revitalization of Mobile Street have been under discussion for years, there was no evidence of any development during the spring of 2004. The street was now mostly residential; the crowds of activists that had once gathered at 507 Mobile Street were gone, along with all the small businesses that had once thrived there. The fire-damaged building was still standing, but it was difficult to imagine the intense meetings held there, or the work done with frantic dedication, and it was almost impossible to imagine Mrs. Woods standing in front of the building, holding her gun and calling out names of men she told to "get to getting." I drove away from Mobile Street regretting that the undeniable economic and social progress in Hattiesburg had meant the sacrifice of that once lively community.

Hattiesburg High School had been desegregated in 1965, and I wanted to see what nearly 40 years of integration had brought about. The high school, a large structure composed of an older and newer section, is in a pleasant tree-filled section of town. I learned that, at the time of my visit, Hattiesburg High School had a population of 1,254 students—1,056 of whom were African American—and a faculty of approximately 150 teachers, sixty per cent of whom were African American. The student population was evenly divided between males and females, classes consisted of 20 to 22 students, and the majority of the high school's graduates go on to higher education. The high school's leadership was shared by two African-American principals: Mr. Johnny Simpson, the co-principal in charge of administration, and Dr. Yvonne Bryant, the co-principal in charge of instruction and curriculum.[5]

My appointment was with Dr. Bryant, and as I passed from one section of the school to the other, I asked directions from a white student. She gave them to me, and then I questioned her about her experience at Hattiesburg High. She assured me that she was being well educated, and looked forward to going to college—she was not sure where—after she completed her senior year. As I walked, I noted the quiet in the hallways; no students were straggling. I glanced through the windows in the doors of classrooms and saw teachers and students engaged in lessons, but I did not see students sitting at their desks while teachers lectured. Often I saw teachers dealing with one group of students, while other groups of students worked together. All the students seemed on task, not withdrawing out of boredom into private conversations.

Dr. Bryant, a lifelong Hattiesburgian, is a graduate of Rowan High School and served as assistant principal there for five years before coming to Hattiesburg in the previous year. She informed me that in the early days of integration, there had been resistance— mostly from adults—but the resistance had decreased over the years. Dr. Bryant expressed satisfaction with the progress she has seen, not only at the high school, but in the entire city. As I left the high school, I stopped to talk with a young white male teacher. I asked him about his experience at the school, and he responded that he very much enjoyed teaching there. However, I was left to ponder the significance of the population shift in Hattiesburg High School from all white to 72 per cent African American.

A recent high school-sponsored event that had set Hattiesburg abuzz was *Freedom Summer*, a play adapted with permission of Frank Kuhn from his dramatic reading *Voices of Freedom Summer* by Theater Arts teacher Michael Marks in honor of the fortieth anniversary of Freedom Summer. The play was presented for three nights in March, and before each performance, a movement activist—James Meredith, Peggy Jean Connor, and Anthony Harris—addressed the audience. One performance was held in the afternoon, so middle school students could attend the play. The students of both races were stirred by the presentation of the city's struggle for justice, in which many of the black students' family members had participated. The young people's growing awareness and appreciation of the civil rights struggle gratified their elders.

The splendid Hattiesburg Public Library lies at the foot of the main thoroughfare, Hardy Street. I learned from Sean Farrell, the cataloging librarian, that Alisa St. Amant, the African-American librarian I met there in 1999, had moved to a new position as branch head of the community library in nearby Oak Grove. However, the five people with professional degrees employed at the library include one African-American librarian, and seven of the seventeen paraprofessionals at the library are African American. Mr. Farrell told me that one of these, Valmina Blackwell, is an alumna of the Mount Zion Freedom School.

On another day, I drove down Route 98, turned left at the landmark drive-in, entered Palmer's Crossing, a community I found difficult to recognize. Indeed, I would have needed help to find the home where Mrs. Jackson had sheltered me, or the home where Delores and I had visited her in 1980. However, I did find the two churches, Priest Creek and St. John. Priest Creek Baptist Church was in a new church building—brown brick with a brown slate roof and a small white triangular vestige of a steeple—by the time I had visited there in 1999, but the old church building where our classes met had been restored and transformed into the Danny Hinton Palmer's Crossing Community Center, named for a city employee known for his love of young people who had died in 2000 at the age of forty. St. John was also in a new building: red brick with a white roof and a vestigial steeple; however, the church building was dwarfed by the adjoining red brick gymnasium. Markers recording the role of the churches in the civil rights movement were posted on nearby telephone poles. As I walked through the community's paved roads, I saw old buildings in disrepair or even in a state of ruin, but I saw a greater number of well-maintained older homes, as well as a development of new, modest but attractive red brick, one-story, single-family homes. The small businesses were gone. However, Henry Naylor, Palmer's Crossing's City Council representative, foresees the homes as enhancing the quality of life for the area, and Hattiesburg officials and Palmer's Crossing residents hope for new businesses and restaurants.[6]

When my former Freedom School students and I visited Dr. McMillen's class in October, 1999, I was struck by the energy of students in that class, as well as among students moving about the campus. The president of USM at the time was Dr. Horace Weldon Fleming, Jr., under whose tenure the School of Nursing had become a college, a master's program in work force training and development had been added in the School of Engineering Technology, a number of other programs had been created, and a plan for expansion of the university throughout the Gulf area had been launched.

After Fleming had served as USM president for two years, the Board of Trustees for the Institutes of Higher Learning in Jackson offered him a one-year contract. Understanding the offer to be a sign of lack of support, Fleming turned it down and took a position elsewhere, In 2002, the Board, despite overwhelming faculty opposition, appointed as USM president Dr. Shelby Freeland Thames, whose career at USM began when he entered as a student in 1955. One of Thames's first actions was to fire Anthony Harris, the only African-American administrator, who has not been replaced. Fortunately Harris, with a B.A. in Spanish and an M.S. in Counseling from U.S.M. and a doctorate in Education in Counseling from Texas A & M University, was appointed Assistant Professor of Educational Leadership and Counseling at Sam Houston State University in Texas.

The energy I found at USM during my stay in Hattiesburg during March, 2004 was driven by a campus-wide furor at President Thames, who had fired two tenured professors, Frank Glamser and Gary Strickland, in midterm because of their opposition to the hiring of an administrator whose credentials they maintained had been falsified. The firings immediately provoked student demonstrations, a vote of no confidence from the faculty and calls for Thames's resignation.[7] In late March the fired professors "were given a deal": they would get paid for two years, but could not teach or criticize the university.[8] However, the settlement did not stop the furor at USM.

Neil McMillen—whose class in African-American history had been a memorable experience for my former Freedom School students and for USM students in 1999—is now retired but teaching part-time at the university. In his view, Thames's goal "is to chill the climate at the university so no one opposes his ideas." McMillen, who joined the faculty in 1969, described the firings as "the darkest hour of the university since I've been associated with it. At no time in its history has the faculty morale been so poor."[9]

In late May the Board of Trustees of State Institutions of Higher Learning in Jackson issued a statement of support for Thames's "plans to improve communication with university constituents, . . . and to work with others to restore trust and support within the institution." The Board declared that it was encouraged by the accomplishments that USM has achieved under Dr. Thames's watch, and would continue "to support the president as he implements this plan,"[10] The Board is composed of twelve members who serve by gubernatorial appointment in rotating positions of twelve years. Most board members are corporate executives and lawyers—a group not known to be concerned about academic due process. The Board members are, however, concerned that order and tranquility be restored to USM, and their statement seem to imply that Dr. Thames must mend fences if he is to maintain his position.

The election of Johnny DuPree in 2001 marked a great distance for African Americans from the struggle to register to vote nearly forty years earlier. Hattiesburg's administration, which changed in the 1980's from a mayor-commissioner form of government to a mayor-council governance, now consists of the mayor and a council, whose members represent the city's five districts. Deborah Denard, representing the predominantly African-American East Jerusalem district, was elected to the Hattiesburg City Council in 2001, the first African American to serve on the Council. In 2003 another African American, Henry Naylor, representing Palmer's Crossing, was elected to the Council, and since then, the Council has decided some key issues—rejecting a school board member, approving a variance for a church that wanted to locate downtown, for example—on a 3–2 vote along racial lines. Nevertheless, most council votes have been unanimous, and when questioned, none of the Council members said they believe race is the sole deciding factor in any decision.[11]

The news about Earl Travillion Attendance Center was also good. The school now serves only grades one through eight; the students then go on to high school in Brooklyn, twenty miles away. Travillion, which had been on the U.S. Department of Education's failing schools list for a decade, was removed in 2002, and near the close of the 2004 school year, its principal, Christopher Furdge, could report satisfaction about the school's progress. With a concerted effort on the part of administrators, teachers and parents, and with access to tutoring support, the targeted goals for the school year in preparing students for the Mississippi Curriculum Tests, improving attendance, reducing student suspensions and establishing discipline had been met.[12]

One improvement that is especially pleasing to me is that the Danny Hinton Community Center is providing important learning experiences to the young people of Palmer's Crossing. Originally offered as a summer recreation program, the program's success led Forrest County Supervisor Rod Woullard to expand it through the entire year, with after-school tutoring added to the other activities such as learning to play chess or using the center's computer lab to work on school assignments. Teachers refer students from Travillion to the center's program, where they are served by about twenty-five USM student volunteers, who play different sports with them, teach them arts and crafts and help them with their homework.[13] That the work Freedom School teachers and students did together is being conducted by a new generation of volunteers and students in the same building where we labored is very encouraging.

The spirit and work of the Mississippi Freedom Schools continues in a number of venues. The Algebra Project, as conceived by Bob Moses, has set the Civil Rights Movement on a new course by establishing math literacy as "a tool for organizing around the issue of access in the economic arena." Moses' children and his Movement comrade David Dennis, along with, "a core group of teacher/organizers" and "autonomous groups of young people," have joined him in setting up the Project's sites around the country.[14]

Another legacy of the Mississippi Freedom Schools is to be found in the summer programs sponsored by the Children's Defense Fund. Founded in 1973 by Marian Wright Edelman, CDF (whose stated mission to Leave No Child Behind has been purloined by the Bush administration) began in 1995 working in partnership with local community organizations, churches and public schools to provide literacy enhancing summer programs in communities where those resources are absent or limited. The CDF Freedom Schools are staffed by college-age young adults who serve students ages five to eighteen for five to eight weeks, in order to promote goals closely resembling those of the original Freedom School curriculum.

The legacy of that summer most meaningful to progress in Mississippi is the work former students are doing in Hattiesburg. Glenda Funchess, as director of Lift Every Voice: Freedom Institute 2004, is passing on the history of the Hattiesburg civil rights movement to high school juniors and seniors through six weeks of class sessions at churches where the original Freedom School classes were taught and through to trips to civil rights sites in Tennessee, Alabama, and Georgia.[15] Jimmella Stokes Jackson has organized Sisters Committed to the Past Present and the Future, a group that includes Shirley Anderson, Gracie Hawthorne, Theresia Clark Banks, Julia Clark Ward, Lillian Jackson Easton, and Carolyn Jackson Preyor, all Freedom School alumnae, and Paige White, Jimmella's niece. Their goal is to preserve the history of the Hattiesburg movement, and their first public event in this area was a celebration of the life and work of Victoria Jackson Adams which was held in St. John United Methodist Church on August 27th, 2004. The Sisters arranged for a small monument to be placed in front of the church identifying it as the birthplace of the civil rights movement in Hattiesburg. Lawrence Guyot returned to Hattiesburg for the celebration, and reminded the community that Victoria Adams had filed the lawsuit that ended poll taxes. Stanley Zibulsky also returned to St. John, where he had taught in its Freedom School, and praised Victoria for her work as a founding member of the Mississippi Freedom Democratic Party that "led to the national publicity that helped change everything." Johnny DuPree said that the civil rights movement brought about the changes that allowed him to be the city's first black mayor. He described Victoria in a proclamation as a "priceless asset to the community." Victoria Adams responded, "Whatever it is that I have given, I have received much more. Nothing wonderful occurred in my life that did not come from this community."[16] Their ambitious long-range goal is to assist women with AIDS, perhaps through the purchase of an old building to remodel as a shelter.

I went in June, 2004 to a memorial for James Chaney, Andrew Goodman and Michael Schwerner in Philadelphia, Mississippi. Mount Zion United Methodist Church has held an annual memorial in June since the murder of the three civil rights workers However, this year the memorial was a sharp contrast to the sad gathering Ben Chaney addressed ten years earlier. For the first time, the memorial was sponsored by the Philadelphia Coalition, a 30-member group drawn from Philadelphia's white power structure, African-American leadership, and the Choctaw Indian tribe of Neshoba County. The Choctaws, led by their visionary chief Philip Martin, were credited with bringing prosperity to the county through commercial development and a casino resort. The Coalition had issued a statement that would have cost them their lives in 1964, and for many years afterward. The petitioners called on "the Neshoba County District Attorney, the state Attorney General and the U.S. Department of Justice to make every effort to seek justice in this case. We deplore the possibility that history will record that the state of Mississippi, and this community in particular, did not make a good faith effort to do its duty."

The service was held in two parts; the first was held in the Neshoba Coliseum, where a gathering of 1,800 people assembled. The Philadelphia coalition invited all of the state's elected officials in the hope that they would join in the effort to move the case for justice in the three murders forward. The Coalition hoped to persuade the Attorney General to pursue a murder case, and in addition persuade the local school district to include civil rights history in the curriculum.

Governor Haley Barbour had been asked to give the welcome. I was sitting among a group from Hattiesburg that included civil rights veterans Ellie Dahmer, Peggy Jean Connor, Clementine Benton, Raylawni Branch, and Jimmella Stokes Jackson. Along with the rest of the gathering, we were stunned when Governor Barbour favorably compared the work done by the civil rights workers, with "the work securing freedom being done by American troops in Iraq." A number of speakers more appropriate for the occasion followed; Dorie Ladner said of the first public honoring of the slain civil rights workers, "I never thought I'd see this day." And civil rights veteran and Democratic Congressman from Georgia John Lewis paid tribute to "three citizens of the world who gave all they had." The speaker that drew the most enthusiasm was former Mississippi Secretary of State and Neshoba Countian, Dick Molpus, who declared, "All of us who are Neshoba Countians or Mississippians have to acknowledge and face our corporate responsibility in this tragedy." Molpus reminded the gathering that those who took part in the killings have told their families and friends what they did, and when "we have heard murderers brag about their killings but pretend those words were never spoken, when we know about evidence to help bring justice but refuse to step forward and tell authorities what they need to know, that's what makes us guilty in 2004."

After the Coliseum ceremony, buses took about 300 of us to Mount Zion United Methodist Church, the site of an earlier church the Klan had bombed in the spring of 1964. The three men had gone to inspect the damage, were arrested and jailed, and when they were released at night, were seized by Klansmen and killed. Again, many people spoke; memorable to me were Carolyn Goodman, 88-year-old mother of Andrew, who said this was the first time she was glad to be in Mississippi; Doug Jones, the prosecutor of the last living suspects in the Birmingham church murders, who said he felt optimistic about achieving justice in this case, and Dave Dennis, whom I had heard at Chaney's funeral in 1964 challenge the congregation to seek justice, for if they did not, he thundered, "God damn your souls." On this occasion, Dennis, who had brought his son, was more reflective. "Forty years later," he said, "I'm hoping something will be done." However, Dennis was less concerned with bringing to justice "some guilty old men," than he was about "building an economic base for our children."

That a practical recognition of the need to establish an economic base has replaced a desperate need to get justice is evidence of the progress achieved in Mississippi since 1964. Hattiesburg has unquestionably undergone a transformation, and many factors account for it, but Freedom School experience certainly is an important one.

Liz Fusco cited the reasons for the success of the schools: students were taken seriously; they were encouraged to talk and were listened to; they wrote and their writing was read with attention to idea and style, as well as grammar. They were challenged to think, to take themselves seriously, to exercise self discipline and to respond meaningfully to situations that confronted them. Thus, they were enabled to envision what houses, schools, jobs, cities, and even federal governments should be. The students had been transformed by their experience in Freedom School, and surely, Fusco believed, it could happen elsewhere.[17]

Fusco's conclusion is echoed by Howard Zinn:

> The Freedom Schools challenged not only Mississippi but the nation. There was, to begin with, the provocative suggestion that an entire school system can be created in any community outside the official order, and critical of its suppositions. The Schools raised serious questions about the role of education in society: Can teachers bypass the artificial sieve of of certification and examination, and meet students on the basis of common attraction to an exciting social goal? Is it possible to declare that the aim of education is to find solutions for poverty, for injustice, for racial and national hatred, and to turn all educational efforts into a national striving for these solutions?[18]

Those questions, along with many others, are not relevant in the ambitiously titled, poorly funded No Child Left Behind (NCLB), a program of reform that assigns control of schools to states, with schools, administrators, teachers and students demonstrating Adequate Yearly Progress (AYP) through students' achievement on tests. AYP operates under the assumption that learning is a regular, mechanical process that transcends economic, cultural, ethnic, and class differences, and therefore learners in all schools can proceed at a uniform pace to achieve proficiency. Under this assumption, therefore, schools that do not achieve the established AYP are labeled "schools in need of improvement."[19] Penalties for under performing require a district to pay for students to attend higher performing schools, or provide them with extra services, such as private tutoring. After three years of less than "adequate yearly progress," a school's staff may be replaced. And after five years, the school can be taken over by the state.[20] The NCLB of 2001 proposes to propel all American students to academic proficiency in reading, language arts, math, and science—social studies, foreign languages and the arts are excluded from the testing. According to a recent report by the Government Accountability Office, the investigative arm of Congress, schools face a rigorous timetable of academic challenges in coming years. Starting with the 2005–2006 year, they must test annually on reading and math, and in 2007, they must also begin testing in science. By 2014, the law requires that all students become proficient in reading and math. However, serious obstacles facing the requirement include unreliable data and lack of clear, timely guidance from the U.S. Education Department.[21]

Parents, of course, support the mom-and-apple-pie concept of "no child left behind"; however, a nationwide survey revealed they are critical of the reform initiative's punitive terms, especially when their children's schools are involved. The high-stakes testing requirement causes parents to worry that too much classroom time is devoted to "teaching to the test." Parents are also alarmed by the threat to stop funding or close low-performing schools rather than to allocate federal funds to improve them.[22]

Furthermore, the heavy reliance on test scores produces odd results. For example, in 2001, the Kilgore School in Cincinnati received a Blue Ribbon Award from the U.S. Department of Education, designating it as an example of education at its best. The following year, Kilgore was designated as a failure, one of

8,600 public schools judged to be performing so poorly that its students must be allowed to transfer to another school. Designation as a failing school also requires the district to transfer students at its own cost. State standards vary widely; a state with ambitious standards, such as Michigan, will have larger numbers of failing schools than states with lower standards. Districts with succeeding schools may become overcrowded when new students transfer and have difficulty maintaining high performance.[23]

Former Secretary of Education Rodney Paige oversaw the implementation of NCLB. Born in Mississippi, Paige earned a bachelor's degree from Jackson State, as well as a master's and doctorate from the University of Indiana. Before becoming education secretary, Paige had taught, coached and served as dean of the School of Education at Texas Southern University. In 1994, Paige became superintendent of the Houston Independent School District, where his achievements led President Bush to select him to implement on a nationwide basis the "Texas Miracle," the plan under which Bush claimed credit for the rise in students' test scores, the narrowing gaps between black and white students and the elimination of dropouts.[24]

Walt Haney, a professor of education at Boston College and a research associate at the Center for the Study of Testing Evaluation and Educational Policy undertook a two-year study in the late 1990s of the "Texas Miracle" that seemed to be revealed by the results of the Texas Assessment of Academic Skills (TAAS) introduced in 1990–91. Haney found the passing scores of the test were arbitrary and discriminatory and that a comparison of reading, writing and math scores with one another and with relevant high school grades raised doubts about the reliability of TAAS scores. Haney's study found that only 50 percent of minority students in Texas had progressed from the ninth grade to high school graduation since the inception of TAAS testing. Since 1982, the rates at which black and Hispanic students were required to repeat the ninth grade had climbed steadily, so that by the late 1990s, nearly 30 percent of black and Hispanic students were failing grade nine. The numbers of students taking the grade ten tests who were classified as "special education" students and therefore not counted in the schools' accountability ratings nearly doubled between 1994 and 1998. According to Haney, Texas educators believe that the enormous time and energy spent preparing students for the TAAS is hurting more than helping them. Haney's study found that during the 1990s, slightly less than 70 percent of students in Texas had actually graduated from high school. The performance of Texas students on the SAT, compared with SAT takers nationally, indicated that the academic learning of secondary school students in Texas had not improved since the early 1990s. Haney concluded that the gains on the TAAS and the dramatic decreases in dropouts were "more illusory than real."[25]

Further evidence of illusory gains was revealed in 2003, when Houston had reported that only 1.5 percent of its students had dropped out, and a state audit of the records of 16 middle and high schools in Houston revealed that 5,500 students who left in the 2000–2001 school year should have been reported as dropouts but were not. The audit in Houston revealed that perhaps the focus on accountability can impel administrators to change data or push out students who may damage the school's profile.[26]

The implementation of NCLB has drawn criticism from parents, teachers, administrators and members of Congress. Labeling a school a failure is devastating to teachers and administrators, who face loss of respect from parents. With high-stakes testing the only criterion of success for students, teachers feel their knowledge and good teaching practices gained from years of experience are being discarded; there is no place for meaningful, inspiring instruction. Teaching to the test and worrying about the impact of low scores on their careers is a disincentive to teachers to stay in the classroom, when what they regarded as a prestigious profession is being reduced to assembly-line work. Education that consists of commercial programs and textbooks cannot provide students with wide-ranging literacy.[27] Many districts have adopted a one-size-fits-all curriculum, and have purchased scripted reading/language arts programs that are uniformly used within a building or across a district. With everyone on the same page at the same time, teachers function as technicians. In some middle schools, teachers are advised to avoid assigning students to read novels and to assign instead poems, short stories, or perhaps a short novel in order to devote more classroom time to preparing for the state test.[28]

Another problem occurs in large heterogeneous districts where students are split into subgroups, a process called disaggregation, to describe breaking down the student population by race, ethnicity, economic background, disabilities, but gifted students are not counted as a subgroup. Many students in these subgroups need supplemental service, but under NCLB, the funding for these services cannot go to the school staff; it must go to outside tutorial services. NCLB, operating under the mantra that factoring aspects of a student's background into the likelihood that the student cannot pass the test is discriminatory or racist, requires that all the subgroups must meet federal performance improvement standards year by year. The failure of one subgroup means the entire school fails.[29] The result is that many schools focus their efforts on students who are not proficient, which begs the question of what efforts are focused on proficient or superior students.

"The building blocks of knowledge," Bush remarked in 1996 as he advised Texas teachers to return to traditional educational practices, "were the same yesterday and will be the same tomorrow. We do not need trendy new theories or fancy experiment or feel good curriculums. The basics work. If drill gets the job done, then rote is right."[30]

The "rote is right" approach to curriculum is in direct opposition to the goal of the Freedom School curriculum to provide a broad intellectual and academic experience, including arts programs and political and social science relating to their own experience. Drilling students to supply the correct test answers is in direct opposition to the Freedom School teachers' pedagogic practice that requires students to ask and answer questions posed by the Citizenship Curriculum. Both the curriculum and the pedagogy were at the heart of the schools' success.

The Hattiesburg Freedom School students were not the only ones inspired by their experience, for I hear occasionally about former Freedom School students elsewhere in Mississippi who have achieved notable success: an award-winning English teacher, a mayor of a city, a college professor. Will NCLB inspire students? Will they remember scripted lessons after forty years as my former students remember the books they read? Will students be inspired to become lawyers, teachers, doctors, social workers, artists, creative writers, and social critics? The likelihood is that gifted teachers who who are compelled to meet the stressful demands of "teaching to the test" will leave the profession. Students who try to perform according to expectations they cannot justify will be stifled and bored; students who cannot or will not meet the narrow standard will drop out of school, and ultimately form the lower tier of a divided society. When such goals as those Howard Zinn cited—to find solutions for poverty, for injustice, for racial and national hatred—have no place in our schools, American society is diminished.

Notes ᔐ

1. MOVEMENT BEGINNINGS IN HATTIESBURG

1. Neil McMillen, quoted in e-mail from Bobs Tusa to author, 31 August 2001.
2. "A Brief History of How Hattiesburg Developed," *Hattiesburg Online*. 5 May 2001 <http://www.hattiesburgms.com/a.html>.
3. "Brief History of Hattiesburg." Report from *Mississippi Democrat*, July 1964, *The Student Nonviolent Coordinating Committee Papers 1959–1972*, Ann Arbor: University of Michigan Research Collections, Reel 69, Frame 26 (Hereafter cited as SNCC).
4. "History of Hattiesburg," *Hattiesburg Online*, 5 May 2001 <http://www.hattiesburgms.com/a.html>.
5. "Report on Housing Conditions," SNCC: Reel 38, Frame 387.
6. Townsend Harris, *Weary Feet, Rested Souls* (New York: Norton, 1998) 299.
7. John Dittmer, *Local People: The Struggle for Civil Rights in Mississippi* (Urbana: University of Illinois Press, 1994) 55–8.
8. Joyce Ladner, *The Ties That Bind* (New York: Wiley, 1998) 129.
9. Josie Brown, quoted in Nikki Davis Maute, "Freedom Summer," *Hattiesburg American*, 28 August 1994, 13A.
10. Dittmer, 80–1; 453.
11. Dittmer, 82.
12. *Ibid.*
13. Dittmer, 83.
14. Charles M. Payne, *I've Got the Light of Freedom: The Organizing Tradition in Mississippi Freedom Struggle* (Berkeley: University of California Press, 1995), 64.
15. Dittmer, 52.
16. Dittmer, 53.
17. Taylor Branch, *Parting the Waters: America in the King Years 1963–65* (New York: Simon and Schuster, 1998) 53, 58; Dittmer, 183.
18. Undated report, SNCC: Reel 38, Frame 104.
19. Cheryl Lyn Greenberg, ed. *A Circle of Trust: Remembering SNCC* (New Brunswick: Rutgers University Press, 1998) 63.
20. Branch, 60.

21. Dittmer, 181.
22. Victoria Gray Adams, remarks recorded in video: "Freedom Summer: A Conversation" at the Parrish Museum, Southampton, New York, 31 March 2001.
23. Branch, 181–2.
24. Payne, 71.
25. Dittmer, 179–80.
26. Dittmer, 184.
27. "Forrest County Voter Registration Movement Report for September 23, 1963," SNCC: Reel 38, Frame 536.
28. Report of September 25, 1963, SNCC: Reel 38, Frame 539.
29. Gerald Bray, "Voice of the Movement," SNCC: Reel 37, Frames 537–8.
30. "Attention Students," SNCC: Reel 38, Frame 564.
31. Dittmer, 202–204.
32. Robert P. Moses and Charles C. Cobb, Jr., *Radical Equations: Math Literacy and Civil Rights* (Boston: Beacon Press, 2001), 76.
33. Dittmer, 209–211.
34. Mendy Samstein, "On the Hattiesburg Situation," SNCC: Reel 38, Frame 551.
35. "Comments on the Hattiesburg Freedom Day," SNCC: Reel 38, Frame 551.
36. Branch, 216.
37. Branch, 217.
38. Howard Zinn, SNCC: *The New Abolitionists* (Boston: Beacon Press, 1964) 111.
39. Branch, 217.
40. Zinn, 114.
41. Branch, 219–221.
42. Pinkey Hall, quoted in Daisy Harris Wade, interview of 11 February 2000, Center for Oral History and Cultural Heritage, University of Southern Mississippi, 764.36.
43. Branch, 219–21.

2. CREATING MISSISSIPPI FREEDOM SCHOOLS

1. Bob Smith, *They Closed Their Schools: Prince Edward County, Virginia 1951–1964* (Chapel Hill: U of North Carolina Press, 1965), 140.
2. Smith, 171, 191, 254.
3. Donald P. Baker, *Washington Post* reporter, quoted in "History of the Civil Rights Movement in Prince Edward County" (1951–1964), an Honors Course paper written by Steven L. Turner, a student at Longwood College in Farmville, in 1996. Among the people shut out of school in 1959 Turner interviewed was William Eanes, who tearfully recalled forty-six years later, "I left school as a child, but I came back as a man. They put me in the eighth grade, but I never caught up. Teachers gave us less instruction and

attention . . . we were so big. It still hurts today . . . . My math is O.K., but I can't spell like I want to."

4. Smith, 255.

5. Smith, 253–255.

6. "Report from Charles Cobb," 31 July 1963, *The Student Nonviolent Coordinating Committee Papers, 1959–1972* , Microfilming Corporation of America (hereafter cited as SNCC): Reel 38, Frame 393.

7. "Prospectus for a Summer Freedom School Program," SNCC: Reel 68, Frame 423.

8. "Overview of the Freedom Schools," SNCC: Reel 68, Frame 424.

9. "From Minutes of the February 13 Meeting of the Summer Steering Committee," SNCC: Reel 64, Frame 547.

10. Lois Chaffee, letter to Jim Monsonis, 1 March 1964, SNCC: Reel 64, Frame 609.

11. Lois Chaffee, letter to Ella Baker, 10 March 1964, SNCC: Reel 64, Frame 570.

12. Lois Chaffee, undated letter to "Dear Friends," with "numerous" enclosures, SNCC: Reel 38, Frames 398–9.

13. "Overview of the Freedom Schools," SNCC: Reel 39, Frame 184.

14. Sandra Adickes, "Mississippi Freedom Schools," SNCC: Reel 67, Frames 758–60.

15. "Mathematics," SNCC: Reel 39, Frames 122–4; Walter E. Gross, "Suggestions for Science Curriculum," SNCC: Reel 67, Frames 761–3.

16. Staughton Lynd, letter to Bob and Dona Moses, 25 March 1964, SNCC: Reel 69, Frame 1231.

17. Lois Chaffee, "Thank You Letters," SNCC: Reel 64, Frames 587–9.

18. Lois Chaffee, Letter to Rachelle Horowitz, 26 April, 1964, SNCC: Reel 67, Frame 256.

19. Liz Fusco, "Freedom Schools in Mississippi, 1964," SNCC: Reel 68, Frame 224.

20. "Summary of Freedom School Curriculum," SNCC: Reel 39, Frame 48.

21. Staughton Lynd, Letter to Freedom School Teachers, May 5, 1964; "Overview of the Freedom Schools, SNCC:" Reel 67, Frames 1183–4.

22. "Notes on Teaching in Mississippi," SNCC: Reel 67, Frames 1179–83.

23. "Materials to Bring With You to Mississippi," SNCC: Reel 67, Frames 984, 1184.

24. "General information on Freedom Schools," SNCC: Reel 67, Frames 930, 937, 150–1.

25. "Dear Freedom School Teacher," SNCC: Reel 67, Frame 1189.

26. *Ibid.*

27. "Summary of Freedom School Curriculum," SNCC: Reel 39, Frame 48.

28. "Unit I: Comparison of Students' Reality with others," SNCC: Reel 67, Frame 834; Reel 39, Frame 42.

29. "Unit II: North to Freedom?" SNCC: Reel 67, Frame 836; Reel 39, Frame 43.

30. "Unit III: Examining the Apparent Reality," 67, SNCC: Reel 67, Frame 837; Reel 39, Frame 44.
31. "Unit IV: Introducing the Power Structure," SNCC: Reel 67, Frame 834; Reel 39, Frame 46.
32. "Unit V: The Poor Negro, the Poor White and Their Fears," SNCC: Reel 67, Frames 798–9.
33. "Unit VI: Material Things versus Soul Things," SNCC: Reel 20, Frames 142–4; Reel 39, Frame 52.
34. "Unit VII: The Movement," SNCC: Reel 20, Frames 87–93.
35. "The Amistad Case," SNCC: Reel 20, Frames 144–5.
36. "Origins of Prejudice" and "Negro Resistance to Oppression," SNCC: Reel 20, Frames 146–8.
37. "Reconstruction," SNCC: Reel 20, Frames 149–53.
38. *Ibid.*
39. "Friends of SNCC," SNCC: Reel 34, Frame 478; Reel 39, Frame 781; Letter from Ruth Schein, 30 May 1964, SNCC: Reel 34, Frame 88; Letter from Lois Chaffee to Penny Vickery, 3 June 1964, SNCC: Reel 67, Frame 268.
40. Volunteer application, SNCC: Reel 39, Frames 791–2.
41. "Guidelines for Interviewing," April 14, 1964, SNCC: Reel 38, Frame 933.
42. "Development of the Mississippi Freedom Project," SNCC: Reel 38, Frames 1162–4.
43. "Memo from Betty Garman to Friends of SNCC," SNCC: Reel 69, Frame 900.
44. "Memo to Accepted Applicants," personal copy.

3. FIRST WEEKS OF A MEMORABLE SUMMER

1. Joe Ellin, e-mail to author, 4 October 2003.
2. Joe Ellin, e-mail to author, 4 October 2003; Nancy Ellin, e-mail to author, 5 October 2003.
3. Joe Ellin, e-mail to author, 4 October 2003.
4. "Mississippi Summer Project Running Summary of Incidents," SNCC: Reel 64, Frame 818.
5. "Summary of Incidents," SNCC: Reel 64, Frame 819.
6. *Ibid.*
7. Richard Wright, *Black Boy (American Hunger): A Record of Childhood and Youth* (1944 New York: Harper Collins, 1993), 3–8.
8. Wright, 243–9.
9. Wright, 252–3.
10. Herbert Randall, remarks recorded in video: "Freedom Summer: A Conversation," Parrish Museum, Southampton, New York, 31 March 2001.
11. "Freedom School Data," SNCC: Reel 39, Frames 975–8.
12. David Dennis, remarks recorded in transcript: "Freedom Summer Roundtable Symposium," University of Southern Mississippi, 7 June 1999.

13. Sandy Leigh, quoted by Sheila Michaels, remarks recorded in transcript: "Freedom Summer Roundtable Symposium," University of Southern Mississippi, 7 June 1999.
14. Staughton Lynd, quoted in Len Holt, *The Summer That Didn't End* (New York: Morrow, 1965), 318.
15. "Special Report—Community Centers," SNCC: Reel 39, 1047.
16. "Palmer's Crossing Freedom News," personal copy.

4. AN EVENTFUL AUGUST

1. Ella Baker, quoted in Dittmer, 282.
2. Staughton Lynd, undated memo to Freedom School Coordinators, SNCC: Reel 68: Frame 320.
3. Joyce Brown, "The House of Liberty," SNCC: Reel 38, Frame 11.
4. "The Declaration of Independence," SNCC: Reel 38, Frame 263.
5. "List of Demands," SNCC: Reel 68, Frames 304–307.
6. Mary Aicken Rothschild, *A Case of Black and White: Northern Volunteers and the Southern Freedom Summers, 1964–1965* (Westport: Greenwood Press, 1982) 136–138.
7. "Library Closed After Integration Attempt," *Hattiesburg American*, 14 August 1964, 1.
8. Lorne Cress-Love, personal interview, 27 August 2003.
9. Phyllis Cunningham, unpublished paper, "Shall We Overcome?" May 1968, 5–7.
10. Ira Grupper, "Labor Paeans 2000," http://motherbird.com/irapope.htm. 28 November 2004.
11. Dittmer, 288.
12. *Intelligence Activities and the Rights of Americans, Book II: Final Report of the Select Committee to Study Governmental Operations, United States Senate,* Quoted in Dittmer, 292.
13. Dittmer, 297.
14. Dittmer, 300.

5. OTHER MISSISSIPPI FREEDOM SCHOOLS

1. Staughton Lynd, "Mississippi Freedom Schools: Retrospect and Prospect," SNCC: Reel 38, Frames 332–8.
2. Pam Parker, "Freedom School Report 18 July 64," SNCC: Reel 67, Frames 432–3.
3. Judy Walborn, letter to Staughton Lynd, 7 July 1964, SNCC: Reel 67, Frame 501.
4. Judy Walborn, "Freedom School Report—July 15, 1964," SNCC: Reel 67, Frames 502–3.

5. Norma Becker, letter to Staughton Lynd, 25 July 1964, SNCC: Reel 68, Frame 394.
6. Wally Roberts, letter to Staughton Lynd, 20 July 1964, SNCC: Reel 68, Frames 666–7.
7. Morris Rubin, letter to Staughton Lynd, 30 July 1964. SNCC: Reel 68, Frame 673.
8. *Ibid.*
9. Sandy Siegel, "Freedom School report—first week, Clarksdale," 9 July 1964, SNCC: Reel 67, Frame 371.
10. Sandy Siegel, "Clarksdale Freedom School," 17 July 1964, SNCC: Reel 67, Frame 372.
11. Sandy Siegel, letter to Lynd, 20 August 1964, SNCC: Reel 67, Frame 514.
12. Anne Marie Williams, "Report from the Pilgrim's Rest Freedom School," 31 July 1964, SNCC: Reel 68, Frame 549.
13. Kirsty Powell, "A Report, Mainly on Ruleville Freedom School, Summer Project, 1964." SNCC: Reel 68, Frame 582.
14. Powell, Reel 68, Frames 582–3.
15. Powell, Reel 68, Frame 583.
16. Powell, Reel 68, Frame 584.
17. Powell, Reel 68, Frame 584–5.
18. *Ibid.*
19. Powell, Reel 68, Frame 585.
20. Powell, Reel 68, Frame 585.
21. Powell, Reel 68, Frame 587.
22. Connie Lee Claywell, letter to Lynd, 9 July 1964, SNCC: Reel 67, Frames 245–6.
23. Claywell, Letter to Lynd, 27 July 1964, SNCC: Reel 67, Frames 246–7.
24. Dan Wood and Gloria Bishop, "Report on Freedom Schools in Rural Madison County," SNCC: Reel 68, Frames 489–90.
25. Wood and Bishop, Reel 68, Frame 490.
26. Virginia Chute, "Gluckstadt Freedom School," SNCC: Reel 67, Frame 239.
27. Chute, Reel 67, Frame 240.
28. *Ibid.*
29. *Ibid.*
30. *Ibid.*
31. *Ibid.*
32. *Ibid.*
33. Chute, Frames 240–1.
34. Marcia Hall, "Canton, Mississippi Freedom School Report" SNCC: Reel 67, Frames 236–8.
35. *Ibid.*
36. *Ibid.*
37. *Ibid.*
38. Hall, Reel 67, Frame 239.
39. Tony O'Brien, undated report to Staughton Lynd, SNCC: Reel 68, Frame 529.

40. O'Brien, Frames 528–9.
41. Florence Jones, "Report on July 16, 1964," SNCC: Reel 68, Frame 406.
42. *Ibid.*
43. *Ibid.*
44. Jones, Reel 68, Frame 407.
45. *Ibid.*
46. Lynd, "Retrospect," SNCC: Reel 38, Frame 335.
47. Hellen O'Neal, e-mail to author, 6 July 2003.
48. Lynd, "Retrospect," SNCC: Reel 38, Frame 335.
49. Edith Moore, "Isn't It Awful?," "Freedom's Journal," 24 July 1964, SNCC: Reel 38, Frame 259.
50. "A Note from the Editors," "Freedom's Journal," 11 August 1964, SNCC: Reel 38, Frame 265.
51. Ira Landess, "Freedom School Report," SNCC: Reel 68, Frames 486–7.
52. Letter from Judy Walborn to Liz Fusco, November 1, 1964, SNCC: Reel 68, Frames 67–8.
53. George W. Chilcoat and Jerry A.Ligon, "Theatre as an emancipatory tool: classroom drama in the Mississippi Freedom Schools," *Curriculum Studies*, 30 (1998) 515–43.
54. Charles M. Payne, *I've Got the Light of Freedom: The Organizing Tradition and the Mississippi Freedom Struggle* (Berkeley: University of California Press, 1995), 305.
55. Gloria X. Clark, e-mail to author, 2 November 2003.
56. Clayborne Carson, *In Struggle: SNCC and the Black Awakening of the 1960's* (Cambridge: Harvard University Press, 1981), 120.
57. Fusco, "Freedom Schools in Mississippi, 1964," SNCC: Reel 39, Frames 5–7.
58. Fusco, "Freedom Schools," Reel 39, Frames 7–8.
59. Fusco, "Freedom Schools," Reel 39, Frames 8–9.
60. Liz Fusco, "Memo to the field from Liz Fusco," August 31, 1964, SNCC: Reel 68, Frame 567.
61. Liz Fusco, letter to Judy Walborn, October 26, 1964, SNCC: Reel 68, Frames 47–8.
62. Rich Miller, letter to Liz Fusco, September 3, 1964, SNCC: Reel 67, Frame 526.
63. Mike Higson, letter to Liz Fusco, August 9, 1964, SNCC: Reel 67, Frame 397.
64. "The First District Newsletter," November 13, 1964, SNCC: Reel 67, Frame 399.
65. Report from David Edmonston to Liz Fusco, October 14, 1964, SNCC: Reel 67, Frame 537.
66. Mary Larsen, letter to Liz Fusco, December 1, 1964, SNCC: Reel 68, Frames 520–1.
67. Nancy Sours, letter to Liz Fusco, December 2, 1964, SNCC: Reel 68, Frames 513–4.
68. "Memo from Liz to Jesse and Dick," 17 September 1964, SNCC: Reel 67, Frame 581.

69. Norma Becker, letter to Liz Fusco, 17 October 1964, SNCC: Reel 68, Frame 38.
70. Liz Fusco letter to C. Michael Bradley, 6 November 1964, SNCC: Reel 68, 90.
71. Liz Fusco, letter to Mrs. William Presser, 4 November 1964, SNCC: Reel 68, Frame 74.
72. Liz Fusco, letter to Mrs. Weil, 25 December 1964, SNCC: Reel 68, Frame 202.
73. Liz Fusco, letter to Ruth, 25 December 1964 SNCC: Reel 68, Frame 202.
74. Liz Fusco, letter to Mrs. Biehl, 25 December 1964, SNCC: Reel 68, Frame 278.
75. Mary King, *Freedom Summer: A Personal Story of the 1960s Civil Rights Movement* (New York: William Morrow, 1987) 450.
76. "Minutes, 5th District Meeting, November 25, 1964," SNCC: Reel 38, Frames 1189–98.
77. Bob Zellner, e-mail to crv, 16 February, 2003.
78. Liz Fusco, undated letter to Kathy, Reel 20, Frames 46, 52.
79. Liz Fusco, undated letter to Kathy, Reel 20, Frame 52.
80. *Ibid.*

6. THE AFTERMATH OF FREEDOM SUMMER

1. Shirley Anderson, personal interview, 20 October 2002.
2. Anderson, interview of 20 October 2002.
3. Jimmella Stokes, letter to author, 16 May 1964.
4. Stokes, letter to author, 17 October 1965.
5. Anderson, interview of 20 October 2002.
6. Anthony Harris, comment in video of Neil McMillen's African-American History Class, 21 October 1999.
7. Clarence Clark, comment in video of Neil McMillen's African-American History Class, 21 October 1999.
8. "Minutes, Fifth District Meeting, November 25, 1964," SNCC: Reel 38, Frames 1190–1.
9. Betty Dwight, personal interview of July 3, 2003.
10. Phyllis Cunningham, unpublished essay, "Shall We Overcome?" May 1968, 9–10.
11. Dittmer, 335–9.
12. Dittmer, 340–4.
13. Dittmer, 344, 351.
14. "Minutes of February 28, 1965 meeting of the Fifth Congressional District of the Mississippi Freedom Democratic Party," SNCC: Reel 69, Frame 353.
15. "Hattiesburg Very Active," SNCC: Reel 38, Frames 556–7.
16. Cunningham, "Shall We Overcome?" 11.
17. Dick Kelly, personal interview, 14 January 2004.
18. Elliot Chaze, "Shinall Murder Trial Under Way," *Hattiesburg American*, 19 July 1965, 1–2.

19. Chaze, "Shinall Given Death Sentence," *Hattiesburg American*, 23 July 1965, 1.
20. Mrs. Clementine Benton, interviews during May and June, 2004. I am grateful for the effort Mrs. Benton made to get this information from Clyde Shinall's family.
21. Dittmer, 341–3.
22. Kyle Marshall, "Night of the Firebombers," *The Daily Mississippian Online*, 23 June, 1999, http://dm.olemiss.edu/archives/99/9906/990623.
23. Vernon Dahmer, Jr., remarks in video, "Pursuing a Late Justice: The Prosecution of Mississippi's Civil Rights Murders," University Forum, University of Southern Mississippi, 29 August 2000.
24. Pinkey Hall, interview, 13 December 1995, Center for Oral History and Cultural Heritage, University of Southern Mississippi, 676. 10.
25. James K. Dukes, remarks in video, "Pursuing a Late Justice."
26. Dittmer, 370–3.
27. Dittmer, 374–82.
28. Shirley Anderson, personal interview, 20 October, 2002.
29. James Nix, interview of 7 March 1993, Center for Oral History and Cultural Heritage, University of Southern Mississippi, 443, 5–7.
30. Daisy Harris Wade, interview of 11 February 2000, Center for Oral History and Cultural Heritage, University of Southern Mississippi, Vol. 764, 4.
31. Doug Smith, remarks in video, "Freedom Summer Roundtable," University of Southern Mississippi, 7 July 1999.
32. Wade, Oral History, 764. 14.
33. Wade, Oral History, 764. 14.

7. FREEDOM SUMMER AS A LIFE-SHAPING EVENT

1. Nick Allis, statement in *Mississippi Freedom Summer: Project Volunteers Twenty-fifth Anniversary Journal*, prepared by Barbara Williams Emerson, Queens College, 1989, 1.
2. Terri Shaw, *Anniversary Journal*, 11; Umoja Kwangvu, *Anniversary Journal*, 44. Douglas Tuchman, *Anniversary Journal*, 49.
3. Dorie Ladner, *Anniversary Journal*, 19; Hollis Watkins, *Anniversary Journal*, 30; Lois Chaffee, *Anniversary Journal*, 38.
4. Gloria Xiafaras Clark, *Anniversary Journal*, 24; Heather Tobis Booth, *Anniversary Journal*, 8.
5. Linda Wetmore, *Anniversary Journal*, 6; Peter Orris, *Anniversary Journal*, 16; John H. Strand, *Anniversary Journal*, 17; Joel Aber, *Anniversary Journal*, 21.
6. Stan Boyd, *Anniversary Journal*, 21; Patricia Barbanell, *Anniversary Journal*, 36.
7. Martha Davis, *Anniversary Journal*, 39; Ruth Gallo, *Anniversary Journal*, 41; Mark Levy, *Anniversary Journal*, 43–4; Gilbert S. Avery, *Anniversary Journal*, 55.
8. Barney Frank, *Anniversary Journal*, 24; Susan Brownmiller, *Anniversary Journal*, 37; Kathie Amatniek Sarachild, *Anniversary Journal*, 47.

9. Elizabeth Martinez, "'On Time' in Mississippi: 1964–1994," *Z magazine*, September 1994, 37.

10. Susan Brownmiller, "The Summer of Our Discontent," *Village Voice*, 19 July 1994, 33.

11. Wilson Booth, "Reflections of Freedom Summer," *Washington Post*, 27 June 1994, D1, D4.

12. Nikki Davis Maute, "Freedom Fighters Reunite," *Hattiesburg American*, 26 June 1994, 1A, 14A; "Freedom Summer: It's Time to Say Thanks to Workers," editorial, *Hattiesburg American*, 26 June 1994, 14A.

13. Jennifer Moore, comments in "Pursuing the Past: the Medgar Evers Murder," PBS Online.

14. Bob Helfrich, comments in "Pursuing a Late Justice: The Prosecution of Mississippi Civil Rights Murders," Then and Now, University Forum, The University of Southern Mississippi, 29 August 2000.

15. Vernon Dahmer, Jr., comments in "Pursuing a Late Justice."

16. Victoria Jackson Gray Adams, personal interview, 15 August 2003.

17. *Ibid.*

18. Bob Beech, personal interview, 21 July 2003.

19. "The Long Walk to Freedom: Portraits of Civil Rights Activists Then and Now," http://communityworksnyc.org/our_programs. 28 November 2004.

20. "LSC Member Helped Start New School," http//www.newstips.org/print.php?section=Successful+Schools+Sub&mainid=103. 28 November 2004.

21. Sheila Michaels, e-mail forwarded to author by Bobs Tusa, 25 May 2001.

22. Joe Ellin, e-mail to author, 4 October 2003.

23. Nancy Ellin, e-mail to author, 5 October 2003.

24. "Village Voices," Lili LeGardeur, 1 December 2004 <http://www.bestofneworleans.com/dispatch/2004-07-06/news_feat2.html>.

25. Bob Moses and Charles E. Cobb, Jr., *Radical Equations: Math Literacy and Civil Rights* (Boston: Beacon Press, 2001), 67.

26. *Ibid.* 136, 146.

27. Dorie Ladner, comments at Memorial Service for James Chaney, Andrew Goodman, and Michael Schwerner, Philadelphia, Mississippi, 20 June 2004.

28. "Joyce Ladner," *Mississippi Writers Page*, http://www.olemiss.edu/mwp/dir/ladner_joyce.

29. Shirley Anderson, personal interviews, 20 October 2002 and 24 September 2003.

30. Gwen Merritt Robinson, personal interview, 9 March 2004.

31. *Ibid.*

32. Lavon Reed Trotter, personal interview, 7 March 2004.

33. *Ibid.*

34. *Ibid.*

35. Jimmella Stokes Jackson, personal interview, 27 March 2004.

36. ———, personal interview, 20 June 2004.

37. *Ibid.*

38. *Ibid.*
39. *Ibid.*
40. Carolyn Moncure Mojgani, quoted in "Freedom Schools: A Page out of History," by Orley Hood, *The Clarion Ledger*, 22 July 2003, 1.
41. Dianne Moncure Sutton, personal interview, 30 June 2004.
42. Antoinette Konz, "Draft Plan Calls for 4 New Lamar Schools," *Hattiesburg American*, 5 February 2005, 1.
43. Dianne Moncure Sutton, personal interview, 30 June 2004.
44. *Ibid.*
45. Julia Clark Ward, personal interview, 7 March 2004.
46. *Ibid.*
47. Theresia Clark Banks, quoted in "DuPree Upsets Morgan," by Scott M. Larson and Kevin Walters, *Hattiesburg American*, 6 June 2001, 10A.

8. HATTIESBURG IN THE PRESENT

1. "Hattiesburg Mississippi, http://www.city-data.com/city/Hattiesburg-Mississippi.html, 8 March 2004.
2. Ed Morgan, remarks in video, "Freedom Summer Roundtable Symposium," University of Southern Mississippi, 7 June 1999.
3. Kevin Walters, "Mobile Street Revitalization Sought, *Hattiesburg American*," 31 May 2002, 1C.
4. Peggy Jean Connor, quoted in Kevin Walters, "Mobile Street Revitalization Sought," *Hattiesburg American*, 31 May 2002, 1C.
5. Sandra McIntyre, personal interview, 7 April 2004.
6. Scott M. Larson, "Palmer's Subdivision Getting 33 New Homes," *Hattiesburg American*, 21 March 2002, 1A.
7. Thomas Bartlett, "Move to Fire 2 Professors Roils Campus in Mississippi," *The Chronicle of Higher Education*, 19 March 2004, 1, 8–10.
8. Donald V. Adderton, "Let reason return to USM campus," Clarion-Ledger online, 18 May 2004.
9. Neil McMillen, quoted in "USM Under Fire for Suspensions," Antoinette Konz and Nikki Davis Maute, *Hattiesburg American*, 7 March 2004, 1, 8A.
10. Statement of the Mississippi Board of Trustees of the Institutions of Higher Learning, 21 May 2004, http://www.state.ms.ud/newsstrory.asp?ID=270.
11. Nikki Davis Maute, "Split Decisions," *Hattiesburg American*, 17 January 2004, 1A.
12. Antoinette M. Konz, "Earl Travillion Principal Happy With Progress," *Hattiesburg American*, 5 April 2004.
13. Antoinette Konz, "Tutoring Proves a Success at Palmers Crossing Center," *Hattiesburg American*, 24 April 2004.
14. Moses, *Radical Equations*, 137, 147.
15. Nikki Davis Maute, "Freedom Summer Stories Passed On," *Hattiesburg American*, 29 February 2004, 1A.

16. Nikki Davis Maute, "Church's Civil Rights Contributions Marked," *Hattiesburg American*, 28 August 2004, 1A.

17. Fusco, "Freedom Schools," SNCC: Reel 39, Frames 8–9.

18. Howard Zinn, *SNCC: The New Abolitionists* (1965; Cambridge: South End Press, 2002), 250.

19. Patrick Shannon, "Adequate Yearly Progress?" in *Saving Our Schools: The Case for Public Education*, Ken Goodman et al., eds. (Berkeley: RDR Books), 2004, 33–5.

20. Teresa Mendez, "Thanks, but no thanks: The No Child Left Behind Law came with too many strings attached," *The Christian Science Monitor*, 25 November 2003, 10 (http://web5.infotrac.galegroup.com/itw/infomark/529/562/54880559w5/purl=rcl_SP02_0. 17 October 2004).

21. Diana Jean Schemo, "Problems Seen for Expansion of Testing of U.S. Students," *New York Times*, 5 October 2004, A17.

22. Mendez, "Thanks, but no thanks."

23. Marjory Coeyman, "Just When You Thought You Knew the Rules," *Christian Science Monitor*, 9 July 2002, 11 (http://web5.infotrrac.galegroup.com/1tw/infomark/529/562/54880559w5/purl=rcl_SP02_0. 17 October 2004).

24. Ken Goodman, "Vanished Without a Trace, Texas Style," in *Saving Our Schools*, 84–5.

25. Walt Haney, 'The Myth of the Texas Miracle," *Education Policy Analysis Archives*, volume 8, number 41, 19 August 2000 (http:epae.asu.edu/epaa/v10n24. 20 October, 2004).

26. Diana Jean Schemo, "Questions on Data Cloud Luster of Houston Schools," *New York Times*, 11 July 2003, A1 (http://web5.infotrac.galegroup.com/itw/136/965/54880319w5/purl=rcl_SP02_0. 17 October 2004).

27. Yetta Goodman, "Teaching Knowledge and Experience: Do They Count?" *Saving Our Schools*, 116–9.

28. Grace Vento Zogby, "Why I Can't Stay (Not Everything That Counts Can Be Counted)," *Saving Our Schools*, 266–7.

29. Roger Rapoport, "A District Sues," *Saving Our Schools*, 268–70.

30. George Bush, quoted in Gerald Coles, "Learning to Read—Scientifically," *Rethinking Schools Online*, Summer 2001 (http://www.rethinkingschools.org/special/reports/bushplan/Read154.shtml. 20 October 2004).

Index

Sours, Nancy, 132, 135
Southern Christian Leadership
  Council (SCLC), 15, 34–35,
  41, 100
Southern Regional Council, 13
Sovereignty Commission, 10
Spears, Lawrence, 63
Spike, Robert, 34, 100
Steinem, Gloria, 170
Stennis, John C., 55, 75, 152
St. John Methodist Church, 14, 64, 71
Stokes, Jimella, 59–61, 65, 68, 77, 90,
  162, 166, 178–79, 191, 193
Stone, Bob, 56, 59, 62, 85, 161
St. Paul Methodist Church, 20, 57,
  68, 71, 81, 85
Student Nonviolent Coordinating
  Committee (SNCC), 1–3,
  13–15, 16, 17–19, 32–34, 39,
  41, 50, 62, 73, 82, 89–90,
  98–99, 127, 135–36, 145, 149,
  157, 160–61, 165–66, 175, 178
  formation of Summer School
    Committee, 3
  Friends of SNCC, 45–46
Sullivan, Minnie, 16
Summer Project Committee, 38–40,
  41, 50, 70, 127

Teachers Committee, 137
Texas Assessment of Academic Skills
  (TAAS), 196–97
textbooks, donations of, 43, 86, 134,
  145, 197
Thomas, Art, 34
Thornhill, Emmitt, 85
Ties That Bind, The (Ladner), 175
Till, Emmett, 9, 66
Tomorrow's Tomorrow (Ladner), 175
Tubman, Harriet, 44, 112, 116

Tuchman, Doug, 59, 69, 71, 95, 99,
  149, 157, 165, 172
Tusa, Bobs, 164–66, 170

United Federation of Teachers (UFT),
  29–30, 35, 49–52, 56–57, 62,
  69, 92, 105, 126, 133, 159
United States v. Lynd, 16

Van Landingham, Zack, 10–11
Vietnam War, 27, 88, 137, 139, 142,
  153, 172
  Gulf of Tonkin incident, 88, 173
Voter Education Project, 13
voter registration, 2, 12–16, 18–19,
  32, 35, 45, 47–48, 62, 69, 72,
  74, 107–8, 112, 121–24,
  126–27, 133, 136, 143, 145,
  147–48, 153, 171–72, 174
  white retaliation to, 65

Walborn, Judy, 104, 125, 129–30
Washington, Booker T., 44, 116
Watkins, Hollis, 13–14, 157, 165,
  173–74
Weddington, Rachel, 30–31, 35
Weinburger, Elaine, 51
White Citizens Council, 63
Williams, Anne Marie, 108
Williams, Sam, 59, 68, 179
Williams, Viola, 124
Williams v. Mississippi, 45
Wood, Dan, 113–14
Woods, Lenon E., 10, 69–70, 185
Woullard, R.W., 11, 13–14

Zellner, Bob, 135
Zibulsky, Stan, 52, 69, 73, 86, 95,
  173, 192
Zinn, Howard, 20–21, 194, 199

CPSIA information can be obtained at www.ICGtesting.com
Printed in the USA
LVOW08s2257100716

495776LV00006B/440/P